What Philosophy Can Tell You about™ Your Dog

Also Available from Open Court

What Philosophy Can Tell You about Your Cat
edited by Steven D. Hales

What Philosophy Can Tell You about™ Your Dog

Edited by
STEVEN D. HALES

OPEN COURT
Chicago and La Salle, Illinois

To order books from Open Court, call 1-800-815-2280, visit our website at www.opencourtbooks.com.

First printing 2008

Open Court acknowledges permission for use of the following pictures.
p. i: ©iStockphoto.com/GlobalP;
p. 1: © iStockphoto.com/Eriklam;
p. 44: © John W. Tucker 2008;
p. 61: © iStockphoto.com/yecatsdoherty;
p. 98: © iStockphoto.com/salihguler;
p. 113: © iStockphoto.com/Jbryson;
p. 134: © iStockphoto.com/kccoffey;
p. 154: © iStockphoto.com/gmnicholas;
p. 165: © iStockphoto.com/Jbryson;
p. 182: © iStockphoto.com/GlobalP;
p. 235: © iStockphoto.com/GlobalP;
p. 298: © iStockphoto.com/suemack.

Printed and bound in the United States of America.

Library of Congress Cataloging-in-Publication Data

What philosophy can tell you about your dog / edited by Steven D. Hales.
     p. cm.
    Includes bibliographical references and index.
    Summary: "Twenty philosophers and dog lovers discuss their experiences with dogs and explore dog-related themes in metaphysics and ethics"—Provided by publisher.
    ISBN 978-0-8126-9653-0 (trade paper : alk. paper)
    1. Dogs—Behavior. 2. Dogs—Psychology. 3. Dogs—Philosophy. I. Hales, Steven D.
SF433.W47 2008
636.7—dc22

                          2008030372

Contents

Kibitz and Bits

STEVEN D. HALES

About ten thousand years ago, dogs decided to do a very surprising thing: they decided to gamble their fortunes on human beings, and throw their lot in with ours.

No doubt wolves, foxes, and coyotes at the time found this plan baffling. Join up with those big-headed hairless apes? Nevertheless, for ten millennia our evolutionary paths have joined together, and on the human side, this arrangement has worked out very nicely. We've used dogs to hunt, to herd, to guard us from our enemies, to pull our sleds across the frozen tundra, to rescue Alpinists with kegs of brandy, and to be our boon companions. We've even trimmed, fluffed, and blow-dried them for dog shows, and the Hollywood glitterati have used them as fashion accessories. For the most part, *Canis lupus familiaris* has done well by this pact, too. When I come home from the grocery store, my dog is sure that I have returned victorious from the hunt, and am now ready to share the kill, which evidently has been conveniently prepackaged into Pupperonis and Milk Bone biscuits. Said kill can be pleasantly enjoyed while lying on an old army blanket over a radiant-heated slate floor.

There are those unfortunate dogs who have fallen into the hands of sociopaths who breed them for dog-fighting, in an effort to compensate for the underendowments of their manhood. While true dog aficionados naturally decry such brutality, it may be that we too haven't sufficiently pondered our own relationships with our dogs. Indeed, the reconsideration of the very familiar is a natural pathway into philosophy. Plato wrote that philosophy begins in wonder, and we would do well to wonder at the lives we have made with our dogs.

There's nothing like trying to train a puppy to take one's head out of the clouds. Young dogs are full of energy, play, and instincts that must be mastered—or at the very least understood and positively channeled—if they are to be fit members of our packs. Training a dog is not for the overbooked, or the faint of heart. Like their owners, dogs have different temperaments and personalities, and training requires figuring these things out. In Part I of the book, our authors consider the philosophical ramifications of training canines.

- **Does your dog embarrass you because his behavior says more about you than you would like?**

- **Is effective dog training impossible unless we assume that our dogs have thoughts, beliefs, desires, and intentions?**

- **How can dog training, crating, and invisible fences enhance your dog's freedom even as they curtail her freedom?**

The classic dogs versus cats joke is that dogs think, "My people keep me warm and dry, feed me good food, pet me, brush me, and play with me. They must be gods!" Cats, on the other hand, think, "My people keep me warm and dry, feed me good food, pet me, brush me, and play with me. *I* must be a god!"

But what actually goes on in that thick furry head? Does my dog really have any thoughts about me? Does he actually think that a parking meter is a pay toilet? Our dogs seem playful, eager to please, aggressive, attentive, or display any number of other personality traits. At least—that's how we interpret their behavior. In Part II, we take a close look at what our dogs might be thinking, if anything, and how we can get inside their heads.

- **Are guide dogs for the blind literally an extension of their owner's mind?**

- **Was French philosopher René Descartes right in maintaining that dogs are mere automata, mindless, soulless, clock-like mechanisms without language or love?**

- **If our dogs think, then do insects think as well? If bees are just robots, then why aren't dogs?**

- **What does your dog think about *you*?**

- **If a dog fails to recognize its own leg as part of its body, what should we conclude about canine reasoning and intellect?**

We hear that dogs are our best friends. Perhaps you're skeptical—after all, how many of your friends have you neutered? Nevertheless, the evidence is in. Dogs do indeed add to our lives and lengthen our days; they insulate us against loneliness and isolation, lift the spirits of the depressed, and cheer sick children in hospitals. Studies have shown that dog-owning senior citizens are more active and live longer than those without canine companionship; throwing the ball all afternoon for Rex is certainly more exercise than watching Lassie re-runs on TV. Benjamin Franklin wrote that "there are three faithful friends—an old wife, an old dog, and ready money." But just what is it to be friends with our dogs, that they should measure up to old spouses and ready money? In the next Part, our professional thinkers ponder these issues:

- **How can your habits and routines with your dog create genuine friendship?**

- **Why do you like your dog more than your teenager?**

- **What does your dog know about being an animal that you don't?**

- **Will cloning bring back your long-lost childhood dog?**

You might think that dogs must be the least logical, the least metaphysically oriented animals there are. Cats might seem inclined to the more abstract, but dogs are here-and-now, practical, action-oriented. At this point in the book our authors have considered what our dogs might be thinking, but next they step off into more rarefied realms—how might our dogs be *reasoning*? The contemplations of my dog seem mostly concerned with effectively making the great tripartite division of the world: is it to be eaten, rolled in, or peed on? As it turns out, there is much to say about logic and metaphysics for dogs.

- In 1615 King James of Scotland and England (of *King James Bible* fame) hosted a debate on the use of logic by dogs. Who won and why?

- Some people think there is no provable difference between a Saint Bernard and a Chihuahua. Why would anyone think that?

- You and your dog have different perceptions, different perspectives of the world. How can you be sure that you and your dog inhabit the same objective world?

- Are there really perfectly bounded, ideal dog breeds, or are they all just a bunch of dawgs?

Affection and friendship are part of our relationships with our dogs, but there's also the more mundane. We have to walk them, make sure they have exercise, clean their yards, feed them, brush them, take them to the vet, give them heartworm pills. Some owners primp their dogs for shows, or breed them for conformity to the ideal Doberman, Cocker Spaniel, or Weimaraner. Others buy their dogs exotic luxuries—trips to spas, doggy day camp, air-conditioned dog houses, filet mignon. We often treat our dogs like furry, four-legged children. But sometimes even the most besotted parent can step back and wonder, "am I doing the right thing?" Is it too much to think that an Airedale is my son? Is an obsession with being AKC-registered respectful of the dignity of our dogs? Do we have any real reason to think that we have moral responsibilities of any sort to our dogs, or are they just sort of hobbies of ours? In the final Part, "Canine Ethics," our authors consider just such matters.

- Why does Friedrich Nietzsche think that we should learn to see ourselves as animals instead of seeing our dogs as little people?

- Do even dogs have a dignity that we must respect?

- Do our dogs really have moral rights, or is it just anthropomorphizing to think so?

- Why does Aristotle think that our dogs cannot be good dogs unless we are good masters?

- Is it wrong to shower our dogs with too many luxuries?

Dogs may have thrown their lot in with human beings, but it is we who have chosen our dogs. To be sure, it is a choice laden with emotional risk, as Rudyard Kipling writes:

> There is sorrow enough in the natural way
> From men and women to fill our day;
> But when we are certain of sorrow in store,
> Why do we always arrange for more?
> Brothers and sisters I bid you beware
> Of giving your heart to a dog to tear.
> Buy a pup and your money will buy
> Love unflinching that cannot lie—
> Perfect passion and worship fed
> By a kick in the ribs or a pat on the head.
> Nevertheless it is hardly fair
> To risk your heart for a dog to tear.

As we take that risk, we do well to consider the richness, the depth, and the wonder that is occasioned by reflection on our life with dogs. And so, enjoy the litter of philosophical pups that follows, and see which one is the first to jump in your lap and lick your face.

I

The *Dao* of
the Dog

1

Why Does My Dog Embarrass Me So Much?

ANDREW TERJESEN

Maybe it's the way she sticks her muzzle into people's crotches. Or maybe it's the fact that she always jumps up to meet people (and occasionally knocks over a very young or very old visitor). Or possibly it's the fact that she drops a toy covered with drool into the lap of all your visitors (totally oblivious to how nicely they are dressed).

It seems that all our dogs have traits that embarrass us. "Man's best friend" can also be our social enemy. In my case, it's the way my dog, Emma, reacts to children. Some toddler will run up wanting to pet her—but as soon as they are within earshot she begins to get skittish and sometimes growls. I know she wouldn't harm a fly, but to the casual observer it seems as if I have raised the next Cujo. And so, I apologize profusely, tug Emma along and hope that my neighbors don't think I'm a poor "parent" (or that I am harboring a menace to society).

It's the same feeling we all get when our dog does something embarrassing—this feeling that we have been found wanting in our dog-rearing skills. This is where philosophy can be of assistance—by reflecting on a situation, we can come to a better understanding of it and, with this enhanced understanding, either correct the situation or come to terms with it.

Sometimes It's Them, Not Us

One source of embarrassment for dog owners is a behavior like crotch-sniffing. In all honesty, this is not usually something we should have to apologize for. Although there are many ways in which dogs are like people, we should never forget that they are not human beings. Dogs have a different biology and as a result of this, they are much more dependent on their noses to understand the world and recognize each other. Moreover, while there are many reasons why it would be inappropriate for Uncle Ted to go around sniffing the crotches of guests, a dog cannot understand that these social taboos exist. Consequently, they lick themselves in full view of your dinner party or molest their children's stuffed animals while you're trying to enjoy the duck *à l'orange*.

A certain amount of training can keep these behaviors reined in, but no amount of training will overcome the fact that dogs are built to experience the world differently and are not equipped to appreciate the nuances of our social etiquette (they have their own). Anyone who is always perturbed by your dog's behavior, probably doesn't own a dog. They're no different than the people without children who expect parents to keep their child under complete control every minute of the day. However, this should not be a free pass for our dogs to indulge in every instance of crotch-sniffing, people-jumping, and toy-molesting. There are some things that even another dog owner would not tolerate—just as parents would not tolerate a child who never stops throwing a tantrum. Behaviors that have developed to this point embarrass us for a different reason than the initial behavior.

In the end, there might be nothing to be embarrassed about—sometimes we have to recognize that dogs aren't able to appreciate our social mores. If anything, our embarrassment in these situations seems to stem from a mistake in thinking of them as like us and being embarrassed *for* them—because we would be embarrassed if we were the ones engaging in that behavior. What we need to figure out are some general principles that will help us separate the behaviors that should not embarrass us from those that ought to make us embarrassed.

Sometimes It's Us, Not Them

Sure, dogs chew (and they *need* to, if they are going to have a healthy mouth), but there are ways to train your dog to associate certain things with "yes, chew" and other things with "no, don't chew." Similarly, dogs greet each other differently and so jumping up is not an inappropriate way for dogs to greet each other (the lack of opposable thumbs really make a handshake difficult); but the instinct to jump up and lick and sniff can be curbed with training.

When I first took Emma home, she was like every other puppy—chewing everything in sight (and perhaps she is a mutant, but that Bitter Apple™ stuff only seemed to make her want to chew on it more) and jumping on every person she met. It was cute when she only weighed ten pounds, but as she got older, it became more and more embarrassing. A seventy-pound dog can go through a lot of molding and furniture and knock over even a spry twenty-something. These behaviors had lots of consequences other than embarrassment, but it was the embarrassment that stung the most.

In a case like this, the embarrassment is not the same as we experience when a dog passes gas in the middle of a dinner party (and in this case, we'll assume it really was the dog). We're not feeling embarrassed *for* the dog when it jumps on people, we're embarrassed *by* the dog. The fact that Emma was jumping on people said something about me and what it said about me was a source of embarrassment. The root of the embarrassment is the fact that I should have trained her not to do that. You'll never train a dog to hold in gas until it is socially acceptable to let it go, or even train it to apologize and show shame when he does so. The former is biologically impossible, the latter is psychologically impossible. However, you can train a dog not to jump on people when they enter the room.

It is here that we see the most important aspect of how we separate the things that should embarrass us from the things that shouldn't. Dog owners as a whole are well aware of what it takes to train a dog not to do something (and they know how likely the dog is to break the training at different stages—and therefore whether a particular instance of behavior might be "understandable" as long as you discipline afterwards). People without dogs don't have this knowledge, so we can't trust their judgments. What we need to do is to consult the judgments of our dog-owning peers and when they're not available, try and imagine what they would think about the situation.

The fact that one hasn't trained their dog to stop behaving a certain way, especially an adult dog you've had all your life, says something about one's character. What it says about us depends on other elements of the equation. In some cases we happen to be willing to tolerate a lot from our dogs—especially the really small ones that can't do much damage. This might be the result of being overindulgent—we love them too much to correct them—or this might be the result of sheer laziness. I must admit that when it came to Emma's chewing, a lot of it could be attributed to the fact that at the time it seemed to be more trouble than it was worth to be constantly watching her, correcting her whenever she went for something inappropriate, and rewarding her when she chewed on the right toys. Laziness and overindulgence are character flaws that we tend to be embarrassed about.

Why do these character flaws expressed in our dogs' behaviors embarrass us so much? The reason seems to lie in an idea that goes back to Plato (428–347 B.C.E.) known as the "unity of the virtues" thesis. People tend to assume that character is an all or nothing thing—if you lack one virtue, you probably lack the other virtues as well. If I am lazy when it comes to my dog, how dependable could I be when humans are involved? What reason is there to think that my laziness only comes in to play when my dog is involved? And if I am lazy in human affairs, then how can one be sure that I will exert myself when morality demands that I do something difficult? Similarly, if I am overindulgent, can I be relied on not to play favorites in other contexts? These concerns are precisely why the dalliances of a president could be of concern to some people.

Even if one is working on the problem behavior, the fact that one has failed to control it, in any instance, suggests some lack of discipline, and therefore virtue, on the part of the owner. I say "suggests" because it seems unrealistic to believe that every canine behavioral problem could be managed by your average dog owner, or that there is no such thing as an inherently aggressive dog.

As I think any dog lover will recognize, pit bulls are not necessarily vicious dogs. However, making sure that the disposition they were bred for does not pose a danger to others requires a skill at dog-training that exceeds the talents of your average dog owner. I've known some truly sweet and submissive pits and rotties, but I don't think *I* could have trained them to be that way. Nonetheless, our failure to recognize when things are beyond our control is a character flaw that people might hold us accountable for—again, this flaw becomes magnified and more embarrassing if one accepts the "unity of virtues" thesis, because it suggests a more general lack of good judgment. So, one source of our embarrassment about our dog's behavior is what it says about our lack of discipline or judgment. It only makes sense to be embarrassed about things we knowingly or knowingly failed to do. However, there's a whole set of embarrassing behaviors that arise precisely because we're not aware of what's going on.

But Sometimes We're Both to Blame

It's Emma's reaction to children that really embarrasses me. Her chewing resolved itself when I began to take her out to the dog park—what a godsend, how could anyone ever oppose having one built in their area—and she burned off the excess energy that went into chewing. It would be several years before I finally got her jumping under control; in fact, it wasn't until my wife, who wasn't willing to tolerate such behavior, came along that I finally gained the resolve to tackle the problem. However, Emma's reaction to children has not been as easy to resolve. Although it does, in part, embarrass me now because it says something about my lack of discipline, even when it first happened it embarrassed me.

Why Emma's behavior embarrassed me, even at the beginning before I could have been expected to manage the problem, has a lot to do with how this particular reaction came about. After all, most dogs are not hostile to children by nature—so it's not likely this is something that I had failed to correct. Instead, it would seem that this is something that I brought about. Which raises the question—do I dislike children as well? That possibility is certainly embarrassing and would reveal a certain flaw in my character, but I'm pretty sure that is not the case. Instead, when I turn to the work of the great Scottish philosopher David Hume (1711–1776), I find the answer to why Emma reacts as she does. Her behavior toward children was something that I had unconsciously taught her. The root of this was not something about me or something about her— as in some of the other cases discussed. The cause of this particular behavior was the connection between us and a feedback loop that went out of control.

This connection is what Hume describes as "sympathy" Here is how Hume describes it in his *Treatise of Human Nature* (1739):

> The minds of all men are similar in their feelings and operations, nor can anyone be actuated by any affection, of which all others are not, in some degree, susceptible. As in strings equally wound up, the motion of one communicates itself to the rest; so all the affections

readily pass from one person to another, and beget corresponding movements in every human creature. (Book III, Part iii, Section 1)

What Hume recognized in the eighteenth century was the psychological process by which emotions can spread from one person to another without any conscious effort. Since it is very much like an infectious disease passing through a population, psychologists refer to the process that Hume described as "emotional contagion." I'll adopt their terminology, since "sympathy" is a term that is used in many different ways and can be misleading. You've probably experienced emotional contagion when a cheerful person enters a solemn room and the mood of the whole room changes.

Hume is talking only about human beings, but there is no reason why we can't extend this phenomena to out pets. Cesar Millan, The Dog Whisperer, likes to talk about how our "energy" is important when training our dog. What he's describing is the process of emotional contagion, albeit with a New Agey spin (presumably to sell it to the Left Coast crowd). We've certainly observed contagion within species—one agitated animal can upset the whole herd—and as far as dogs are concerned we are a part of their pack. This may seem far-fetched, but consider how you tell what someone is thinking (and that they are thinking at all). In philosophy, this question is known as the problem of other minds. When you think about it, you can't see that I'm thinking, and yet you're pretty sure that I am. The English philosopher Bertrand Russell (1872–1970) offered the most straightforward solution to this problem. I can tell that you're thinking because you act like I do when I'm contemplating something and I can usually tell what you're thinking because you make the same gestures and sounds as I do when, for example, I ask someone to pass the salt. This likeness between my behavior and your behavior causes me to draw an analogy between me and you—and since I think "I want the salt" when I ask someone to pass it, I infer that when you ask you also are desiring the salt. Dogs are no different—they use the same analogical reasoning. They look to behavioral cues in order to tell what other dogs are thinking—whether they want to play or are territorial—and they'll do the same with their human pack leader. In fact, this tendency to associate certain behaviors with certain feelings might explain why we are embarrassed for our dogs—we can't help but make the connection between how we would feel in their situation and how we think they ought to feel.

How We Teach Our Dogs Without Trying

Emotional contagion is not a conscious process—all these inferences are going on at an unconscious level as we quickly make connections between behavioral signals and feelings. With Emma I sent the wrong signals about children without being aware of it, but in order to figure out what I did wrong and therefore needed to do differently, we have to understand how this process works. It is to Hume's credit that the process he identified almost three hundred years ago, based upon eyeball observations and some reflection on his experiences, has been confirmed by modern science. Emotional contagion is only one part of story, though, about how we teach our dogs without even thinking about it. The entire process is called "social referencing" and it has been studied in primates and infants.

It begins with some object that is unfamiliar appearing before the baby. Unfamiliar objects draw the attention of babies—as we can tell from the fact that they stare at those objects longer than anything else. After looking at the unfamiliar object for a while they then look to their parent and track the parent's gaze. If the parent's gaze is focused on the unfamiliar object, the baby will then look at the parent's behavioral cues—usually just a facial expression—and mimic them. As the Harvard philosopher William James (1842–1910) noted (and some psychologists given evidence to support this counterintuitive supposition) having a certain facial expression can lead to feeling the emotion associated with that expression—in other words we can cheer ourselves up by smiling and bring ourselves down by frowning. Try it, you'll see. So, a baby that copies the parent's expression will learn to associate the unfamiliar object with that emotion. The phenomenon of joint attention—made possible by the capacity for gaze-tracking—is very important for early child development.

If one accepts that dogs and humans are capable of emotional contagion with each other, it follows that it happens by a similar process. Facial mimicry is pretty much out of the question, but other cues could be associated with the object of joint attention, including cues humans are not sensitive to, like smell. On the human end of the relationship, the process is probably a lot more cognitive-oriented and less contagious. After all, we try and simulate in our heads what the baby is thinking and figure out what the baby wants. This is because we have the mental capacity to do so and so we do the same with our dogs—rather than relying on the quick cues that our dogs do. Thus, the mistakes we make are more inferential, resulting in emotions that aren't there (like attributing shame to a dog because it passed gas), while the mistakes that dogs make are the result of an incomplete transfer of the content of our emotions to the dog.

Once I had this model in mind, it became pretty clear to me what I had done wrong with Emma. Emma was my first dog and when I was growing up most dogs I encountered barked at children—at least they barked at me when I passed by their yards. So, when I got Emma, I was very worried about how she would behave around children. But being a young graduate student, I did not know any children, so the only children Emma and I encountered together were strangers. We would meet a small unfamiliar person that Emma needs to figure out how to react to. She looks to me and I'm anxious, because I'm worried about whether she'll act like the dogs from my youth. After a couple of times, Emma begins to associate this anxiety with those small two-legged creatures and reacts as any dog would when she's anxious—by barking and growling at the source of anxiety. At this point though, my worst fears are realized and I become even more upset and Emma picks up on that, creating a vicious feedback loop. Without realizing it, I've taught my dog to be afraid of children. And that loop only gets further reinforced when the children begin to exhibit fear because they are being barked at and Emma picks up on that anxiety too.

The Problem Is that My Dog Misses the Point

Once I realized what I'd done wrong, it became clear what I needed to do to at least mitigate the problem. I needed to be more aware of how I was reacting to the presence of children and try and send a different message to Emma through emotional contagion. Or as the Dog Whisperer might say, "Change my energy, change her behavior." And it certainly has helped some. It helps even more that I now know some people with children and can expose Emma to them, and I'll be more relaxed because these children aren't strangers.

Still, this cross-species contagion has a lot of potential to go awry because human emotions are different from animal emotions. One difference is that it's not clear that humans and animals have all the same basic emotions. After a decade of living with a dog, I'm leaning in that direction. When I took Emma to obedience school, they told us that dogs couldn't feel guilt. I've definitely seen a guilty dog slink out of the hallway after she has made a mess of one sort or another. I think dogs feel guilt; I just don't think they feel it for very long. I think that is why they tell us not to scold dogs after the fact—not because they can't feel guilt or shame, but because they live in the moment and don't make the cognitive leaps necessary to understand what behavior was bad. Scolding Emma as a puppy did not teach her not go to the bathroom in the house—it taught her to make sure that when she had to go she went somewhere the evidence wouldn't be found. Only months later, did it start to click.

What this illustrates is something that a contemporary philosopher, Martha Nussbaum, writing on the emotions has tried to emphasize (and she is actually trying to revive the way that the ancient Greeks and Romans had looked at the emotions). Nussbaum is challenging the view that the emotions are irrational feelings and nothing more. To make her point she refers to the works of a number of ancient thinkers. For example, the ancient Roman Seneca (around 4 B.C.E.–65 C.E.) in his essay *On Anger* makes it clear that he thinks all emotions are judgments about the world—in the case of anger, it's the judgment that I have been wronged unfairly by someone. Nussbaum and Seneca may go too far in suggesting that emotions are no different from the judgment that "My dog is brown," but they do draw our attention to that fact that emotions have a cognitive component even if there is more to an emotion that that. There are two reasons for accepting the view that emotions are cognitive processes. The first reason can be traced to the notion of "intentionality" (or the "aboutness" of our thoughts) put forward by the philosopher Franz Brentano (1838–1917) in his work *Psychology from an Empirical Standpoint* (London: Routledge, 1995). As Brentano puts it, "every mental phenomenon includes something as object within itself . . . in judgment something is affirmed or denied, in love loved, in hate hated, in desire desired and so on" (pp. 88–89). I don't just think, I always think about *something*. Emotions are usually about things too. I don't just experience fear, I'm afraid of *something*. And when I do experience an emotion without intentionality—maybe because I got it by contagion—I quickly try to figure out why I'm afraid. Intentionality does not travel very well through contagion, so there's a lot of room for mishap. If all emotions were just physiological feelings, they could not have intentionality.

The second reason for thinking that emotions are cognitive is that we usually distinguish emotions by different thoughts. Indignation, the thought that "a wrong has been done," is what Seneca seems to have in mind when he describes anger, but another form of anger might be accompanied by the thought that "I should bring harm to this person"—your basic savage rage. Many emotions might have the same physiological feelings associated with them—for example anxiety and lovesickness—but are accompanied by different objects and different thoughts which is how we usually tell the difference. Many of our most complex emotions— like sublime awe, *ennui*, or *Schadenfreude* (that wonderful German word for taking pleasure in the misery of others), only make sense because they are associated with certain thoughts about the world.

Once we recognize that emotions have a cognitive component, it's easy to see how they can be miscommunicated to our dogs. Dogs can't form those complex thoughts about the world that are attached to our emotions—at best they probably only get the most basic elements like fear or joy. So it's no surprise that Emma does not catch my anxiety concerning how she'll behave around children or my embarrassment when she doesn't behave properly. All she gets is my basic fear and she connects it as best she can to the object we're jointly attending it to. But in this particular case, a lot of nuance got lost and she completely misunderstood that my fear was about her, not the children.

My Dog Is a Window into My World and that Is Very Embarrassing

Perhaps the embarrassment I experience when Emma drops a slobbery chew-toy on my sister-in-law's dry-clean-only black pants and insistently nudges her leg doesn't stem completely from the lack of discipline that behavior might reflect on me. Perhaps it stems more from the thought that this behavior indicates the lack of attention I give to Emma daily. Many of the most embarrassing aspects of canine behavior can be linked to the fact that our dogs often end up expressing those attitudes and behaviors we usually self-censor or things that we are in denial about. A dog that obsessively wants to play tug of war could be the result of an owner who is not very attentive, and so the dog needs to drop the doll in someone's lap in order to get any attention.

I suspect that I am not only embarrassed by the implication that I am not as attentive as I thought I was, but also because Emma's social ineptitude is partly the result of a lack of practice. Her behavior highlights the fact that people don't drop in to my apartment often. One of the reasons Emma's greeting and play behaviors have not been addressed more thoroughly is the lack of opportunity in my hermit-like existence. Or maybe my more relaxed attitude towards fashion meant that I was less aware of the dangers Emma posed to rayon blends. So we see that our dogs' behavior can say a lot about the way we live our lives.

Because of our close contact with our dogs, and the fact that they regard us as their pack leader, it is no surprise that their behavior makes us self-conscious when we see it as a mirror reflecting our own tendencies and traits. Though I can't speak to this from experience, I imagine that a parent's attitude towards their child is much the same way—every aspect of their child seems to be a reflection on them as a person. (Who taught Cayden *that* word?) The difference is that children grow up and are supposed to learn complex emotions like embarrassment. When they act in a manner that shows shamelessness, there is a sense in which their parents can be scrutinized for not passing on this bit of social awareness.

Dogs, on the other hand, could never conceive such a complex emotion. Therefore, the only reason we have to feel embarrassment is when their behavior truly says something about us. And even then, as these examples have tried to illustrate, whether it is something we need to be embarrassed about depends on what we did and how much we think we contributed to the embarrassing behavior.

I've suggested that we judge how embarrassed we should be by referencing what another dog owner would think. This is certainly helpful in determining whether you are doing everything you can to manage a problem with your dog's behavior. However, this world is not populated by dog lovers only. We share this world with cat people, too. And so, we need also to consider how they are affected by our dog's actions and try to strike a balance between their impossible standards and what we can get away with. We certainly can't carry the shame they think we should feel around with us all the time.

As it stands, I would hazard a guess that most of the time we are embarrassed *for* our dog, as opposed to being embarrassed *by* him or her—but in those instances we may be over-reacting (if they're not going to feel the embarrassment in two minutes, why should we?). The moments of true embarrassment *by* our dogs can provide an opportunity for serious reflection, as we ponder what it is about our dog's behavior that bothers us and then consider changing the message that we've sent to our dogs and the rest of the world.

2

What Your Dog Can Teach You about Philosophy of Mind

EDWARD MINAR

Poco, a beautiful, muscular red-and-white Australian Shepherd, was what they call "difficult" from the outset.

Endowed with startling intelligence—distinctly a mixed blessing—Poco quickly learned to determine the means to get what he wanted and to avoid what displeased him. His preferred method was to use his teeth. By the time he was six months old, despite my wife's and my best efforts to curb his "mouthiness," he had advanced to serious biting—no mere puppy nips. As he matured, the problem only got worse, although fortunately he found that he didn't need to resort to using his mouth with other people. Only my wife and I were getting in the way of his calculated courses of action. We were, to say the least, distraught by the whole situation.

Before bringing Poco home, we had done our research, studied up on raising a puppy and training a dog, visited all the local training schools, thoroughly versed ourselves in the lore about his breed and his particular pedigree. Once we got him home, Poco's many talents shone through. The first thing he had learned was "be nice to the kitty", and he had a love-fest going from day one with our male cat. He was the star of his puppy and basic obedience classes and did "heel" and "come" wonderfully. He turned into a true young gentleman with other dogs and was civil if rather distant with other people. We thought we had done everything responsibly, meticulously, and by the book. We had a brilliant, affectionate, well-trained young dog on our hands. But, in certain circumstances in which Poco apparently felt challenged, he bit. There really was no way around it: He was dangerous, and it was scary. On the other hand, we were determined that we could not give up on him.

What's on Poco's Mind?

We worked hard with Poco and tried to make sure that his obedience was spot-on. We exposed him to as many different environments as we could, and he was well-habituated to all kinds of situations that might have put him on emotional overload. We read as much as we could on the basics of dog training and particular protocols for dealing with aggressive behaviors.

We sought help from recognized experts on aggression, nationally renowned as well as local dog trainers, long-time breeders of Australian Shepherds, knowledgeable and sympathetic friends. Diagnoses of Poco's problems from expert quarters were not providing much help, however. Whether he was breaking skin from fear (but of what?), or because of aggression ("my dog bites because he's aggressive"—hmm, sounds like "the sleeping potion puts me to sleep because it possesses a dormative virtue," that is, the power to put one to sleep), or out of a drive to dominate (really? meaning what?), or because he had a screw loose (thanks!), this kind of explanation of Poco's behavior came to seem rather beside the point.

People tended to want to assign blame, generally to us or to Poco's breeder, although sometimes to the dog; or to settle on a label ("dominance aggression," "fear biting," "sport biting"); or to propose a generic solution—"put him down" or "train your dog" being the two most popular. The latter I found particularly disheartening. Nobody who saw Poco could exactly deny that the dog was very well-trained, except for the biting. Beyond doubt, this comprised a major hole in his training! It wasn't going to be addressed, however, by improving his basic obedience or by trying to set up situations in which he would try to bite but be thwarted or persuaded otherwise. In the end, both admonitions to train the dog and speculation about the sources of Poco's behavior underestimated the seriousness of his case. They were disengaged from the particulars. *Where* was the fear or the dominance or the aggression? THIS dog and his relationship to his environment were being left out of these explanations.

As we continued working with Poco, eventually a corner was turned. No single thing transformed Poco into a dog we could live with, just a lot of hard thinking and hard work. A key step was consulting with Brian Kilcommons, who along with Sarah Wilson is co-author of quite possibly the best general-purpose dog book out there.[1] We sent Kilcommons video of a training session and some day-to-day interactions with Poco. We've never met Brian, and it seems to me that his not knowing us (or the dog) "personally" enabled him to discern features of what was going on that had escaped the notice of those closer to home. Egos weren't getting in the way.

Kilcommons pointed out several circumstances in which Poco and I were at cross-purposes. For example, at crucial points, I treated the dog's confusion as willful inattention. As Poco's feeling confused gave way to his feeling backed into a corner, he would become unsure of his alternatives and then turn to his most effective tool for temporarily easing his anxiety—his teeth. A quick learner to say the least, he soon began to anticipate that he could avoid getting into such predicaments in the first place. Bites became pre-emptive strikes. To address the problem, I'd have to learn to distinguish confusion and misunderstanding (usually, on both the dog's part and my own) from disobedience.

The particular lessons from Kilcommons's observations were less important than the general moral I began to appreciate as I became more attuned to the kind of thing he was pointing out: Often, in my eagerness to set things aright, I was trying so hard to do things by the book that *I* was neglecting the dog. In fact, everyone would be better off keeping in check the impulse to regard him as if he were a troubled adolescent human in wolf's clothing. This anthropomorphic projection of our categories and value judgments onto the dog seemed to be tied up with an all-to-human desire to control our dogs by categorizing them according to their "personalities" or characters. And as such, it represented an obstacle to our ability realistically to assess Poco's actual needs and circumstances.

The problem lay *not* in anthropomorphism *per se*, but in the particular form it took here. I was in the process of learning that I had to listen to the dog, let him tell me what was going on. I would have to get better at heeding the terms in which he experienced

---

[1] Brian Kilcommons with Sarah Wilson, *Good Owners, Great Dogs* (New York: Warner, 1992).

and regarded the world. To do so would involve embracing "critical anthropomorphism,"[2] in this case by attending to the relationship between the person and the dog as communication between two minds. Before realizing how to put this critical anthropomorphism into practice, I might well have regarded a training breakdown as a failure of communication. But I had been conceiving of that failure as a matter of a botched attempt to "get through" to the dog—my failure to *seize* control.

Communication, however, is a two-way street, and as often as not its vicissitudes would turn out to lie in my inability or refusal to hear, even to grant that whether I was really listening could be at issue. Hearing the dog, obeying the dictates of the situation, called for more than knowledge of the "inner" ingredients of dog psychology—for example, the elements of dog sensory experience or the content of doggy concepts. All of that would be nice. But the first step toward a more enlightened anthropomorphism would lie in the willingness to *cede* control, in effect to grant that dogs have minds, to recognize their autonomy.

There was nothing like a light bulb moment in dealing with Poco's aggression. No magic words set him on the straight and narrow. If there was a key to his improvement, it lay in realizing that for whatever reason he lacked confidence in the reliability of his environment. Proceeding to build his confidence was an arduous process. He recovered as he came to regard *us* as responsive both to his environment and, I dare say, to his take on it, his point of view. As Poco and we came to terms with the conditions of leading civil lives together, I became increasingly involved with training dogs. Here the focus of my concern could not rest with the abstract, abidingly interesting—perhaps seductive—philosophical questions: "Do dogs have minds? How could we know?" My question became: "What is this dog telling me about what he or she is thinking?" In what follows, I shall try to convey some of what I am learning about dogs' minds after more than ten years of intensive engagement with dog training.

---

[2] Gordon Burghardt, "Cognitive Ethology and Critical Anthropomorphism: A Snake with Two Heads and Hognose Snakes that Play Dead," in Carolyn A. Ristau, ed., *Cognitive Ethology: The Minds of Other Animals—Essays in Honor of Donald R. Griffin* (Hillsdale: Erlbaum), p. 73.

The Dog Trainer's Take

]In our day-to-day dealings with dogs, we talk and think about their beliefs and desires, their pains and pleasures, their feelings and emotions. We wonder at their motivations, ascribe to them character traits, virtues and vices, and sometimes try to think about things from their points of view. In other words, we indulge in anthropomorphism—"the use of human characteristics to describe or explain nonhuman animals."[3]

From various scientific and philosophical quarters, we have been warned of the dangers of anthropomorphizing. Ethologist Marc Hauser cautions that at some point in your experience with animals, "you probably interpreted the event as if you were inside the animal, assuming that the animal thought and felt as you did."[4]

The potential problems with overreaching the limits of our understanding of other animals via this route are obvious. We risk imposing, on the basis of little or no evidence, our ways of thinking and feeling on our non-human animal acquaintances. Certainly we need to be cautious and critical about our projections. Once we begin with this train of thought, a short path beckons toward a far-reaching skepticism about the general "assumption" that animals think and feel more or less as we do. What, after all, do we *really* know about their experiences, let alone the workings of their thought processes (if any)?! In considering how animals act, we had better start from the ground up—carefully observing and describing their behavior without helping ourselves to explanations that presume some kind of knowledge of the mental equipment supposedly lying behind it.

Hauser calls the tendency to anthropomorphize "natural, compelling, and almost irresistible" These predispositions may be more prevalent with respect to dogs than to any other creatures in our ken. Dogs are our familiars, they inhabit our world; to a remarkable extent we share interests and activities with them. In any case, in our day to day dealings with dogs, anthropomorphism runs rampant. Dog owners notoriously humanize their beloved pets, and the notion that Fifi does her obedience "tricks" because she loves us or

---

[3] Alexandra C. Horowitz and Marc Bekoff, "Naturalizing Anthropomorphism: Behavioral Prompts to Our Humanizing of Animals," *Anthrozöos* 20: 1 (2007), p. 23.

[4] Marc Hauser, *Wild Minds* (New York: Holt, 2000), p. xiv.

that Fido urinates on the living room sofa because he is rebellious is more likely to lead to serious training problems than to solutions.

Again, we are tempted to treat dogs as little children in wolves' clothing. For the dog trainer, strictures against the excesses of anthropomorphism are indeed most welcome in the context of dealing with the aforementioned Fifi and Fido. Insisting that a certain dog wants to please its owner or that he or she doesn't like his or her collar is likely to represent a piece of fantasy on the owner's part, a refusal actually to engage with the dog. The cost often turns out to be an "untrainable" dog who learns to ignore what we try to teach him or her.

From the animal trainer's perspective, however, caution can be only one side of the story. Consider what Stanley Coren, psychologist and dog writer, recounts from a conversation with Donald Hebb, an early pioneer of behavioral neuropsychology. Working with chimpanzees during the 1940s, Hebb strove to observe the strict behaviorist, anti-anthropomorphic prohibitions that were *de rigueur* in the scientific study of animal behavior at that time. But things did not go smoothly:

> The truth of the matter is that when I did try to objectively describe the temperaments and behavior patterns of the animals without using the words we use to describe human emotions, all that I ended up with was a giant mess. . . . You really couldn't find any order, pattern, or meaning in that kind of data. . . . I nearly had some fingers bitten off—or worse. . . . I couldn't help but notice that the staff . . . didn't seem to have any problems. They used the same kind of intuition that we normally use when we observe the behavior of people. Because of that they could describe one animal as having a 'dominant personality', another as being 'nervous', another was considered to be 'a friendly beast', still another was 'shy' and there was even one that they claimed was 'bashful'. These were clearly anthropomorphic statements which suggested that, like people, the animals had distinct and individual personalities and that you could use their personalities to predict the animals' future behaviors.[5]

When the trainer reaches the kind of impasse we imagined with Fifi and Fido, he or she must ask, not "Does this dog have something like a human psychology?" but "What's going on with this dog?"

---

[5] Stanley Coren, *Why Does My Dog Act that Way?* (New York: Free Press, 2006), pp. 252–53.

Careful effort must be made to understand the dog's point of view—to partake of that openness to taking the dog seriously that I earlier labeled "critical anthropomorphism." A good example of what this openness entails comes from dog trainer and National Public Radio personality Patricia McConnell. In the human context, *we* interpret hugs as tokens of affection, but, she says, "a dog's version of hugging is a display of social status." Most dogs will, of course, tolerate their humans' excess shows of affection, but some will "take our hugs as serious violations of canine social rules, and lash out in protest."[6] To disabuse ourselves of our anthropomorphic and sentimental desire for the dog to express his or her love in basically human ways, we do not banish anthropomorphism, but strive to be more mindful about it: We take into account what dogs will and will not tolerate as violations of their mores and attempt to be tuned in to the ways they express affection.

Like Hebb's chimp handlers, the dog trainer will not have much use for general skepticism about dog minds. He or she is engaged with the animal from within a particular "form of life," a background of interactions, practices, and interests in relating to dogs, in which the possibility of dogs' not having minds is not taken seriously. Here, as in the case of the gamut of our dealings with human beings, for the most part the trainer is "shutting [his or her] eyes in the face of doubt".[7] In other words, in the dog training context, skepticism gets no real foothold, any more than it gets a grip on my interactions when I am dealing with other human beings. I am no more overcome by doubts about whether my ascriptions of psychological attributes to dogs might represent a fool's game that I am generally worried about whether my family, friends and colleagues might on closer scrutiny turn out to be automata. Skeptical scruples postpone the important business of saving the dog from our failures to talk with him or her.

An Elementary Lesson

The trainer has plenty good reason to turn his or her back on generalized, philosophical skepticism about dog minds. The practice of

---

[6] Patricia McConnell, *For the Love of a Dog* (New York, Ballantine, 2006), p. 16.

[7] "Form of life": Ludwig Wittgenstein, *Philosophical Investigations* (New York: Macmillan, 1953), pp. 174, 226. "Shutting [his or her] eyes . . .": the same book, p. 224.

dog training is bound to make unapologetic (but also severely critical) use of a rich mentalistic toolbox of concepts in understanding the dog. In order to provide a sense of the extent to which this is so, I want to reflect on a relatively simple example of obedience training in action. My youngest Australian Shepherd Bess understands "Sit!" She knows how to sit, and what "Sit!" means, which is to sit where she presently is and not to shift her position until instructed that it's okay to do so. She knows what I'm asking of her when I give her the command, and I'll give her the concept, or anyway a concept, of sitting. For not only does she get that "Sit!" means to sit whenever the command is given, she also distinguishes "Sit!" from "Down!" and other actions in her repertoire—the behavior is under what is called "stimulus control." Moreover, her performance is fluid; she'll sit when told pretty much anywhere, she doesn't have to relearn the command in new contexts. She will hold her sit-stay indefinitely, and if I leave the study where she sits now and go to the kitchen to load them the dishwasher or drive to the store to pick up some milk, she'll be there when I return—although if I'm being sensible, I should leave her in a more comfortable down-stay. She's mostly undaunted by the cats and the other dogs.

Occasionally Bess will break her sit-stay. If I leave her on a sit for a long time, or if her mind wanders, she may decide that it's alright to go down. When this happens—it's virtually always when I'm in sight—I go over and give her a correction, generally a finger in her collar and an upward popping motion with my arm which places her back in the required position, accompanied by a verbal "no, sit." If she's excited at the start of an agility run, she may creep forward toward the start line a bit, not quite getting all the way up but not remaining in place either. What I should do here is to return to her and correct her for this movement—I could be more consistent about doing so, largely because I'm pretty keyed up at the start of a run too. Invariably, in either case, she clearly knows that she's done something wrong. She expects and understands the correction, and in fact will generally return to her assigned position before the physical correction happens, thus putting matters right herself. Also, contrary to how the sit-stay may look, Bess understands that in sitting, she is *doing* something—her performance is not just the accidental, undisturbed continuance of this particular sitting position. For one thing, she will maintain a stay against substantial physical pressure.

As my reference above to "stimulus control" suggests, the training process here could undoubtedly be described in terms of simple behaviorist learning theory—positive reinforcement (reward in the form of treats or play with a toy or praise) increases the likelihood of the desired performance (holding the stay); punishment (collar correction) decreases the likelihood of an undesirable behavior (getting up, thus breaking the stay). What counts as reinforcement and punishment will be defined by the dog's specific needs and preferences, so to intervene effectively in the process, the trainer must actively take these aspects of the dog's mental life into account.

The fluidity of the behavior and the dog's ability to generalize it to new circumstances speaks of intelligence. Training will go more smoothly when the dog comprehends for what he or she is being reinforced and for what he or she is being punished. The attentive dog who's attuned to the training process will be quite savvy about all this. Bess, moreover, sits with *intent*. She knows what she's doing; you might say that her sitting is backed up by right thought about what she is supposed to be doing. I know this because occasionally I pick up hints—some obvious, some fairly subtle—that her mind is not on the sit. Again, she may be thinking about lying down or about charging toward the agility jump directly in front of her. When I catch on to this, I will correct her *before* she moves to break her stay—and she clearly understands that the purport of my doing so is to bring her mind back to the activity at hand.

Understanding is a normative concept. In attributing understanding, and not mere correct performance, to Bess, I grant her something like a grasp (in these contexts, for purposes of sitting) of the difference between right and wrong. The ramifications of this normativity are most readily seen if we consider training errors. There are all kinds of ways the "Sit" exercise can go wrong. The dog may be inadequately clued in about what "Sit" means"; disoriented by an unfamiliar environment; distracted by things going on around her; more interested in something else at the moment.

Perhaps the dog may simply have misheard (although most dogs are not hard of hearing, contrary to what owners appear to believe when their repeated delivery of an ignored command gets louder and louder). Connie Cleveland, dog trainer and columnist in *Front and Finish*, the pre-eminent obedience training magazine, makes a useful distinction between "effort" and "lack of effort" errors.[8] Effort errors involve confusion; the dog is trying, but fails to grasp what is being asked of him or her or to understand the situation in context. Lack of effort errors entail inattentiveness or lack of interest on the part of a dog who knows perfectly well what he or she is doing.

It's of paramount importance that the trainer make this distinction by attending to the dog's state of mind when an error occurs. Where there is a lack of effort error, it makes perfectly good sense to hold the dog accountable for what he or she is doing and to correct the performance with, for example, a collar correction. Here it's important that the correction be well-timed and unambiguous, as the dog needs to be in a position to understand for what specifically he or she is being corrected. With an effort error, on the other hand – the dog is trying but confused—it's not only unfair but unintelligible for the trainer to correct the dog. Obviously, in making this discrimination the trainer judges how things are from the dog's point of view—how the dog perceives the circumstances, what the dog does and does not understand, what the dog's attitude is. Worrying about whether the dog's mind is capacious enough to have an understanding of right and wrong would get in the way of the crucial step of trying to figure out where the dog's mind is at the moment and what to do about it.

Cleveland emphasizes that we need to communicate with our dogs when they go wrong: "Your dog deserves to know that he made a mistake." In saying this, she joins a tradition which does not shy away from what poet and trainer Vicki Hearne calls "the trainer's habit of talking in highly anthropomorphic, *morally* loaded, language"[9]—a language of authority and obedience, rights and responsibilities. For Hearne, this tradition culminates in the writings of her mentor William Koehler, author of the much-reviled but indispensable *The Koehler Method of Dog Training*.

Koehler writes:

Following Nature's precept that creatures be permitted to experience the consequences of their own actions, my methods follow the practice of rewarding the favorable acts and correcting a dog when he knows what he should do but refuses to do it.[10]

---

[8] Connie Cleveland, *Dogs Are Problem Solvers: Handlers Should Be* (2006), p. 3.

[9] Vicki Hearne, *Adam's Task* (New York: Skyhorse, 2007), p. 6.

[10] William Koehler, *The Koehler Method of Dog Training* (New York: Howell, 1996), p. xiii.

There is more meaning and awareness of living in a life that knows the consequences of both favorable and unfavorable action. So let's not deprive the dog of his privilege of experiencing the consequences of right and wrong or, more definitely, punishment as well as praise.

Hearne insists in no uncertain terms that the notion of training as teaching the dog right and wrong is fully meant and not reducible to some behaviorist or mechanical paradigm, where what is really at stake would be managing the dog by checking his or her impulses. For one thing this paradigm leaves out the relationship to the trainer, who on Hearne's view must, for the dog genuinely to obey, exercise his or her authority in commanding the dog in such a way as to allow the dog the consequences of his or her actions. Through training, in obeying, the dog becomes a genuine actor, and thus training makes the dog a citizen of the moral realm.

This gives a whole new weight to the idea that sitting is something that Bess *does*; it is not that she has been coerced or cajoled into controlling her wanton desire to chase the squirrel or to go say "Hi" to the cat, but that she is working, she is doing her thing, and she can be trusted to do so on her own. And (as Hearne has it) this trustworthiness, this respect for the moral law, constitutes her autonomy. Because she takes responsibility for her actions, Bess enjoys the freedom to do as she pleases when she is not working. Part of her becoming a citizen is that, like all right-thinking citizens, she recognizes and respects that there are limits to what her freedom entails. For example, she is not allowed on the dining-room table, despite the cat food that beckons from up there—and it is hard not to think that the range of her understanding here goes well beyond her direct conditioning. Bess enjoys the freedom to work off lead, including walking off lead at heel even amidst the hustle and bustle of large crowds of people, because she sees the necessity of obedience to the law.

Hearne's descriptions of training language have a richer vein, involving the authority of the trainer to give commands, which my account so far leaves out, and Hearne is sublimely aware that many will find her commitments here, in the words of one sympathetic reader, "over the top."[11] "If it sounds queer to talk this way, to suggest a connection between commanding and granting rights," she

---

[11] Raimond Gaita, *The Philosopher's Dog* (New York: Random House, 2002) p. 41.

writes, "it is only because we have failed to be sufficiently anthropomorphic."[12] The "proof" of Hearne's descriptions is that they lend
coherence to the practice of training. The dog obeys. Does the dog
really have a conception of obedience to the law? Must we regard
the dog as an autonomous being? To those who would answer neg-
atively, Hearne provides further description: What licenses talk of
the dog's rights and responsibilities is the trainer's ability and willingness to exercise legitimate authority to command (rather than to
coerce or cajole) the dog. This in turn makes available to the dog
the autonomy to obey. The trainer responds to the dog, but with
the impersonality of legitimate authority, and not out or his or her
own fantasies or needs. Thus the dog acts in response to the law,
not to the arbitrary will of the trainer. The locus of freedom, we
might say, lies in the relationship.

To those who balk at all this—and admittedly, we seem to be
going in a fairly small circle here—Hearne's response, if she does-
n't go on to tell us more stories about training, is terse and *ad
hominem*: What do you know about dogs that entitles you to be
sure that the morally loaded language I have used to make the
point and success of training intelligible doesn't truly apply?

Resistance here is turning one's back on the fact that a human
being relating to a dog is relating to another mind. Hearne's view
of mind is influenced by the philosopher Ludwig Wittgenstein, who
says, with respect to how he perceives another person, "My attitude
towards him is an attitude toward a soul. I am not of the *opinion*
that he has a soul."[13] Similarly, I am not of the opinion that my dog
has a mind. In other words, the trainer's conviction in dog minds
is not some skeptic-proof form of certainty that happens to attach
to a certain hypothesis, but a willingness to go on with the dog on
the path toward autonomy—the path leading to a responsible sit-
stay. Denial that autonomous minds are relating to each other here
is insisting that there must be some kind of hook on which to hang
talk of freedom and responsibility "inside" the mind. We want to
find signal proof of autonomy in some inner ingredient of consciousness rather than in the actions of the dog seen in the context
of the form of life set up by the training. We should expect to do
no better in the parallel search with human beings.

---

[12] Hearne, *Adam's Task*, p. 49.
[13] Wittgenstein, *Philosophical Investigations*, p. 178.

How should we be critically anthropomorphic in training our dogs? As we have seen, we must try to figure out what the dog wants; think through what the dog perceives in a given context; concern ourselves with how the dog understands our desires and intentions and how this affects his or her estimation of his or her responsibilities. We need to know who the dog is. Our successes in training show us that we *can* know this. There will be limits and obstacles, but these present challenges to the imagination—not metaphysical barriers to genuine understanding.

The Status of Dog Psychology

As a dog trainer, I can't do without thinking about what's going on in the mind of the dog I am training. I must utilize the vocabulary of the mental or the resources of folk psychology in order to understand what is going on in the training. I unabashedly embrace anthropomorphism. I counterbalance this confidence with the hope that I have learned from trainers I value to be a critical anthropomorphizer; I strive not to impose my prejudices when trying to grasp what is going on from the dog's point of view.

This simple point has some complex ramifications:

1. To label the trainer's openness to the minds of dogs "anthropomorphic" is somewhat misleading. The trainer's acceptance is not taken on reluctantly; rather, the trainer finds another mind already present in the here and now, no less so than we do in our everyday dealings with each other. Bess and I went on a hike recently. She had fun. She flushed a wild turkey from the high grass in the meadow. She was excited and happy for the rest of the walk. I don't need the rigors of a "theory of mind" to make a particularly difficult inference about her mental state; the complications of interpretation or "mind-reading" don't arise. I saw she was quite pleased with herself. If the notion of anthropomorphism amounts to the idea that we take concepts that are *in the first instance* applicable to human beings and decide to use them with reference to some other beings (dogs), worry about whether to apply them to some (flies), and determine to withhold them from others (stones), then the trainer will be quite baffled by what "in the first instance applicable to human beings" means here—applying my concepts of fun, excitement, happiness and pride to Bess were not "second instances."

Hesitancy about the label "anthropomorphism" is part and parcel of what makes me find the idea of bringing "the vocabulary of the mental" and "the resources of folk psychology" to bear on dogs a little off-putting—as though we make a prior calculation that such tools, at home with respect to human beings, will prove useful in dealing with this alien species. In many cases, understanding the training environment already puts us in relation to other (dog) minds. Here we ought not to think of ourselves as lacking something of great epistemological significance in the absence of a well-justified *theory*. For example, there's no pressing need to back up our mental-state attributions by investigating the complexities of canine neural structure. Nor should we put any particular credence in the notion that in the absence of a theoretical justification for the trainer's stance toward dogs, we make an ungrounded decision to treat them as if they really have minds.

2. The trainer finds a commitment to dog mind indispensable, even unavoidable. To think, however, that such talk is of *merely* pragmatic or instrumental value, and so (somehow) not to be taken literally, seems to me to misrepresent the kind of use that mental talk has in relation to the dog in training. As we have just noted, there is no prior calculation of the advantages and disadvantages. Behavior may be difficult to read, or its significance may be obscure, but this by no means precludes further inquiry into what is really going on. Problems with particular attributions of beliefs or desires to dogs, taken in contexts in which we are trying to motivate the dog or to understand his or her confusion, will be problems of interpretation or technique. Here we may concern ourselves which understandings will *work* to get the dog headed in the right direction. We encounter particular doubts, and resort to particular pragmatic resolutions, only against a background which already grants the reality of what is going on in the dog's mind—which acknowledges that there is really something in particular at issue, that is, what this dog is thinking and feeling and doing. There's training to be done, and to speculate about some further question taking us beyond the particulars to a general doubt about the overall reality of dog minds demotes the *kind* of reality enjoyed by dog minds, a reality that shows up in obedience, to second rate status. At this point this skeptically-minded probing appears to cast doubt on dog minds either by fiat, or as a result of privileging a particular set of descriptive terms—those acceptable to a behavior-

ist, say—as having an exclusive purchase on reality. At this juncture, this insistence begins to seem rather forced and arbitrary.

I've just been voicing my suspicion that skepticism about realistic construals of psychological ascriptions to dogs is based in considerations that would lead to skepticism about other minds in general, and in particular about other *human* minds. If so, we have no reason to single out the trainer's anthropomorphism as in principle confused or mistaken or overblown; the skeptic's sights, that is, are no longer focused on *animal* minds. And then we might say: The other-minds skeptic wants to step outside of the forms of life which give meaning to our understandings of ourselves and others; and, as consideration of training dogs and other animals shows, these forms of life include relations to non-human minds.

Dogs Do Have Minds

I've been saying that the trainer's perspective should suggest that dog minds are, though different, real; or anyway that we have no compelling reason to assert otherwise. Putting this another way, there is no privileged perspective from which we could determine that in training a dog we are not *really* dealing with a mind. The burden is not to refute the skeptical voice about dog minds that we harbor within us, but to let the allegedly anthropomorphizing practices of trainers show us something about what it is to know dog minds, and thus something about the kind of things dogs, and at least their minds if not also ours, might be.

Dog minds show up in the patterns of significance that constitute the particular relationships trainers and dogs forge. We are blind to something if we keep insisting that what the dog might *really* be thinking remains at best beyond our reach, a hidden inner ingredient.

What Happened to Poco and Me

Poco's idiosyncrasies remain. But his story has a good ending; he's had a rich, full and happy life and he's contributed immeasurably to mine. In the meantime, through classes and seminars, books and articles, innumerable conversations, and above all work with our dogs (Poco and two other Australian Shepherds, Guinan and Bess who understands "Sit!"), my wife Diana Nagel and I absorbed an immense amount about dog training, dog thinking, and dealing with "problem" dogs.

Eventually we took over the training classes at the obedience school we had settled on as a supportive environment in which to work on Poco's issues, and we're now the training directors at a dog school we helped to open. Each dog we work with presents us new challenges; even more interesting is helping people figure out their relationships to their dogs.

This chapter is written in gratitude to the many people involved with dogs to whom I owe an intellectual debt, and to Poco, still amazing me in his otherness and thrilling me with his brilliance. At the risk of being presumptuous, I leave you with an invitation: If you want to learn something about what mind is, and some of mind's limits and possibilities, train your dog. Your efforts will not disappoint.[14]

---

[14] Thanks especially to Randall Havas and Diana Nagel. To a remarkable extent, writing this chapter has become an effort to come to terms with the writings of the late Vicki Hearne. Her *Adam's Task* should be considered essential reading for philosophers interested in dogs and in the provinces of mind.

3

Bitches Gone Wild: On Canine Liberty

WEAVER SANTANIELLO

I had an hour to kill at the mall while Sears was fixing my flat tire, so I wandered into a pet store to buy some toys for Turbo. A miniature dachshund, with a cardboard sign above her cage reading "Dawn," caught my eye. The clerk asked: "Do you want to hold her?" "No," I replied, "I need to go pick up my car." In an afterthought, I shrugged: "Oh, why not." The gate was opened and Dawn was taken out and placed into my arms. Her eyes were glazed and watery, she had a week's worth of tears caked on her face, and the adorable but sickly dapple barely weighed four pounds. She placed her head on my left shoulder and sighed.

Tempted to take her from that place, excerpts from *The Complete Idiot's Guide to Choosing, Training, and Raising a Dog* rang in my ears:

- *Never* **buy a puppy from a pet store—they buy from puppy mills**

- **When buying from a reputable breeder, check to see that the dog's eyes are alert and clear, if not, choose another pup**

- **Don't choose the runt from the litter—they often have a Napoleon complex**

- **Spend a sufficient amount of time observing the puppies—if necessary, visit the breeder several times**

before making a final decision. Do *not* be hasty—your choice will lastingly affect your life.[1]

I turned to the clerk and said: "I'll take her." I then urged: "Hurry up; I need to pick up my car before they close at nine." She scrambled for a cloth and wiped Dawn's face. I found a crate, asked if they had a cardboard box I could put her in to take her home (like they have for parakeets), and fled the mall with "Plato" in tow.

tire change from Sears:	**$148.00**
new pup from the pet store:	**$750.00**
pet supplies and accessories:	**$95.00**

—one hundred and eighty-seven dollars per pound: priceless.

She sat on my lap in the car all the way home chewing on a smoked pig ear.

Crating and Canine Liberty

Ever since I can remember, the sight of dogs in pet stores in small crates behind steel bars has distressed me. Even to the point of rescuing Plato. When obtaining Turbo, I had planned for him. But Plato was a whim, based partly on pity for her and the prison-like conditions I sought to free her from. This is not to say that I had not pondered getting another pup—a friend for Turbo. But I never imagined it would happen like that!

When Turbo joined the household a year and-a-half before Plato, I struggled with the notion of crate training. I researched and pondered the ethical pros and cons of the issue. One side argued that dogs are meant to be free, and that containing them in crates was akin to putting them in jail. An information sheet from the vet held that placing dogs in crates was not inhumane, but that it would be cruel to allow a puppy to wander around the house unsupervised, subjected to all types of dangers, such as chewing on electrical cords. The pamphlet noted that the crate served several purposes:

---

[1] Sarah Hodgson, *The Complete Idiot's Guide to Choosing, Training, and Raising a Dog* (Alpha, 1996).

- **It cuts down the time it takes to housebreak a pet.** The puppy quickly learns that his crate is his instinctual den that he wants to keep clean. The notion of inside and outside extends to the actual home, and he tries not to eliminate until he's outside.

- **It allows the owner peace of mind when not at home, and the pet also feels secure.**

- **It allows owners to travel with their pets. Many hotels allow pets with crates, and pets on airlines must be crated.**

- **The pet can enjoy the security and privacy of his den when stressed out, sick, or tired.**

Many other sources that supported crating were uniform on their rules concerning proper use. Most importantly, they held that the dog should not be confined for more than four to six hours at a time; that the crate should be large enough for the dog to stand up and stretch on its side; and that the dog should also enjoy lots of freedom *from* the crate. The two main points were that the crate should be used as a special place for the dog, and *never* as a place of punishment.

Two Concepts of Liberty

At Oxford University in 1958, political philosopher Isaiah Berlin delivered his famous lecture, "Two Concepts of Liberty." Based on that lecture, later published as an essay, many philosophers have commented on Berlin's distinction between two types of freedom: negative and positive liberty.

Negative freedom is the absence of coercion or restraint by other people (freedom *from*), whereas positive freedom implies the notion of choice and possibility (freedom *for*). Negative freedom is the traditional and classical liberal notion of liberty: freedom means things that no one, especially the government, may hinder us from doing. So, free speech is purely negative: the government may not stop us saying what we feel like saying. A classic statement of the case for negative freedom is John Stuart Mill's *On Liberty* (1859), arguing that "the only purpose for which power can be rightfully exercised over any member of a civilized community, against his will, is to prevent harm to others."[2] According to Mill, an individual's own good, either physical or moral, is not a sufficient warrant for outside intervention.

Positive liberty refers to an individual's opportunities to fulfil the potential of his or her authentic self. Berlin associated positive liberty with the idea of self-mastery and autonomy, major concepts previously employed by thinkers fundamentally at odds in their respective philosophies, such as Immanuel Kant (1724–1804) and Friedrich Nietzsche (1844–1900). Kant stressed personal autonomy, good will, and moral duty toward others; Nietzsche praised self-mastery, individual creativity, and separatism from the mob.

Kant's systematic approach elevated the primacy of reason as that which clearly separated humans from animals. A more passionate and intuitive Nietzsche, writing in a Darwinian era, stressed that humans are animals but that we can rise above the beasts with our ability to overcome our "herd instincts," and free ourselves from conventional ways of thinking. According to Nietzsche, decadent mass movements, especially Christianity and other religions, tend to inhibit any human progress over the animal realm: "humanity does not progress . . . it does not even exist."[3]

Crating Dogs for Their Positive Freedom

Is it morally acceptable to restrict dogs' negative liberty by putting them in crates? Following the standard definition of jail as short-term incarceration (usually less than one year), and prison as long term confinement (usually a sentence of more than a year), the crate can serve as all or none of these.

Puppy mills can be regarded as cruel oppressive prisons, where breeding operations are perpetuated solely for financial gain. In the mills, dogs virtually spend their entire lives crated and are prone to filthy conditions, infections, and parasites. They are force-bred and there is no concern whatsoever for their physical health or psychological well-being. The animals get so bored and stir crazy in small crates, they often chase their tails in circles for hours and even days at a time. As pack animals, they receive no affection. The mills typify the harshest form of solitary confinement for innocent studs and bitches. And, yes, the dastardly mill entrepreneurs often

---

[2] John Stuart Mill, *On Liberty* (Indianapolis: Library of Liberal Arts), p. 13.
[3] Friedrich Nietzsche, *The Will to Power* (Vintage, 1967), section 90.

sell their stock to retail pet stores. Behavioral problems and illness often plague these puppies.

The cages in pet stores can be seen as jails; a temporary holding cell that contains a pet until a consumer provides bail. And finally, the crate at home, if used properly, can serve as a humane constraint to keep the puppy—or dog—safe and free from need, danger, and fear.

Granted, dogs will react differently to crates. Some dogs simply cannot tolerate them and shouldn't be forced to. But for the most part, crates can serve as safe havens for pets if owners use them correctly. Turbo tends to go to his crate for peace of mind when stressed out (usually when the vacuum appears); Plato uses her crate much less and only when she's sick (usually with a back ailment). But the point is that crates are viewed by the dogs as welcoming dens. Humans can also use the crates as forms of punishment, oppression, and torture that canines should be free *from*.

Sometimes I wonder if I did the right thing by buying both Turbo and Plato from pet stores. Next time, I'll seek out a trustworthy breeder and visit them in person. With that said, I take solace in granting two fantastic dogs independence, but fear that I contributed to the systemic oppression of the dreaded mills. To ease my conscience, I once wrote a sincere note to Turbo's breeder in Lebanon, Missouri, thanking them for producing such a great, cool dog. I included his one-year-old birthday picture, splashing in his new, blue, kiddie pool.

They never wrote back.

Lady, Tramp, and Scamp

Walt Disney's film *Lady and the Tramp II: Scamp's Adventure*, is a wonderful illustration of Berlin's two concepts of liberty. Tramp and Lady's mischievous puppy, Scamp, has a good home but wants to be a "real dog" that can run wild. Longing for independence during the week of July 4th, Scamp ventures far from home and meets a stray named Angel, who introduces him to the Junkyard Dogs led by Meanie Buster, whose motto is: "Every dog for himself."

Scamp is thrilled to escape the rules of the house, all fences and boundaries, dreaded baths, visits to the vet, and his human and canine guardians who "crush" him with hugs. Scamp reasons: "What good are teeth and claws if you can never use them?" Free to "wet where he wants," and from the absence of coercion and restraint from his family (negative freedom), Scamp attains the positive freedom of choice and possibility with his decision to join the Junkyard Dogs.   However, before he's accepted into the pack, Scamp has to prove himself to them. He has to demonstrate that he is not an elite house dog and that he can survive on the streets as a rugged, underclass hound. After successfully completing several trials and rituals, Scamp is joyful when he finally becomes footloose and collar free.

Berlin's notion of positive freedom also includes the freedom from want and fear: this is the element of liberation that Scamp is unable to attain as a fugitive. Every day he has to fetch his own meals, dodge dog catchers, fight off canine bullies, even while romping bountifully with Angel. However, as time goes by, Angel laments to Scamp that he, unlike her, was lucky to have had such a nice home. And Scamp's apprehension and danger continues to increase: he is almost hit by a train, nearly drowns, ends up in a dog pound, and finally comes to realize that he prefers the comforts of home and family to his free-wheeling, yet endangered, life. He retrieves his collar and badge of honor (dog tag) from the junkyard, and returns home (bringing Angel along).

When Scamp apologizes for running away, his father responds that they can "go down to the river" once in a while and bay at the moon. Tramp understands more fully that his son needs a bit more adventure than his well-behaved daughters who love their baths. And Lady, appalled by Scamp's junkyard stench, tempers her disgust and fondly says that his bath "can wait" for awhile. The film ends with Scamp scowling in a bubble bath, but he is happily at home for good.

The film paints an accurate portrait of the way dog owners typically have to juggle positive and negative freedom with regard to the health and safety of their pets. For example, reducing a dog's "freedom to" (run into the street, jump on guests, eat your dinner off the table when your back is turned), we at the same time increase the dog's "freedom from" (the risk of getting hit by a car, the dislike of guests, and so on).

Scamp initially attained *negative* freedom from virtually all constraint when running away from home; chose *positive* freedom for independent living with the Junkyard Dogs; was unable to attain *positive* freedom from want and fear on the hazardous streets and alleys; and finally again chose *positive* freedom involving some restraint, by returning home to a more secure life. After living on both sides of the railroad tracks, Scamp concluded that he could still be self-autonomous with constraints, and that some constraints actually allowed him greater freedom from danger.

All Tied Up with No Place to Go

One day in class when discussing animal ethics, a student proclaimed that taking wolves from the wild and domesticating them with collars and leashes was similar to slavery. I had to stop myself from laughing out loud. His remark assumed a master-slave relationship between owner and pet. And I smirked because I instantly thought: "My dogs have it *made. They* rule the roost." Further, when discussing mercy killing earlier in the semester, this same student told a story of life on a farm with a very ill rabbit who was plagued for years with blindness, chronic arthritis, and then cancer. He proudly stated that he refused to honor his mother's wish to euthanize the pet, because he saw the rabbit's continuous suffering as somewhat romantic and religiously redemptive. He concluded: if pets can persevere, humans should too. I found it implausible that on the one hand, he had no problem prolonging his rabbit's horrid, painful life. Yet on the other hand, sternly objected to domesticating dogs because placing them in homes was "cruel" and unnatural. Also, his radical statement about collars and chains not only demeaned victims of slavery, it was similar to the controversial ad by PETA (People for the Ethical Treatment of Animals) which compared factory farming to the Nazi Holocaust.

Several years ago, inspired by a girl who was attacked by a family dog chained in the backyard, PETA launched an "Unchain a Dog" campaign aimed toward educating people about the connection between tethering and aggression. Armed with slogans such as "Keep Your Family Safe: Chain Your Door, Not Your Dog," PETA elevated national awareness toward "Breaking the Chain of Cruelty and Danger." PETA stressed that keeping dogs chained was cruel; it violated dogs' nature as social pack animals, confined to a lonely, unsupervised life. PETA also stressed the danger of chained dogs to humans and other animals within their striking range. Not free to romp with other dogs or people, and not free to retreat in the face of danger, many animal experts agree that aggression and stress increase over time, and can very well lead to mauling. According to Karen Delise, author of *Fatal Dog Attacks*, canines are "fight or flight" animals. A chain limits the dog's space; when confronted with a threat, the animal cannot flee so she must fight. Consequently, tragedies often occur to humans (especially small children), and frantic dogs often hang themselves off decks and backyard cable runs.[4]

Many years ago, my friend's neighbor kept their large dog chained in the front yard 24/7. With each passerby, the dog snarled and flailed itself wildly, often jumping on the hood of a dilapidated car that was parked in their dirt driveway. I felt bad for the "mad" dog that lived its life on the end of a chain, but was scared shitless of him. I knew if he got loose he'd be deadly. Over time, I chose to avoid him on my path at all costs. But I should have reported his crazy owners to the Animal Protection and Rescue League.

I applaud PETA's mantra: "Friends Don't Chain Friends. Bring Your Dogs Inside." We should give our animals freedom by walking them daily or containing them safely with fences. Many communities throughout the United States now have safe, legal and enclosed dog runs and dog parks where well-mannered puppies and dogs can play together off-leash. But my student's argument was not only that we should free dogs from chains and collars. His point was also that we should never have domesticated wolves to begin with—approximately 12,000 years ago—and that now we should unshackle dogs from their chains and let them "run wild" again. In this sense, he opposed domestic unions between humans and canines.

Shock Collars: The Sounds of Silence

I won't waste time arguing that collars, tags, leashes, and even microchips are essential for a pet's autonomy and safety: *every two seconds a family pet is lost.*[5] But electric shock collars may pose more of an ethical issue. These collars emit a small shock and are typically used for training dogs, keeping them from barking, and, in conjunction with underground wire fences, to keep

---

[4] Karen Delise, *Fatal Dog Attacks* (Anubis, 2002).

[5] http://www.sherlockbones.com/Keeping_Pets_Safe.php. Approximately every two seconds a dog or cat is put to death because there are not enough homes for our current pet population. Having pets spayed/neutered will save lives: www.cheyenneanimalshelter.org/animal_control.aspx.

them contained. Adopting the notion that collars, like crates, are not cruel in themselves, I'll try to sort out their positive uses and abuses.

In training dogs, dog handlers can use a remote control to instantly correct a dog's undesirable action. In most cases, the electric stimulation can be increased at the handler's will. Dogs can be controlled not to dig, chew furniture, jump on guests, bark, chase cars, *ad infinitum*. I suppose that if a handler wanted a dog not to eat steak, she could accomplish that too. Advocates of these training devices, well aware of their potential for misuse, insist they should be used sparingly, especially when conventional methods have proven ineffective. They also claim that the collars don't cause any physiological or neurological harm. Opponents of these devices beg to differ.

Barking collars vary (from training collars with remotes), in that the device is preset to deliver a shock after the dog starts to bark (yet they can also be controlled by remotes when their owners are present). And finally, proximity collars designate an electric current that warns the animal that it is near another device (usually a wire fence) in order to prevent or deter the animal from entering or leaving any land. Often, proximity collars emit a warning sound. Animals only receives a shock if they cross a particular boundary.

When pondering the use of a bark collar for Turbo, who is prone to nuisance barking, the first question I asked was if shock collars actually "hurt" a dog. Not surprisingly, the manufacturers and sellers of the collars said that the dog would not feel pain but a slight "sensation." A sensation of what?

I used a bark collar on nineteen-pound Turbo several times and it seemed to work without causing him undue distress. I then used it once on ten-pound Plato, while we were sitting on the front porch. As a dog passed by she barked. Then she yelped. Then she twitched off all fours into the air. I instantly tore it off her neck and threw it away. Plato's reaction scared me; her response led me to believe that the collar actually harmed her. My father, who was also present, said that the shock just scared *her*, but that it didn't "hurt" her. And my mother scolded both of us: "How would *you* like it if every time you talked you received a shock in *your* neck." My mother anthropomorphized Plato's incident, but her point was well-taken: there was national outrage when a ten-year-old boy from Toledo was forced by his parents to "wear a remote-controlled shock collar and was repeatedly zapped by the device meant to train animals."[6]

Renaissance mathematician, physicist, and philosopher, René Descartes (1596–1650), believed that animals don't feel pain. He even performed vivisections on dogs without anesthesia! Descartes, a dualist, thought that humans consist of body (matter) and soul (mind-spirit). The "body" ticks like a clock; for instance, our heart beats on its own and we need not consciously do anything to keep it ticking. Our souls are conscious spirits; the soul is eternal while the body is not.

Descartes held that animals don't have souls; thus, concluded that they can't feel pain. Descartes was aware that dogs yelp when their feet are stepped on or when he cut them open, but viewed their response as automatic stimuli similar to that of a ticking clock. Like a clock, a dog can't be self-conscious of its pain so dogs can't really feel it. Put another way, perhaps on some level the pain is felt by the dog, causing it to react. But the dog isn't aware that *they* are feeling it because they have no soul (or self-consciousness). Thankfully, today, we know that animals indeed feel pain. But along with modern science, contemporary philosophers, such as Peter Singer, have constructed arguments against their counterparts, such as Descartes.[7]

The modern-day controversy regarding shock collars somewhat resonates with medieval thought regarding dogs and pain. As stated, companies who manufacture collars typically argue that shocks don't hurt dogs; animal activists insist that they do. Perhaps the notion of "hurt" is problematic.

For instance, when I accidentally touched the prong of Turbo's collar, which was on the lowest setting, I received an uncomfortable buzz on the tip of my finger. It was similar to the time I received a shock when touching a live electrical wire changing a smoke alarm. Unlike getting blood taken from my arm with a needle, the shock didn't "hurt" locally like that. But in some senses the shock was worse; it sent a rapid, chilling surge throughout my entire body that was petrifying. I was spooked to death and was barely able to finish installing the alarm. I certainly never wanted to get shocked again.

---

[6] www.cleveland.com/news/plaindealer/index.ssf?/base/news/1178268346121040 .xml&coll=2.

[7] "Animals Do Feel Pain," Peter Singer, www.animal-rights-library.com/texts-m/singer03.htm

I suppose that if the shock level of a dog collar is turned up to higher levels, it would resemble my experience with the smoke alarm. If the collar levels went even higher, perhaps it might feel like getting hit by lightning (which I have not experienced). If the shock collars went as high as we could possibly make or take them; well, I have never been electrocuted but I bet it would hurt!

An alternative to the shock collar is the citronella collar. When a dog barks, it emits a scent that the pet finds offensive; distracted, they cease barking. A sonic collar is also useful; it emits a high pitched sound that deters barking. These collars have been very effective for Turbo and Plato. Plato does not yelp with these collars; and the sonic collars are suggested for use with "small" dogs.

If asked, I would discourage electric barking collars (for dogs of all sizes) in favor of more humane alternatives, such as citronella collars and those that emit sounds. With caution, I would approve (electric) proximity collars. They adequately warn dogs and keep them free from danger, and also provide freedom of choice for a dog not to cross a particular line. However, when asking Turbo's groomer her views concerning proximity collars, she told me a true story about a golden retriever who defied an underground fence chasing a deer. The long prongs on the collar burned two holes into his neck.

With that said, oftentimes the best case scenario is a good ol' fashioned fence: it keeps things out of your yard, and keeps the dog in. For those unable to build conventional fences (for geographic, financial, or other reasons), underground wire fences with proximity collars are a fine choice. I would criminalize the use of training collars with remotes, for they can easily promote an abusive master-slave relationship between insensible humans and their pets, as I discuss in the next section.

Masters, Slaves, or Best Friends?

Research has and continues to be conducted on the physiological and neurological effects that electric shock collars have on dogs.[8] Even in the unlikely event that scientists conclude that electrical currents have no ill effects, a *philosophical* point should address the consequences that these devices may have on the *relationship*

---

[8] For a summation of results, see http://en.wikipedia.org/wiki/Shock_collars, "Shock Collars," Reference.com (2007).

between pets and owners. In *Beyond Good and Evil*, Nietzsche laments that philosophy has been taken over by science and reduced to a "theory of knowledge." In a section entitled, "What is Noble?" he speaks at length about the "order of rank" involving the ruling group and the ruled. Conceding that master and slave moralities can exist within a "single soul," he nonetheless makes clear distinctions between the noble person, who knows how to command, and the "doglike people who allow themselves to be maltreated."[9] Nietzsche's insight, although addressing human societies, applies to the situation concerning the control of dogs through the use of remotes and electric shocks: there is something fundamentally bizarre imagining a reckless pet owner sitting on a couch pushing remote control buttons to make Fido mind—or to fetch his beer from the fridge. By Nietzsche's standards, the owner is not a noble, but a slave with no authority to command. And according to Nietzsche, those who cannot command should obey.

To clarify: regarding bark collars, I prefer citronella and sonic collars to shock collars. I approve proximity collars that emit warning sounds before delivering a shock. I would ban shock training collars with remotes, because of their enormous potential for abuse by humans (including children), who could shock a dog whenever they wanted for whatever reason. Training a dog should be akin to guardianship, not mastery or ownership. And remote controls that are able to zap dogs from far distances without adequate commands or human instruction could very well hinder pet-owner relationships. Who would want to train a dog like that? Granted, some people might use the remotes wisely, but I suspect many others would not.[10] For instance, it seems to me that "training" a family puppy with a shock remote, at minimum, suggests human slothfulness and a need for immediate gratification through power and control. The shock remote tends to instantly assert the handler's ultimate authority over the pet, as opposed to developing a gradual give and take guardianship through trial and error. (Even an

---

[9] Friedrich Nietzsche, *Beyond Good and Evil* (Vintage, 1966), Section 260.

[10] For an example of one who advocates electric training collars, see Ed Frawley's philosophy of electric collar training: http://leerburg.com/qaelectric.htm. He sells remote shock collars ranging from $174.95 to $664.99, with detailed instructions for use. Even if he has (humanely) attained mastery with the collars, the brief do's and don'ts listed on his site seem complicated for the average pet owner. For an opponents' view of electric training collars, see www.naturalmatters.net/newsview.asp?news=1850.

infant could inadvertently have power over a Doberman Pinscher by randomly pushing shock buttons.) Put another way, the remotes can easily pass from the innocent, to the inexperienced, to the sadistic—and beyond—causing dogs unwarranted distress.

Let's be honest: sometimes we use modern technology because we either can't command our dogs or don't have the time or inclination to do so. In this respect, an over-reliance on technology can hinder a healthy relationship between pet and owner. Even with the many positive uses of technology at our disposal, we should still continue to uphold our relationships with pets based on classic philosophical notions of friendship, dating back to Plato and Aristotle.

The Beginning of a Beautiful Friendship

Seven years ago, before buying Turbo, I read *The Idiots Guide to Choosing, Training, and Raising a Dog*. While growing up, we had several beloved dachshunds in our household; however, I never owned a pet (except for a parakeet), and wanted to be fully prepared as a guardian. Recovering from a life-threatening illness prompted my desire for a new, loyal companion. I thought it was time to commit responsibly to a long-term relationship, but was worried that I'd pick a dog I'd end up disliking. After doing research for several weeks on various dog breeds and temperaments, I decided to buy a miniature schnauzer because they are good, compact watch dogs who don't shed. So, after more deliberation, one summer day I picked up the phone and took the plunge. I asked the pet store if they had a *miniature* schnauzer. They did. My girlfriend and I arrived there fifteen minutes later. I went into a small room with the little black pup. He was adorable. Although very friendly, he naturally seemed a bit frightened. After ten minutes or so he was calm and we were having a pleasant visit. I liked him well-enough, but kept asking myself: "Is this the right dog for me?"

My friend poked her head in the door: "Weave, come here. You need to see this dog—he's crazy." I entered another small space. A wheaten-colored pup was running and barking, sliding wildly across the floor chasing a ball. As he romped after the ball, I vied for his attention. Minutes later I was laughing to the clerk: "A Cairn terrier? I've never heard of them."

Today, he's as super-charged as he was then.

4

Mess With My Dog and You Mess With My Mind

PAUL LOADER

What's the difference between a man and a dog? Answer: A man wears trousers, a dog—pants.

This used to be one of my favourite jokes but it may be under threat from philosophy, for if one takes certain philosophical considerations seriously the joke might have to be changed to: "What's the difference between a man and a dog? Answer: Not that great in certain circumstances where the dog might be viewed as part of the man's mind."

This version of the joke, despite possessing a certain surreal quality, has the disadvantage of not being funny. Lack of humor, however, does not necessarily make for lack of truth. So, is there any truth in this view of dogs and their human owners, or is this just a bad joke?

Otto and His Notebook

We begin with a story that does not feature any dogs at all but rather two human beings called Otto and Inga. The story was told by Andy Clark and David Chalmers in a well-known article called "The Extended Mind" (1998) and goes like this:

> Otto has Alzheimer's Disease and his memory suffers as a result. His strategy for dealing with this is to write down important information in a notebook that he carries with him. Inga, unlike Otto, doesn't have Alzheimer's and so has normal memory function. Both Otto and Inga hear separately of an exhibition at the Museum of Modern Art on 53rd Street and both decide that they would like to go. Inga pauses to recall

where the museum is before heading off there. Otto looks up the location of the museum in his notebook before he too heads off there.

This is more or less all there is to the story. Admittedly it's somewhat lacking in character development or narrative complexity. However a certain amount of 'drama' is created by the authors' subsequent analysis of it. Clark and Chalmers make several claims about the events in this story.

Firstly, they claim that, just as Inga wanted to go to the museum and believed it was on 53rd Street, so the same can be said of Otto. This seems relatively uncontroversial. Slightly more contentious is their second claim which is that both Otto and Inga believed that the museum was on 53rd Street before they consulted their information repositories (Inga's memory and Otto's notebook). This might seem like an odd thing to say. However if we consider how we usually talk about beliefs then it might seem less unreasonable, at least in Inga's case. It's not part of our ordinary conception of 'beliefs' that someone necessarily has to be consciously entertaining a belief in order to be said to have that belief.

Tony (another character, who doesn't appear in this story) might be said to 'have the belief' that the first dog in space was called Laika but this doesn't mean he is currently entertaining such a belief, and indeed he might have to pause to think when asked who the first dog in space was. Likewise the fact that Inga pauses to recall where the museum is, need not imply that she didn't always believe it was on 53rd Street. So far so good.

And what of Otto? This is where things start to get tricky. Clark and Chalmers's position seems to be that the only difference between the case of Otto and the case of Inga is in the location of the item looked up. Otto looks up information in his notebook and Inga 'looks up' the information in her head. There's no reason, they then argue, why the mere physical location of the item looked up should make any difference to how one describes their mental states. Therefore if Inga can be reasonably described as having had her belief before she looked in her memory then Otto can be reasonably described as having had his belief before he looked in his notebook.

There are a number of assumptions that a reader might like to take issue with here. Does Inga really 'look up' information in the same sense that Otto does? Doesn't she really just 'look things up' in a derivative sense? And even if she does 'look things up', is the information that she looks up literally located 'in her head' in the same way that Otto's information is literally located in his diary?

We will pass such objections by for the time being on the grounds that we will never get to talk of dogs if we start to consider them now—though admittedly this may constitute one of the lamest excuses given for avoiding thorny issues in philosophy. However, disgruntled readers might like to know that others before them have shared their disgruntlement and committed it to print.[1]

To continue, then: If we're able to say that Otto had his belief before he looked in his notebook, this is only because that belief was itself contained in his notebook—for where else could it be? Just as Inga's belief was "sitting somewhere in memory waiting to be accessed" so Otto's belief was sitting somewhere in his notebook waiting to be accessed. We thus have a situation where "a belief is simply not in the head" but is "constituted partly by features of the environment." The notebook, in short, is part of Otto's mind. Otto's mind has become extended beyond his skull and now includes the notebook.

It's not entirely clear from Clark and Chalmers's story whether the notebook itself, or the information it contains, is part of Otto's mind. There's also some ambiguity as to whether this information constitutes part of Otto's 'beliefs' or his 'memory', or both.

Here again readers might feel more than a little annoyed. Those in possession of large dogs might even feel like turning them on Clark and Chalmers. Are we seriously suggesting that just because Otto uses a notebook as an 'aide-mémoire', it should literally count as part of his mind? In that case why aren't the books on my bookshelf, or for that matter all the information on the internet, part of my extended mind? Suppose I tie a knot in my dog's tail to remind me to feed him when I come home from work—is that knot part of my extended mind?

Clark and Chalmers have answers to these and similar questions. Otto's notebook is only usefully viewable as part of his mind because it fulfils certain other conditions not fulfilled by the internet, the books on my bookshelf, or my dog's knotted tail. These conditions include:

---

[1] See Andy Clark's own "Memento's Revenge" (2003) for an attempt to respond to similar objections, as well as to many other objections.

- **The item in question must be 'reliably available'. Otto's notebook, for example, is generally kept about his person (just as Inga's head is kept about her person).**

- **The information 'stored' within the item must be 'readily accessible'. Otto has no more problem opening his notebook and perusing its contents than Inga has recalling information from memory.**

- **The item must be 'typically invoked' as a source of information and any information retrieved be 'automatically endorsed'.** Otto will typically check in his notebook before answering that he doesn't know something, and once he has retrieved information from this source he does not doubt it but uses it as a 'guide to action'. In the same way Inga relies on her memory in her everyday dealings with the world and will typically accept its verdict without question.

Looking at these conditions, then, it might be suggested that the Internet, even if 'reliably available' on a portable device, would be less likely to count as part of someone's extended mind because, as Clark and Chalmers say, one would not generally want to automatically endorse any information found via Google. As for the other examples, neither the books on my bookshelf nor the knot in my dogs tail fulfil the condition of being 'reliably available' (and hence of being 'readily accessible') in most circumstances.

Otto and His Dog

At this point we might be struck by the following thought. Supposing, instead of a mere knot in my dog's tail I had a whole dog that fulfilled all of the above conditions—a dog that was 'reliably available', and that I would typically turn to for 'readily accessible' information which I would then 'automatically endorse'. Would that dog count as part of my Extended Mind according to Clark and Chalmers's account?

Initially one might think it hard to find such a dog. Indeed one might be skeptical about whether dogs generally do much 'information providing' at all. Many dog-owning readers might think that their own dog provides them with scant information about the world other than that the universe contains at least one dog and that that dog smells a bit musty.

A moment's reflection, however, reveals that a dog will quite often provide its owners with different types of information about the world. A clear example is the dog who barks when he hears someone coming up the driveway. Here the dog might quite reasonably be seen as conveying the information that there is someone coming up the driveway. Our only problem in this situation is with the reliability of the information conveyed, for sometimes that same dog might just jump up and start barking his head off for no apparent reason. (Anyone who has lived with a dog can confirm this.) Thus one wouldn't want to 'typically invoke' nor 'automatically endorse' the information provided by such a dog. Nor would one have him constantly in one's company as sole provider of important information about the world.

However the situation's different if we have a dog who has been trained to provide information about the world in a reliable and dependable fashion to an owner with a sensory impairment. Such is the case with guide dogs for blind people. ('Hearing dogs' for deaf people are another example.)

Let's reimagine the Otto scenario then. This time Otto does not have Alzheimer's Disease or a notebook. Instead he is blind and has a guide dog. Here, as we have suggested, all of Clark and Chalmers's conditions seem to have been met:

- **The dog would probably accompany Otto for much of his day and so be as 'reliably available' as the notebook.**

- **The dog would provide Otto with a variety of types of information such as where obstacles are, where the kerb is and whether a passageway is too narrow to fit through.** Strictly speaking, he would not be able to tell Otto whether it's safe to cross the road because he could not, for example, decipher changes in traffic lights. Nevertheless he would have been trained to selectively disobey instructions such as 'forward' if obeying them would involve stepping into oncoming traffic or other dangerous situations, and thus he would effectively be able to provide the information that it's not safe to cross the road.

- **This information would be 'readily accessible' because the dog's extensive training would have equipped it to provide such information in an efficient manner, for example by ignoring distractions and through**

appropriate acts of leading, avoidance, and stopping.
Likewise Otto may have had up to a month's orientation in
getting to know how to use a guide dog and in getting
acquainted with the particular personality of the dog allo-
cated to him. Eventually he will have become adept at interpreting his dog's signals. He will be attuned to its way of
conveying information to the extent that 'getting information'
from his dog may well be as fluid and automatic for him as
looking something up in a notebook had been for
'Alzheimer's Otto', or as looking something up in memory
had been for Inga.

In a similar vein we might also claim that the information provided
by the guide dog would be 'typically invoked' and 'automatically
endorsed' by Otto. Otto would depend on his guide dog for obstacle detection and he would not usually question the information
provided. This 'automatic endorsement' would show itself in
action, for example by avoiding an obstacle that his dog has sig-
nalled by its own movements. It may take time for Otto to get used
to the idea of 'automatically endorsing' what his dog tells him.
Guide dog owners will sometimes tell how they had to learn to
trust the information provided by their dog—indeed it may take
several collisions with obstacles before they are willing to do so—
but eventually automaticity is achieved.

Otto and his guide dog, then, seem to have all the requisite similarities with Otto and his notebook. Does this mean that Otto's
guide dog is part of Otto's mind?

It seems likely that many readers will be skeptical about this.
Some will be skeptical because they are unwilling to take seriously
Clark and Chalmers's analysis of the original Otto story and so don't
want to compound this absurdity by extending it to the world of
dogs. Their position might be something like this: "Look if Otto's
mind extended into his notebook then it would make sense to say
things like 'Otto left his mind behind the sofa today', but it obviously doesn't make sense to say things like that so Clark and
Chalmers must be wrong."

Another group of skeptics may be more circumspect. They will
let Otto leave his mind behind the sofa if he wants to. However
they will not be happy with the idea that anyone's mind ever walks
around with its tongue hanging out, or that it customarily pees
against lamp posts. Below we will look at some possible objections

from this second group of sceptics—those who are willing to accept the original extended mind argument but are unwilling to swallow the doggy version—although a few general considerations of interest to the first group will also be touched upon.

Objection #1. Doesn't the Guide Dog Help Otto See?

Surely, say the skeptics, if there's one clear analogy between the notebook and guide dog scenarios then it is that whereas Alzheimer's Otto uses his notebook in place of memory, blind Otto uses his dog in place of sight. Therefore if the guide dog instantiates anything at all it is 'sight', not 'mind'.

This is a good point. It's true that guide dogs are often said to be the 'eyes' of their owner—an idea that is reinforced by the use of the term 'Seeing Eye' dogs in the U.S. But does such a point count against a dog-mind hypothesis? Might it not even be said to strengthen it?

Many philosophers have tried to understand sight on the model of touch and if we adopted such an approach we might claim that the vibrations and other sensory stimuli that Otto feels through the harness constitute a kind of 'seeing'. It's debatable whether the use of the term 'seeing' here can ever be more than metaphorical and some readers, blind or sighted, might think it a bit of a stretch to suggest that guide dog usage literally gives sight. What's clear, nevertheless, is that use of a guide dog can enhance sensory experience of the world for its owner. It's not merely that the owner feels vibrations and makes inferences about the world around him— rather, he can have a direct experience of the world different to that had without a dog.

Rod Michalko, an academic and guide dog user, refers to an enhancement of the 'distance sense' and remembers being taken aback by his first experience of this:

> I experienced an expansion of my immediate environment . . . Leo [the dog] seemed to bring my physical environment closer. (Rod Michalko, *The Two in One*, Temple University Press, 1999, p.26)

At one point he declares that "it was as though I could 'see' several feet ahead" although he elsewhere suggests that a better analysis is

that "the tactile sense becomes the distance sense." This observation harks back to the work of the philosopher Maurice Merleau-
Ponty who offered a similar description of the experience of using
a cane:

> The blind man's stick has ceased to be an object for him and is no
> longer perceived for itself; its point has become an area of sensitivity
> extending the scope and active radius of touch, and providing a par-
> allel to sight. (Maurice Merleau-Ponty, *Phenomenology of Perception*)

We might agree, then, that guide dogs, like canes, can enhance
their owners' sensory experience. Does this jeopardize the
'extended mind' interpretation? Clark himself (in other writings)
suggests the opposite. He takes such facts to be part and parcel of
a more general account of human extendedness into the world
according to which portions of the world are used by human
beings to extend their subjective sense of spatial presence. Clark is
more interested in high-tech examples like remotely controlled
cameras and robot arms, but, following suit, we could add the
humble guide dog to this list. We could say that not only is Otto's
dog part of his mind in the ways previously outlined, there is also
a subjective dimension to Otto's mind extension. Otto feels himself
to be spatially extended into the environment thanks to his dog.

Objection #2. Walking Around Isn't Thinking

Okay, say the skeptics, we'll accept that the guide dog's role as a
kind of sensor need not count against its status as part of Otto's
extended mind—and on a particular interpretation might even
count for it. But this is not the sort of 'extended mind' we were talking about earlier. That 'extended mind' was a 'mind' in a stronger,
more literal sense. It had to do with things like information and
beliefs, as exemplified by Otto's use of the notebook. It wasn't just
about sensing stuff but was, we might say, more 'cognitive'—by
which we really only mean 'more *mind*-like', but we're trying to
avoid repeating ourselves here! We maintain that a guide dog could
never be part of Otto's extended mind in this strong sense, even if
its use can be described in such a way that it meets all of Clark and
Chalmers's conditions.

This can be seen (continue the skeptics) if we consider a particular difference between the role of Otto's notebook and the role

of Otto's guide dog. Although both notebook and dog can be char-acterised as supplying the information Otto needs to get from A to B they do this in different ways. Otto's notebook will tell him the location of the museum whereas his dog will 'tell him' the location of things *en route* to the museum. (Actually a guide dog who is used to a route may well be able to 'tell' his owner the location of a place as well, in the sense that he could take him straight there given the appropriate command.)

In the first case we have a process of information retrieval which takes place over a distinct time period prior to the physical act of walking and which is the focus of Otto's attention. In the sec-ond case, there is no such separation between the alleged 'telling' and the physical act of getting from A to B. Everything is all mixed up. Moreover, whilst they are walking around, at no point need blind Otto or his dog even be thinking about what they're doing. Otto might be anticipating the delights that await him at the museum, hoping that at least some of the exhibits are accessible to the visually impaired. His dog could be thinking about bones.

Insofar as Otto and his dog are engaged in a shared activity, then, this activity does not seem to be 'cognitive' enough to count as the activity of an extended mind.

My reply to this is that the most such arguments can show is that there's more than one way of being 'cognitive'. It's not necessary that an operation be done consciously, or that it be fully separable from physical activity, for it to count as cognitive. We might even go further than this and argue that the majority of cognition is only ever intermittently conscious and that it is inextricably bound up with physical activity. This view of things has had a resurgence in popularity in recent years, particularly amongst more philosophi-cally oriented cognitive scientists (a group which may include Andy Clark) who—under the influence of the philosopher Martin Heidegger—are fond of using terms like 'smooth coping' and 'embodied know how' to describe the seamless interface between mental and physical activity in everyday life.

The point, as far as Otto and his dog are concerned, is that they represent a perfectly respectable version of 'cognition'. Navigating hazardous walkways is every bit as cognitive as remembering or looking up the location of a museum. Indeed the account of cog-nition which tries to keep apart conscious, purely mental acts and unreflective, merely physical acts, is perhaps the more unrealistic one. In the real world even Inga's act of remembering might be relatively unconscious and bound up with physical activity. She might not, for example, pause to recall where the museum is but may just feel that she 'knows' where the museum is and head off for it. If she is anything like the average person she may then use various environmental prompts to steer her in the right direction en route.

Conversely, blind Otto's negotiation of the sidewalk with his guide dog might contain many acts of concerted conscious attention, particularly if it is a new route or if Otto has recently acquired the guide dog and is not yet accustomed to its ways.

There seems to be no good reason, then, for describing what Otto does with his guide dog as 'not cognitive enough'.

Objection #3. What Part of My Mind Is My Dog?

Alright, say the skeptics (who don't give up easily), let's forget about things not being 'cognitive'. One point we were trying to make when we used that word is that we don't have (and the implication is, 'nor could we have') a name for the mental property or act that Otto's guide dog represents. In the original Otto story it was easy to see how the notebook could be a stand in for 'memory' or its contents for 'beliefs'. What's the equivalent with the guide dog?

In response to this we might want to question whether there has to be a single nameable mental property that the dog represents in order for it to count as part of Otto's mind. It's true that the notebook example works well because there is a one to one correspondence between two unambiguous and discrete acts—Inga's recalling something and Otto's looking something up in the notebook—and so it's easy to transfer terms like 'memory' or 'belief' from one to the other. But this example was deliberately designed with the idea of keeping things simple so that the extended mind argument could be made in a relatively clear fashion. Clark and Chalmers would be the first to admit that things are more messy in the real world and that finding a label for the mental properties or activities constituted by the extended part of an individual's mind might be difficult.

Nevertheless, if we had to give a name to that portion of Otto's mind which is constituted, at least in part, by his guide dog then we might plump for a term like 'navigation system'. It's true that this term doesn't sound as straightforwardly mind-like as 'memory' or 'belief', and there is also the danger that it could be interpreted as meaning nothing more than 'sensor'. However such difficulties are surmountable if we argue that by 'navigation system' we mean something which includes other more basic mental properties. Navigation clearly does, for example, involve *beliefs* about the location of obstacles.

If Alzheimer's Otto's beliefs can be said to be partly constituted by his notebook because he relies on the notebook to find out the location of the museum, then likewise blind Otto's beliefs can be said to be partly constituted by his dog because he relies on the dog to find out the location of obstacles.

That should keep the sceptics quiet . . .

Objection #4. It's a Dog, You Idiot!

No, no, no, say the skeptics, (becoming quite exasperated), now things are getting hopelessly muddled! If we were able to say that Otto's notebook in some way constituted or contained Otto's beliefs, that was only because there was no one else around whose beliefs they could have been. But a dog is a living creature. Any additional beliefs in the Otto–guide dog story will therefore belong to the dog and the dog alone. If blind Otto, following his dog, swerves to avoid an obstacle, he doesn't do so because he has a belief in his extended mind that there is an obstacle there. He swerves when his dog swerves because the dog has that belief and communicates it to him by swerving.

In reply to this we might say that it certainly seems reasonable to point out that, unlike the notebook, the dog is a living creature. However, if the idea of extending one's own beliefs to other entities makes any sense at all then there seems to be no good reason for excluding other living creatures as possible candidates. Clark and Chalmers themselves argue as much when they consider the possibility of other human beings becoming part of an individual's extended mind:

Could my mental states be partly constituted by the states of other thinkers? We see no reason why not, in principle. In an unusually interdependent couple, it's entirely possible that one partner's beliefs play the same sort of role for the other as the notebook plays for Otto. Otto and his dog (who is surely a 'thinker') could be an example of just such an interdependent couple. In the same way that Alzheimer's Otto had problems retaining beliefs about the location of buildings and so offloaded these to his notebook, blind Otto can be seen as having difficulties acquiring beliefs about the location of obstacles and so delegating these to his dog.

In both cases (it could be argued) the beliefs are still Otto's because of the tightness of the relationship had with the item or animal in question (see earlier arguments about ease of retrieval and automatic endorsement.) In saying this, of course, we are not denying that the dog has his own beliefs, it is just that these beliefs also play a role in an over arching system called 'Otto's mind'.

Objection #5. Whose Mind Is It Anyway?

At this point our skeptics might be expected to have packed up their bags in disgust and left the building. Even without their help, however, we can see room for a potential problem here. If a couple are truly 'interdependent' what grounds have we for saying that any shared mind which emerges from their relationship belongs to one party rather than the other? Why have we been talking in terms of Otto's mind rather than his dog's, or some combination of both?

Clark and Chalmers's answer to this question seems to be based, in the main, on their perception of existing power relationships—it's the dominant partner whose mind gets extended:

> . . . the waiter at my favorite restaurant might act as a repository of my beliefs about my favourite meals . . . In other cases one's beliefs might be embodied in one's secretary, one's accountant, or one's collaborator.

Here, despite the reference to a 'collaborator', it is clear that a subordinate work role is seen as an indicator of one's position in the extended mental hierarchy. If I work for you I may become part of your mind. This could constitute the beginnings of a critique of society, except for the fact that Clark and Chalmers present it without any irony whatsoever. Many readers might therefore take exception to this passage, especially if they are secretaries or waiters.

Extremist dog-loving readers—perhaps those long since disillusioned with the world of *Homo sapiens*—may be more concerned to know where this leaves guide dogs. The answer would seem to be that because Otto's guide dog works for Otto he is doomed to be subsumed into Otto's mind.

But this may not be the only possible answer. Although what we might call a 'single ownership' description of the extended mind dominates Clark and Chalmers's paper, they sometimes favour other ways of talking. They allude, for example, to cases where

> the human organism is linked with an external entity in a two-way interaction, creating a *coupled system* that can be seen as a cognitive system in its own right. (p. 2)

The idea of a "coupled system," at least as used here, seems to be a more democratic one than that of 'one-way mind extension', insofar as it's neutral on the question of ownership. Both parties to the arrangement are dependent on and reciprocally influence each other resulting in a new formation which is reducible to neither.

How, then, does this relate to Otto and his dog? Well, if we can make a case for 'reciprocity' between the two of them then it's good news for the dog. He'll be able to throw off his chains (if not his harness) to become an equal partner in a coupled system. Such reciprocity is fortunately not hard to find, forming, as it does, the bedrock of the guide dog–owner relationship.

Rod Michalko is clear that the relationship he has with his dog, despite involving some sacrifice on the dog's part, is more one of give-and-take than of dominance and submission. He says at one point that he and his dog "are almost literally extensions of each other" (p. 5) a conception that he reinforces by the use of terms like 'dyad' and 'two-in-one'. to refer to the unity of the owner–guide-dog team. In places he offers an almost transcendental account of this relationship, making reference to

> something dynamic and fluid that flows from one partner to the other and back again . . . (p.72) . . . a fluid relation that does not apply when leader and follower are understood as static and completely separable entities. (p. 185)

This is not an idealization of the guide dog–owner relationship but a description of the nitty gritty of their daily operations together. It refers for example to the 'turn taking' involved in activities like crossing the road, where first the dog will signal that the curb has been reached by stopping, then the owner (after listening out for traffic) will signal back that it is safe to cross by issuing a command to do so, to which the dog will then respond either by moving off or by not moving off according to his visual assessment of the situation. It also refers to the continuous and more subtle interplay of signals between owner and dog through the medium of the harness.

The coupled system version of the extended mind thesis, then, seems to apply quite well to the guide dog–owner dynamic and has the benefit that it need not imply any loss of status for the dog.

Does Any of This Matter?

Okay, say the skeptics, who seem to have returned for a final assault, you've done your best to try to accommodate Otto and his dog into the extended mind framework, albeit by use of some fairly suspect reasoning, and you've even tried to make the arrangement comfortable for the dog. But is anything to be gained from this exercise? What hangs on it?

Perhaps not very much—but even slightly bizarre sounding philosophical theories can have practical consequences. Clark, in a separate publication (Andy Clark, *Being There*, MIT Press, 1997), talks of the dependence many Alzheimer's sufferers have on a structured home environment. They may rely not just on a notebook, as in the Otto example, but on a whole range of reminder notices distributed about the house. Clark says of such a set up "this really is a case of using the world as external memory" (p. 66). In making such a claim he's describing the scenario in a way which could have concrete implications for the lives of Alzheimer's sufferers. Increased awareness of the integral nature of the relationship between an Alzheimer's sufferer and his home environment makes less likely the undertaking of actions, or introduction of policies, which could disrupt such a fragile arrangement.

Likewise with the guide dog–owner relationship. Although disability legislation has had a considerable impact on the everyday lives of guide dog users in many countries, they can still face a number of unnecessary inconveniences. These can range from well intentioned but potentially distracting dog petting by passers-by, to more serious limitations of freedom imposed by managers of public premises and amenities. Such inconveniences might be less common if those responsible were to conceive of interference with the dog as interference with the owner, or if they were to conceive of interference with both as upsetting the flow of interaction in a finely tuned coupled system.

The slogan "Mess with my dog and you mess with my mind" perhaps suggests itself.[2]

―――――――

[2] Thanks to Deniz Loader and Luke Hewitt for their comments and suggestions. In memory of Tony's dog Vicky and my mother's dog Jane.

II

Getting Inside Your Dog's Mind

5

Two Canine Dogmas: Language and Love

GLENN STATILE

Dogs are not our whole life, but they make our lives whole.

—ROGER CARAS

President John F. Kennedy once challenged us to think more in terms of what we can do for our country than of what our country can do for us. Turn around is also fair play when it comes to the relationship between philosophy and dogs. While philosophy can tell us a great deal about our canine friends, we still should not lose sight of the fact that dogs can easily return the favor, shedding light upon and showcasing the worth of some of our most valuable philosophical ideas. For dogs comprise a still largely untapped resource that can and should be put at the disposal of philosophy.

Consider the problem of free will, one of the staple topics within the branch of philosophy known as metaphysics. The French philosopher René Descartes, who himself denied that dogs possess any of the higher faculties, asserted that while our powers of judgment and intellection are finite, the scope of our will is infinite. By this he meant that there is no limitation upon our human ability to affirm or deny any possible belief.

A well known principle of ethics stipulates that "ought implies can"—we can't be morally obliged to do something we don't have the ability to do. Yet while many people might acknowledge that we ought to love all human beings, most of us, short of sainthood, simply cannot manage the task.

But that the ethical and religious mandate to love many more people than we customarily do is not necessarily beyond our capacity is suggested, although by no means proven, by the ardent dog lover's facility in loving such a large number of dogs. Thus our shortcomings in regard to the lack of love many of us feel toward so many of our human acquaintances are better explained by the complications which mark human interactions than by any handicap placed upon our natural affections toward members of our own species.

When it comes to the human affection for dogs: it might fairly be said that once loved, always loved. We owe to dogs, perhaps more than to any other creature, our recognition of the fact that the call to universal love is not necessarily an unattainable ideal. Concerning the pedagogical value of dogs for humans I think that James Thurber put it best when he referred to that "strange and involved compulsion" humans have "to be as happy and carefree as a dog." He called this predilection the "Dog Wish."

Most if not all canine admirers would concur that dogs are capable of love and can effectively communicate their feelings to humans. Such convictions are nearly (pardon the pun) dogmatic to anyone who has ever lived with and loved a dog for any significant length of time. There are many cynics who would claim that the human love for dogs is nothing more than an expression of our anthropomorphic sentimentality. But we, the friends of dogs, must unite to dispel such sloppy thinking. Such cynics might be surprised to learn that the very word "cynic" itself derives from the Greek word for 'dog'. The Cynics were followers of the Greek philosopher Diogenes of Sinope, who was famous for pursuing virtue with a dog-like tenacity.

A Tale of Two Dogs

Literary insight into the deep emotional bond and communicative rapport between dogs and their masters is provided by Homer in Book 17 of the *Odyssey*, where we encounter the moving reaction of the aging Argos to the return of his heroic master Odysseus. After twenty years of separation from his globetrotting master, and neglect at the hands of the household staff in Ithaca, the old and ailing Argos once again detects the voice of the person whose memory has presumably kept him alive for so many years. At that precise instant Homer tells us that "a dog that had been lying asleep raised his head and pricked up his ears." Upon hearing his master's voice one last time, and wagging his tail in farewell to the faith-filled love which empowered his long-suffering life, he dies a happy death.

The ecstatic vision of his master was the dog's just reward for a life lived in accordance with the virtue of fidelity. With this touching episode Homer (not only an epic poet, but perhaps also an astute precursor of early Greek philosophy, as philosopher Seth Bernadete argues) provides us with a perfect example upon which to model any examination of the relationship between dogs and philosophy. Homer teaches us an important philosophical lesson about how characters, both human and canine, can be molded and motivated by what the poet John Keats described as the "power of unreflecting love." With this pathos-laden canine death scene Homer is presenting an image of love in poetic language that is pure, simple, unswerving, and divorced from any rational weighing of utility, and which is completely unlike any of the personal and group alliances and oaths of allegiance sworn by the many boastful and unforgiving characters which populate his epic terrain. It's a love that stands out in stark contrast to the ongoing cycles of revenge which inhabit the literary landscape of ancient Greece so artfully portrayed by Homer.

While Aristotle tells us that humans are rational animals, most of us would simply not settle for such an undervaluation of what we are all about. We're much more complicated than any capacity for logical inference can convey. Our exalted capacity for love, for example, is often obscured by the complex machinations of the human heart. Homer however allows us to see in a very moving way what can come of the saga of love when it is not mediated through the emotional maelstrom that is the human heart, with its hubris and passions, but is nurtured quietly and unseen in the soul of man's best friend, the dog.

The purity and power of love, as exhibited in the dog, stands out much more clearly as a result. In his own way Argos speaks to the reader. With utmost eloquence he reveals his soul to us. Students of analytic philosophy, which deals with the logical analysis of words and concepts, are familiar with the notion of using language in a performative manner. For example, the issuance of a promise functions as a linguistic utterance which provides information, while at the same time enacting the information which is expressed. As a kind of reversal upon the performative theme in which a locution is equated with an act, the dying pantomime of Argos speaks eloquently of his love for Odysseus, a love, one might easily contend, which flies in the face of reason, while at the same time enacting the deepest stirrings of his canine soul.

Language is a form of communication. That dogs do not speak our language does not force us to conclude that their actions and vocalizations are devoid of meaning. One possible response to the dilemma of meaning is to enlarge our conception of what is meant by language. Meaning is larger than what normally falls under the auspices of the syntactic rules which govern the structures of human languages.

As the philosophy of language has taught us in recent years, human language is plagued by various logical problems which follow from attempts to translate sentential structure (syntax) into units of semantic meaning. The philosopher Ludwig Wittgenstein espoused the view that the possibilities of language are endless, and cannot be confined by any straitjacket of logical rigor. We do injustice to language when we limit it to the rules of a strictly human eloquence. Many readers will no doubt recall true stories of dogs who have grieved tirelessly for their dead masters. A famous Skye Terrier, now immortalized in the reputedly true story of Greyfriars Bobby, spoke volumes when keeping a faithful vigil upon the unmarked grave of his master John Gray for fourteen years, departing only for nourishment, until his own death in 1872. One might say that this dog did Elizabeth Barrett Browning one better, whose famous love sonnet to her poet husband Robert concludes with the memorable verse "I shall but love thee better after death."

To Beg or Not to Beg

The mechanical philosophy of the Enlightenment inaugurated by René Descartes and others, which taught that all physical things and events can be explained by reducing sensible reality to microscopic particles and their collisions, led to the dissemination of the view that dogs and other animals are to be equated with machines. Prior to Descartes the tradition stemming from Aristotle at least conferred living status—if not much else—upon dogs and other animals.

Since the time of Descartes (1596–1650) we have slid quite some way down the slippery slope of existential worth toward the daunting prospect that perhaps we humans are no better than machines ourselves. Consider the fact that the Artificial Intelligence community at Carnegie Mellon University has even gone so far as to host soccer competitions in which robotic contestants are designed to resemble dogs. The reason for such a choice should be apparent to any salesman: to convert our mostly apprehensive feelings toward robots and what they stand for into warm and tender feelings toward dogs.

Not even the proponents of the downgrading of both human and canine status are completely comfortable in what they're trying to do. What lover of dogs does not rebel at the awarding of a Nobel Prize to Ivan Pavlov, who achieved his experimental results at the price of canine torture, one of the ultimate degradations of the mechanical mindset? To those who favor a higher metaphysical status for dogs than the degrading tail wagging automaton of Enlightenment propaganda, the post-Cartesian philosophical resources are plentiful. The enrichment of philosophy in areas such as science, language, and consciousness, to name but a few, can also be harnessed for other, including canine, purposes. Voltaire issued a stern reprimand to Descartes in one of the entries included in his *Dictionnaire philosophique* (1764) by praising the poorly treated dog who "surpasses man in friendship."

If material reality is all there is, then both dogs and humans are nothing more than mere contraptions, marvels of natural engineering. By virtue of the logical principle of transposition however it follows from this proposition that if dogs are more than mere automatons, then material reality does not exhaust all of cosmic significance. While all dogs beg, those who assume that reality is to be equated solely with a materialistic outlook, or insist without evidence that dogs fall upon the material side of the metaphysical line, beg the question. As Jeremy Bentham pointed out in protest at any categorical denial of the rights of animals in Chapter 17 of *The Principles of Morals and Legislation* (1789), the "dog is beyond comparison a more rational, as well as a more conversable animal, than an infant of a day, or a week, or even a month, old."

Man's Best Friend

Centuries have not dimmed the kinship of feeling between humans and their proverbial best friend, the dog. Everyone who has ever been visited by a therapy dog in the hospital will realize that the physiological and psychological health systems which safeguard human life respond palpably to the presence of dogs. And while it is often said that laughter is the best medicine, there are many who would testify to the even superior healing power of canine companionship. Concerning canine love for human life no less an authority than Charles Darwin in *The Origin of Species* said that "It is scarcely possible to doubt that the love of man has become instinctive in the dog."

For Aristotle, the love which signifies true friendship must be mutual. It would be ridiculous to speak of our friendship for wine he says since a mere beverage cannot love us back. While wine may age better than the best of us, and its consumption may allow for remarkable insights into the nature of truth, as in the old adage *in vino veritas*, it undoubtedly lacks a soul. Aristotle however did regard animals as possessing souls which befit their nature as sentient beings. Saint Paul goes even further in *Romans* (8:21), asserting that "the nonhuman creatures are eagerly awaiting to be liberated from corruption to share in the glorious freedom of the children of God."

Aristotle's analysis of friendship in the *Nicomachean Ethics* may seem as if it offers no breathing room for the possibility of any true friendship between dogs and humans. But this isn't so. While Aristotle is correct in thinking that friendships based upon utility and pleasure are inferior to reciprocal relationships between equals based upon a profound sense of civic virtue, the contemporary philosopher Alasdair McIntyre and others have argued that any incorporation of the virtues into the theoretical framework of modern ethical theory requires the realization that the Aristotelian sense of virtue, which was rooted in the Greek *polis* or city-state of his time, needs to be both updated and expanded. For when we consider the reciprocal relationship between humans and dogs, built upon a bedrock of both love and virtue, who can really deny that it meets the requirements for true friendship? Gratitude, unselfishness, fidelity, an unlimited willingness to forgive, a thorough lack of dissimulation, undying affection, these are all timeless virtues brought by the dog into the lifetime contract of love shared by a dog and his master. The dog does not realize that we humans get much the better of the deal.

Dogs and Their Discontents

The book of *Genesis* speaks of a time when the entire Earth was home to one universal language. Since at least the time of Descartes, however, it is fair to say that the pedigree of existential superiority has been held hostage by the activity of what we call thinking, which in turn is said to be intimately linked to the various forms of human language. During his early period, Wittgenstein even argued that language is a necessary condition for thinking, while in more recent memory Jerry Fodor created quite a stir with his hypothesis that a language of thought exists.

Whatever the case, an eternal veil of inscrutability blocks us at every pass whenever we try to close the gap between human and canine consciousness. This should come as no surprise, nor is it in any way unique, given the longstanding philosophical intractability of the problem of ascertaining the mental content of other human minds. The famous American philosopher William James put it quite well when he wrote that "marvelous as may be the power of my dog to understand my moods, deathless as his affection and fidelity, his mental state is as unsolved a mystery to me as it was to my remotest ancestors." Canine skeptics however would do well to avoid the double standard of being more doubtful about dogs than they are about themselves.

The metaphysically sponsored prejudice against dogs by both Descartes and Aristotle was by no means unanimous. Among the ancient Greek philosophers, the Stoics are best known for their belief that the goal of existence is to live in harmony with both nature and reason. Among their many philosophical achievements was their extension of the logical principles compiled and consolidated by Aristotle. Stoic logic included an example of a dog following a trail in pursuit of some quarry. Upon reaching a fork in the road the dog pauses to sniff at one of two alternative pathways. Discerning nothing with his hypersensitive sense of smell the dog then immediately proceeds down the remaining pathway. What is the moral of this logical parable? According to the Stoic interpretation the dog in the story is to be credited with implicit knowledge of one of the basic principles of logic. The dog is said to have performed an inference known as the disjunctive syllogism, which is one of the most fundamental of argument forms in the entire logical canon. The dog presumably realized that if the first of two possible pathways or disjuncts did not promise a successful resolution to his quest, then the remaining choice had to be correct. He did not need to detain himself any longer in order to gather further olfactory evidence. According to this logical scenario the dog exhibited a perfect intuitive understanding of the principle known as the excluded middle. If two possibilities exhaust the spectrum of choices at one's disposal, then the falsity of one guarantees the truth of the other.

Experimental results involving the language acquisition skills of various non-human species have long been hailed as a failure by those who are skeptical about any attempts to elevate the cognitive status of the higher animals above that of the lowly beast. The civilized Greeks once thumbed their noses at all those foreigners who did not enjoy the advantages of Greek culture, dubbing them collectively as barbarians. Over time the Greeks would rudely discover that it was difficult to keep a good barbarian down.

Perhaps this lesson should not be lost on us in the case of animals. For decades chimpanzees have been at the forefront of experimental efforts to gauge the potential of animal rationality and linguistic competence. After all, they are our closest genetic cousins. But as everyone knows, and as philosopher Donna Haraway has long argued, dogs are our evolutionary partners. One might say that humans and dogs have domesticated each other. Haraway espouses the view that our knowledge of dogs is intertwined with our knowledge of humans. Employing the language of phenomenology, which deals with the intersection between consciousness and the environment, it is fair to say that dogs and humans share the same lifeworld. The saga of human history and culture is much more bound up with the dog than with any other animal, discounting of course those creatures whom we consume as nourishment in order to survive. Mark Twain once quipped that were we to cross a man with a cat the man would be greatly improved. I would add that by living at close quarters with dogs for many generations mankind has improved immeasurably. Chinks in the Cartesian wall of prejudice against dogs abound. Like Donna Haraway we must continue to expose and enlarge them until it comes crashing down.

Brave New World

In recent cognitive studies dealing with animals it is fair to say that dogs may be the new apes. While dogs are made to jump through hoops in agility trials and in the circus, recent evidence has confirmed what all dog lovers have always known. Canine intelligence is of high caliber. The philosophy of mind has long distinguished between folk psychological knowledge, which is our common wisdom accumulated over time, and knowledge gleaned from empirical studies. While there is no certain verdict as to the worth of such folk psychological knowledge in comparison with hard experimental evidence, it is nevertheless taken quite seriously by a significant percentage of philosophers. Why then should the common wisdom about dogs not receive an equivalent amount of respect?

While the term *speciesism* was first coined by philosopher Peter Singer to refer to the last frontier of discrimination, the violation of the natural rights of animals, I would argue that its meaning can also be extended to include any *a priori* or indiscriminate rejection of superior canine intelligence. While dogs may not be our linguistic and cognitive equals, their abilities for language and thinking differs from our own only by degree, not kind. This is one of the philosophical lessons to be learned in our evolutionary era. Moreover, as the philosopher Willard Quine argued in a famous article entitled "Two Dogmas of Empiricism," empirical methods are insufficient for establishing an infallible method of translation in the case of human language. According to this thesis all meaning is at best indeterminate. If this is so then we must learn to be more patient as well as more creative in our assessment of what dogs know and what dogs mean. Recall the words of Franz Kafka in his "Investigations of a Dog." "All knowledge, the totality of all questions and answers, is contained in the dog."

The case of the eight-year-old border collie named Rico was reported in the June 11th 2004 issue of *Science*. Rico was successful in learning the names of unfamiliar toys after only one exposure with about a seventy percent accuracy rate. A new and unfamiliar toy was then added to a group of seven toys whose names were already familiar to the dog. When the dog was asked to retrieve the new toy by name he was able to do so even though its name had not yet been disclosed to him. It seems then that the Stoics were quite on the mark with their judgment in regard to canine intelligence. Rico's feat is analogous to the human cognitive skill known as fast mapping, which is posited as the means by which children are able to quickly formulate hypotheses in relation to new word meanings. In this case Rico was able to formulate the hypothesis that the unfamiliar word referred to the unfamiliar object. Whatever the brain structure which supports such learning, it is not unique to humans. Philosophers of science working in the area of the logic of discovery and the psychology of learning would do well to extend their horizon of research to include dogs, assuming that they do not in any way demean the dogs in the process.

Linguist Noam Chomsky, whose own work on the innateness of language is heir to the project begun by Descartes, was wrong in his insistence that language is unique to humans. He has said that attempts to teach animals to speak are doomed to failure, just as humans who practice flapping their limbs will never be able to soar much beyond the record for the Olympic high jump. While dogs, like chimpanzees, may lack the vocal apparatus to make a variety of modulated sounds, this does not mean that true canine education is a lost cause. As philosopher Paul Churchland argues in his book *The Engine of Reason,* our own language skills may not be completely hardwired into our brains but may also be the result of learning. The counter-evolutionary perspective known as social constructivism endorses a similar view. Such a perspective on learning is reminiscent of the later view of Wittgenstein, who held that language transcends the mere abstract correspondence between arbitrary symbols, sounds and objects. Language, he thought, is a social act embedded in a situation. And dogs, as we all know, are quintessentially social animals.

Closing Down the Cartesian School

Various post-Cartesian intellectual developments provide us with an invigorated confidence that the initial Cartesian basis for discrediting dogs and other animals as mere mechanical contraptions is doomed. As Newtonian science, which represented the consummation of the Cartesian mechanical project, has been eclipsed by the probabilistic uncertainties of the quantum theory, it is therefore, according to one way of looking at the evidence, no longer scientifically or philosophically tenable to simply describe the actions of humans, or dogs for that matter, as entirely predetermined. One might counter that since even machines are subject to quantum indeterminacy there is still no good reason for elevating dogs above machine-like status. But the crucial point here is that the Cartesian paradigm of what it means to be a machine is no longer viable. No Cartesian-style mechanical argument against the possibility of what animals can feel or know continues to have any merit. The Cartesian school, with its militant anti-canine propaganda based upon a naive form of mechanical thinking, is simply out of business.

With the demise of the mechanical model that was emblematic of the Cartesian school, practitioners of philosophy have at least two important ways by which they can attempt to justify a higher regard for dogs and their abilities. The first way involves employing the resources of the philosophy of science so as to better interpret the results of various forms of canine research. Those who too quickly overrate or undervalue what tests on dogs show do more harm than good. Explaining what such tests mean requires the diagnostic tools of measurement theory, as well as many other resources customarily employed by philosophers of science in the evaluation of experiments. Secondly, if we bracket those religious arguments which favor an ontological distinction between humans and animals, then there is no genuine genetic basis for adopting a philosophical double standard, one for animals and one for humans, unless such a standard is to be based upon measurable differences in degrees of genetic, or perhaps cerebral, complexity between one species and another. For example, to deny that dogs can love because they lack free will is to adopt a standard that we do not usually apply to ourselves. Humans assume that they are free as a logical prerequisite which enables them to love as well as to sin; otherwise we are automatons. But where's the proof that we choose freely? Despite quantum indeterminacy, recent experimental work by Benjamin Libet and others, which reveals that specific act related activity in the brain may predetermine our behavior, challenges the very existence of free will altogether. So it is not philosophically legitimate to deny to dogs something that we do not really fully understand in relation to ourselves.

One of the original injunctions of philosophy, which appeared over the portal of the priestess of Apollo at Delphi, is to 'know thyself'. Only by knowing more about our human capacities—which is the province of philosophy—can we establish models by which we can better understand dogs and other species. Consider the fact that arguments against canine ability most often focus upon the linguistic and hence cognitive limits of dogs in comparison to humans. Except for sociobiological explanations of love, which ascribe evolutionary or ultimately selfish motives to the behavior of both humans and animals alike, very little attempt is made to deny that dogs can love. One good reason for this is that the evidence for canine love, especially in the form of forgiveness, is too overwhelming to take its denial seriously. That dogs love humans is a conclusion which equates to what philosophers would call an inference to the best explanation. That humans love dogs, while equally true, also functions as a line of moral demarcation for how we feel about and treat our fellow human beings. As Saint Francis, the patron saint of animals, so eloquently states: "If you have men who will exclude any of God's creatures from the shelter of compassion and pity, you will have men who will deal likewise with their fellow men."

Dogs Never Lie

Regarding the issue of what dogs can learn I would suggest that a greater emphasis needs to be placed upon the overall *education* rather than the mere *training* of dogs, the latter being a legacy of the Cartesian mindset. Such an attitude is in conformity with the general thrust of the philosophy of human education over the last half century or so. Stimulus training and behavior modification produce dogs who conform to our human whims. Our dogs deserve better. It was Plato who first introduced the idea that education is an exercise in self-discovery, involving the development of one's inner potential and innate talents. What Michelangelo did with marble, in liberating the hidden form from within the block of stone, we need to do in sculpting the untapped talents of our canine friends. This is a difficult task and requires no less than a complete transformation in our pedagogical mindset toward dogs.

We must not treat dogs as slaves who must repetitively respond to the imperative of external stimuli, but as beings with inner resources awaiting cultivation. It is undoubtedly true that dogs will never be our intellectual equals. They will never compose symphonies, write sonnets, solve differential equations, or even tell tall tales that titillate the imagination. But let us never underestimate that one unique talent, one might even call it a virtue, with which dogs have been especially blessed. Unlike humans, dogs never lie about love.

6

What Thoughts Can Your Dog Think?

LAURA DUHAU

> Recollect that the Almighty, who gave the dog to be companion of our pleasures and our toils, hath invested him with a nature noble and incapable of deceit.
>
> —SIR WALTER SCOTT, *The Talisman*

My dog Kibbles is particularly keen on eating the cat's food whenever I turn around to answer the phone, and very fast in disappearing from view as soon as I hang up. He's usually a loud and clumsy dog, but he is extremely careful when stealing the cat's food; he avoids making noise and tries to hide from anyone that could see him.

Whenever I tell this story, people normally agree with me in that he is trying to deceive me. We all explain his actions by saying that he believes that if he disappears from view before I hang up I won't know that he is guilty. We attribute lots of beliefs and desires to our dogs, and also complex emotions such as guilt and shame. But do dogs really have beliefs and desires? Do they think the thoughts we attribute to them and feel the sort of emotions we feel? How can we be sure?

Philosophers disagree with each other regarding these questions. Positions often go to the extremes. On the one hand there are those, like the American philosopher Donald Davidson (1917–2003), who claim that dogs don't think because they don't have a language. Languageless creatures, claims Davidson, can't have any beliefs and desires, or any emotions that depend on them. On the other hand are those, like the contemporary British thinker Peter Carruthers, who believe that dogs (and even bees and spiders) have beliefs and desires because they represent and respond to different aspects of their environment in a systematic manner.

You probably disagree with Davidson and also with Carruthers. You want to believe your dog thinks, but you also want to believe that there's a difference between your dog's mental capacities and those of a bee or a spider. You probably think that bees and spiders don't think. Am I right? Let's take a closer look.

No Talk, No Thought

Suppose your dog is chasing a cat, and suddenly the cat climbs up a tree, escaping. The dog has been distracted by your call just that second, misses this move, and starts barking towards your garden's fence. How do you explain its behavior? Would you say something like 'The dog thinks that the cat climbed over the fence'? Well, according to Davidson, you really don't have good reasons to attribute this thought to your dog, or in fact, you don't have good reasons to attribute *any* thought to your dog. Why not? Because your dog doesn't speak, and therefore you can't know whether it believes that the cat climbed over the fence, or over that thing he can't reach, or over that obstacle that the cat climbed the last time the dog chased it.

The idea is that there are many different thoughts your dog could be having, but because he can't tell you which he in fact has, you just can't attribute one. This happens all the time. Also, claims Davidson, you can't attribute thoughts to the dog because to do that you have to be able to attribute many different thoughts, since thoughts are all connected, and there's no way you can do this for a languageless creature. For example, if you are going to attribute any thought about the cat and the fence to your dog, you should also be able to claim that he has other thoughts about cats and fences; not any fixed thoughts, but quite a lot of them. A creature can't have only one belief about cats, it has to have many, such as the beliefs that cats are animals, cats climb things, cats run fast, cats scratch and make noises. Yet there's no way for you to know which thoughts about cats your dog has, because he won't tell you, so you can't say he has any.

Maybe you have already thought of a reply. Davidson, you may think, is claiming that something about us as interpreters—the fact that we have difficulties saying *which* thoughts and concepts our dog has, implies that our dog doesn't have thoughts or concepts. But that's not true. There is no implication. I can have difficulties saying what thoughts *you* have, but that doesn't mean you don't have them.

Bees, Dogs, and Us

Davidson hasn't really given us enough reasons to accept that our dogs don't think. His criteria rely on something about our own practices in attributing thoughts. What we need are some conditions for thought that we can apply directly to our dogs, something that *they* can either meet or not.

Carruthers has given some such conditions. The problem, as we will see, is that they are so lenient that not only do we and our dogs meet them, but even bees meet them as well. For Carruthers, there are two things we have to observe in a creature's behavior to say that they have beliefs and desires. The first one is that we have to observe some behavioral patterns of constancy—but within significant variation—in the creature's responses to different situations, so that we can say that attributing different concepts and thoughts to the creature helps to explain its actions.

This makes sense. If a creature invariably responds to a variety of situations with the very same behavior, all we can conclude is that it is simply responding to a particular stimulus that is common to all those situations. We don't have reasons to attribute any concepts to the creature.

Suppose that your dog encounters different cats on different occasions, let's call them Pussy, Missy, and Tussy. Pussy's behavior on one occasion might cause your dog to treat her as a toy, while an encounter with Missy makes him treat her as something to chase, and an encounter with Tussy derives in him acting as if she was as a dangerous threat. But then on further encounters, the cats may act differently. Pussy may become more aggressive and constitute a threat. If your dog acts differently towards her and towards the other cats if their behavior changes, that means that he can represent each cat as being different from each other and he can attribute different properties to them. We can say that your dog has distinct abilities to represent Pussy, Missy, and Tussy, and to represent toys, things to chase and threats, and he can combine these different representations.

The second condition Carruthers suggests is that these different abilities to represent different things should underwrite transitions between different mental states in virtue of their common contributions to them. For example, your dog's ability to represent his bowl of food could appear both in his belief that the bowl is in the kitchen and in his desire to get to it, and the combination of these two states could derive in your dog going to the kitchen to get his food. But the representation of the bowl could also appear in other mental states of your dog; for example, your dog could believe that you took the bowl to the back yard. In this case, this belief could interact differently with the dog's desire to get to the bowl, making him to go to the back yard instead of the kitchen. In this way Carruthers defends the idea that bees have concepts and think, on the grounds that bees have representations that can appear in different mental states to produce different behaviors.

Bees are amazing, there's no point in denying that. They have impressive navigational abilities, and they dance to communicate information of various sorts to other bees, such as where a rich nectar source is. According to Carruthers, bees have a suite of information-generating systems that construct representations of the relative directions and distances between a variety of substances and properties and the hive, and they use these representations to decide where to fly and when. A bee's desires can interact with the information it has collected to create a potentially unique behavior, never before seen in the life of that particular bee. Bees think, he says, because they have mental states– beliefs and desires– that interact with one another to determine behavior in a ways that are sensitive to the structure of those states. In his own words:

> For if one and the same item of directional information can be drawn on both to guide a bee in search of nectar and to guide the same bee returning to the hive, then it would seem that the bee must be capable of something resembling the following pair of practical inferences (using BEL to represent belief, DES to represent desire, MOVE to represent action—normally flight, but also walking for short distances— and square brackets to represent contents).

(1) BEL [nectar is 200 meters north of hive]
BEL [here is at hive]
DES [nectar]
MOVE [200 meters north]

(2) BEL [nectar is 200 meters north of hive]
BEL [here is at nectar]
DES [hive]
MOVE [200 meters south]

These are inferences in which the conclusions depend upon structural relations amongst the premises.[1]

So this is it, bees fit the criteria for thought. Your dog does too, of course. Maybe you've been convinced by Carruthers and you agree that bees think. No problem. But maybe you're feeling, as I do, that something extra is needed for *real* thought. Bees, you may think, do all that they do because they are pre-programmed to do it, and they are much more rigid in their behaviors than your dog. You wouldn't attribute the capacity of deception to a bee, as most of us do in cases like the one of my dog stealing the cat's food. What's going on here? What else is needed for us to say that a creature really thinks?

Mix and Match, and Detach

Carruthers is right in that, if we are to say that a creature thinks, it should at least be able to recombine different concepts in different thoughts, and this should reflect in its behavior. This idea is quite intuitive, if you think about it. Thoughts are composed of concepts, and the concepts that compose thoughts are such that they can figure in many different thoughts. For example, the thought that dogs are animals is composed by the concept DOG and the concept ANIMAL, and these can figure in different thoughts. Carruthers asks only for a few possible recombinations, that's why bees turn out to be thinkers under his view, because they can recombine a few different representations to generate some variation in their actions.

But contrast this with what we humans do. There seems to be no limits as to how many thoughts we can have. We can always get to think thoughts that we have never thought before. Just now, for example, I can join two concepts I have never joined before in one thought to generate a thought that I have never had before, such as: 'My computer is a jerk'. You may think this is nonsense, but at

---

[1] Peter Carruthers, "On Being Simple Minded," *American Philosophical Quarterly* 41 (2004), p. 216.

least you understand what this thought is about, and with a little bit of effort you can give some sense to it. Although maybe we shouldn't think that this unlimited capacity for creating new thoughts (only limited by the fact that we are finite creatures and there are only so many thoughts we can entertain in our lives) is a necessary condition for thought. Maybe a little recombination is all that's needed. It's difficult to draw a line. However, it does seem that the line should be somewhere else, at a place that makes dogs thinkers and not bees. Because it's difficult to draw a line only with this criterion of the ability to recombine, we should maybe try to see if there is anything else we could add.

There's another characteristic of thoughts, which together with the fact that they are composed of different concepts that can figure in other thoughts, makes them peculiar. You don't need to be in the presence of the things your thoughts are about in order to have them. Thoughts float free. I can think now of pink elephants, and I swear I'm not only not seeing one now, but I have never seen one. This idea is very intuitive if you think about it. If a creature can picture a red ball only when it is seeing a red ball, should we say that the creature can think something like 'This is a red ball'? It seems that if the creature can't represent a red ball unless it is directly watching it, it can't really think of red balls. It can perceive them, but it doesn't have any thoughts about them.

I bet I know what you're thinking. Bees do represent things in their absence. Bees dance to communicate to other bees where nectar is, and they do this without directly watching the nectar source. They have a memory of where the nectar was, and that's it. So bees are still on the team. Okay, that's true. We should fix our criteria a bit.

Maybe what we should say is that it's not only that thoughts don't depend on what we are seeing at any given moment, but that they also don't depend on what we have actually seen. I don't have to have seen a pink elephant to be able to think about one. If a creature can only picture a red ball because it has seen one, then all it has is some memory of a perception of a red ball, but it's not really combining the different concepts BALL and RED to form a thought. What would make a creature to have these two different concepts is that it can mix and match them in different thoughts, but can do this independently of a present or past perception of red balls.

So, if we're going to say that our dogs think, two things should be true. First, dogs should be able to mix and match different representations to form different thoughts. Second, they should be able to have representations that are detached from what they perceive or have perceived.

Now that we've come up with some (hopefully!) clear criteria for thought, what remains is to test our dogs to see if they fit them. How can we do this? They can't tell us, so we have to decide what kind of behavior on their part would indicate that they are mixing and matching and detaching.

Dog Thoughts

Let's first consider my dog Kibbles's cat food stealing behavior. Does it show that Kibbles is mixing, matching, and detaching representations? In order to act as he does, does he need to combine representations in new ways and have any representations of things he hasn't directly observed? Sadly, he doesn't. All that has to have happened is this: The first time he stole the cat's food, I was watching and I hit him with the newspaper (oh, yes, I can be a bit harsh). The second time, the same thing happened. Next time, however, I was suddenly distracted when the phone rang, and I didn't see him stealing the food; therefore, he got away with it. He's a fast learner, so he only needed one more time to learn to associate my speaking on the phone with his getting away with stealing the food. From then on, he would only steal the food when I wasn't watching.

The thing is, he just learned a new association, and this is something lots of animals do. If he had planned this scheme *without* having had the experience before, then we could say he was representing a succession of facts that he had never observed before, we could say that he was *planning* what to do. Plans are the sort of thing that require *real* thinking. To plan some course of action in the future you have to be able to imagine situations you've never experienced before.

Can you think of any situation in which your dog has planned a course of action, one in which he came up with a new behavior, one you weren't expecting, one that he didn't learn out of experience? If you have, then you'll be able to claim that you have a thinking dog.

Now, don't get desperate. We don't have to be so stringent on our criteria for thought. We can say that there are degrees. We can say that dogs aren't thinkers to the same degree we are, but that they are thinkers to *some* degree. They can recombine some of their representations, as in the example of the dog's representations of different cats and different qualities of cats. We can also say that they can detach representations to an extent. They can remember many different bone hiding sites. We can claim that this is enough for us to say that our dogs think. But then, unfortunately, we have to accept that our dogs are at the same level as bees, maybe the only difference being a matter of quantity: our dog can think a few more things than a bee can. Dogs can learn more things, they can surprise us, they are not as rigid in their behavior.

If you still feel uncomfortable putting your dog at the same level as bees, we need to find some other difference between them. Maybe you're also thinking that dogs have feelings and emotions, and bees don't. Although this is somehow another issue, there is something to say about it, since some emotions and feelings are connected with representations of things we cannot directly observe. Think for example of shame. Shame depends on our representations of someone else's opinions. We feel shame because we think that other people will judge us badly. Something similar can be said about jealousy. We feel jealous when we think that the object of our jealousy prefers someone else. To feel shame and jealousy then, we have to be able to imagine other people's thoughts, and thoughts are not something we perceive. Dogs, then, probably don't have this kind of feelings, since there's no evidence they can imagine or represent things they have not seen.

We can say that dogs have basic emotions like fear. Fear is a gut reaction, it doesn't require its subject to represent anything that cannot be seen. But we should be careful in attributing any emotion or feeling to dogs that depends on representations of things that are not directly observable. A dog can't be jealous of you petting another dog, because he can't think about what you think, he can't think that you prefer the other dog. He will probably beg for your attention and he will even probably show some signs of distress or sadness, and you may interpret this as jealousy, but the truth is that your dog is acting like this because he has obtained a response from you in the past when acting this way, and not because he is jealous.

Something similar can be said for cases in which your dog's behavior seems to indicate he is trying to deceive you. Real deception requires the deceiver to think about what the subject of the deceit has in mind. To deceive you, your dog would have to be able to know that you believe one thing and will keep on believing that same thing while he is doing another that you won't believe. If the dog's cat food stealing behavior is an example of deception, then he should think that you believe that he is not the one stealing the food. But as we saw, there is a much simpler and compelling explanation of this case: your dog doesn't read your mind, but has merely learned your reactions (and lack of them) on previous occasions, and acts accordingly.

Dog Intelligence

We could say that dogs are concrete thinkers. They think about the things they can perceive, and the things they are practically interested in. They can think of bones that they have hidden, and of you when you are not there (probably), so they have some capacity to detach their representations from their immediate perceptions. But they can't think of pink elephants (not even of gray elephants, if they haven't seen one). They also can't read your mind; so they can't do things that depend on that capacity. They can't trick you or deceive you, and they can't be jealous or proud, since these are emotions that depend on access to other subject's thoughts. Maybe it's true that your dog can sense when you're sad. But that's because there are some readily accessible cues that he can directly perceive: he can lick your tears and see you moaning. He learns to act accordingly.

Not Almost Human

I don't want you to finish reading this chapter with the feeling that your dog is more stupid than you thought. All I've done here is to compare dog's conceptual capacities with our own. This is usually the method, since we are the paradigmatic example of creatures that have concepts and can think. Still, this method is a bit unfair. The truth is that our dogs possess certain capacities that we are unable to grasp completely, because their brains are built differently from ours, so that they adapt to their own ecological niche. You just have to take your dog for a walk and you'll notice that all he does is smell everywhere. Smell is a dog's chief sense, so their world is a world of smell. Smell in us, by contrast, is a more subordinate sense. A dog's perceptual world is in a way quite different from ours, and we can't really claim to know what dogs' thoughts are about.

Dogs have their own kind of intelligence, one that allows them to survive among other dogs and among humans, one that lets them do impressive things, such as returning home from miles away even if they have never been released so far away before. They can detect strangers before they've cross the door, and they know about every dog in the neighborhood with an accuracy that we probably couldn't get even for our closest relatives. Dogs are clever, yes, it's just that they're not human, and they're rated unfairly when their thinking capacities are judged by our own standards.

As expert dog trainer John Holmes writes in his book *The Farmer's Dog*, "a dog is not 'almost human', and I know of no greater insult to the canine race than to describe it as such."

7

Does Your Dog Know What You're Thinking?

MIKOLAJ HERNIK and MARCIN GOKIELI

"So, where do you think that bone is that you want me to find?" thought the dog.

"So, why should I think that you think that I think?" thought the man.

What if I call you by your name, look into your eyes, say "Hey, look over there!", and point? I bet you'd turn around and look where I pointed. Why? Because you'd probably think that I noticed something interesting, amusing or scary, and that I want you to see it, too.

If I call a dog by its name and point, she will probably not just stare at my finger. She will follow my pointing. Can this mean that the dog—just like you—has some understanding of seeing, wanting and thinking, as these are understood by humans? For some people, this would be a bold and dubious claim. For others, it's just obviously true.

Philosophers have a reputation for questioning things that most people treat as self-evident. A philosopher will try to understand whether what people instinctively take for granted is actually *true*. So philosophers may wonder whether your common-sense understanding of what's going on inside your dog's head is right. Do we really have good grounds to believe that your dog understands your reasons for pointing at things?

For humans, thinking about other people's thinking is so ubiquitous, effortless, and automatic that it takes some reflection to realize what an amazing skill it actually is. When interacting with others we're constantly taking their minds into account: we're working out what people mean, we're trying to convince them, or we're just sharing our own thoughts to let them know what we think; we're trying not to hurt their feelings (though sometimes we're hurting them deliberately), and so on and so forth. We are dealing with other people's mental states on an everyday basis just as if thoughts were a kind of thing which actually can be dealt with. Well, are they?

I Think, but Should I Think that You Think?

René Descartes, a famous French philosopher of the seventeenth century, was worried whether other people have any minds. He was convinced he had one, as he knew his own sensations and thoughts, but maybe people around him didn't have any, maybe they were just machines devoid of any mental life whatsoever. You never see or feel someone else's sensations, do you? Perhaps other people are just some sort of automata that perform their tasks with no internal life.

Descartes's follower Nicolas Malebranche applied those worries to dogs. What's even worse, he based his practice on those doubts: he kicked dogs. When some good person passing by told him to stop, as he's hurting the animal, Malebranche claimed that dogs are just machines. "What do you mean?" the man replied, "It's nonsense! He's hurt! He screams every time you hit him!" This didn't make much impression on Nicolas. "That's exactly what I mean! He screams *every time* you kick him! His behavior is automatic! The dog has no soul!"

Malebranche's problem is behind us now. We'll assume what we hope is obvious to most of the readers of this volume: that dogs actually do feel and do think, that they remember, consider, believe things, and aim for various objectives. The reader should keep in mind though that there are still some scholars who disagree. However, these philosophers are usually suspicious of all thinking-for them, not just dogs' thinking. Some philosophers are reluctant to grant any serious mental life to anybody.

But we're going to look at a different issue: can dogs *think that we think*? Before we can investigate this question, we first have to explain what thinking is all about.

What Do You Suppose Thinking Is?

Nowadays many cognitive scientists, including philosophers and psychologists, have offered a theory of what thinking is. It's called the Representational Theory of Mind (RTM). It's not universally accepted, though it seems fair to say that the majority takes some form of RTM for granted, even if sometimes unknowingly.

Some say the Representational Theory of Mind has been around at least since the seventeenth century and that Descartes should be considered its godfather. Nowadays, its most famous proponent might be the philosopher Jerry Fodor, whose work aims at explaining the general structure of RTM.

RTM recognizes that the mental life can be roughly divided into two parts: one is thinking that . . ., hoping that . . ., worrying that . . ., and the other includes feelings, perceptual images, sounds, and so forth. The former are collectively known as *propositional attitudes* (the term will become clear in just a moment). In our everyday lives, propositional attitudes are not separated from the rest of what's going on in our minds. When we hope that the lunch will not turn out to be too expensive, we have images in our minds, various feelings, and so on. But it's useful for psychology to treat propositional attitudes separately from other aspects of mental life, just as it's usually useful in physics to separate the information about the velocity of a body and its mass from the information about its color.

While our knowledge of what dogs' sensations are like is rather limited (can you even imagine what it's like to have a sense of smell as refined as dogs have?), many people would readily assume that dogs do have at least *some* propositional attitudes: that they *think that* they will get food soon, that they *want to* go for a walk, and so on. Dogs do notice and remember things and they do pursue goals. They seem to base their actions on their beliefs, their wants, and their memories.

The view that dogs do have such mental states is perfectly consistent with the main claim of the RTM: subjects behave the way they do because there are things they believe in, and some things they want. If a human wants money, and if she thinks that in order to get some she has to either work or steal, and she does not want to steal, she'll go get a job. And it seems fair to say that if a dog wants a bone, and he thinks that by barking he will get one, he'll bark. Whether he'll succeed is another story: the dog can overestimate the effect the barking has on you, and be shouted at instead of being rewarded with what he wants.

You can *want* what you *believe in* and *vice versa.* If you were not able to do so, how could you know that you had gotten what you wanted? According to the RTM, you can do this because the propositional attitudes are composed of two parts. One determine what kind of *attitude* you have—whether it's believing, wanting, seeing, or fearing—while the other determines what *is* believed, wanted, seen, or feared. This object of thought and wants is called the *content* (or the proposition) of the propositional attitude. You can think of *the attitudes* as mental 'boxes' for the propositions. Thinking is in a sense filling those boxes with content: you never *just believe*, period, nor *just hope*, period; you believe *that it's time to walk your dog*, or you hope *that your dog will not tear apart your carpet*. You need propositions for your propositional attitudes and you need *concepts* to build some.

Concepts are mental primitives, images of things in the world, tiny little symbols out of which an image is built of what the world is like according to you and of what you'd like to happen, and so on. So, if you have the concepts DOG, EAT, MEAT, you can think that *dogs eat meat*. You put the concepts in the right order (it does make a difference—think about *dogs eat meat* versus *meat eats dogs*), and then into in the proper mental 'box'—voilà! Here you are, thinking fondly that *dogs eat meat*. And something like a proposition *I eat meat* gets into your dog's wishing box quite frequently. Now it should be clear why the theory is called the 'Representational Theory of Mind': complexes of concepts *represent* the states of things in the world.

Finally, representation doesn't have to be faithful and our mental representations don't have to correspond to what is real. Just as you can build false sentences from your words, you can form false beliefs from your concepts. But this doesn't mean that you (or your dog) are completely left on your own. There are mechanisms which help both of you to co-ordinate your world view with reality. That's what your nose, eyes, and ears are for: they inform you about what's happening around you.

Just the evidence of your senses won't get you very far. But you can draw on the knowledge you already have, and get much further. In a normally functioning adult human mind this knowledge includes understanding that there are things called *mental states*. We can't see or hear other people's mental states, but we can use them to help us explain what makes those people behave the way they do.

Sounds Familiar? It's Supposed To

The RTM follows quite closely our usual common-sense idea of mental life. In our ordinary life, we very often explain both human behavior and dog behavior by appealing to what those humans or dogs want, and how they act to obtain what they want, given what they believe the situation is. We don't just *believe* and *wish and so on*, but we also have the concepts BELIEF, WISH, and so on, and therefore we can think about what *other* individuals think.

We characterize the contents of other individuals' beliefs and wishes, for instance by putting a sentence after the word 'that' in contexts such as *believes that*, or *wishes that*. You may not care so much about concepts, content, representations, and stuff, but you surely say things like 'Both Sam and Mary think that the Democrats will win the next election' and 'Fido wants to go for a walk'. The RTM is *a philosophical theory of mind*, but it's also a refined and systematized version of our everyday thinking about thinking—an ability often referred to as a *common-sense theory of mind*.

Our beliefs about mental states of others aren't always true. For example, some people attribute intentions to ordinary objects, like cars (they say the engine doesn't *want* to start), while others act like Nicolas Malebranche and refuse to accept that dogs have thoughts.

Minds in the Dogs' World

Assuming RTM is true of dogs, then dogs have some concepts. But what are the concepts they have? They surely do not possess every one we do. Humans tend to miss that point. And so, on a Christmas day, the father of one us wanted to feed a dog some cake. He was asked not to do it, because cake is not good food for a dog. 'You're cruel, let him know it's Christmas!' the father replied. Well, he might have wished well—but dogs don't care about Christmas, they just don't have the concept CHRISTMAS as we know it. And cake is still not good food for a dog.

Dogs deal with food, walks, and so on, so they may have the relevant concepts FOOD, WALK, and so on. They deal with humans and human actions too, on an everyday basis. According to archaeological evidence, the dog was the first species domesticated by our ancestors. It surely would be beneficial for dogs to develop some understanding of human behavior and to acquire knowledge about what causes it. Using concepts like BELIEF, SEE or WANT could enable them to predict our behavior better and even to influence it—that's what *humans* use their commonsense theory of mind for.

Dogs' knowledge and concepts can be quite different from ours. We surely shouldn't expect them to understand the human psyche the way we do. It seems probable, for example, that dogs do not have the idea of as many attitudes as we do: they may understand just WANTING and SEEING but not BELIEVING. Or it may turn out that dogs' ability to represent the content of mental states in others is constrained in ways it is not in humans.

For some researchers and thinkers the claim that dogs may have some understanding of the mental life of humans is not just a biased conviction taken for granted by the majority of the dog-lovers. It can be a subject to theoretical considerations and experimental scrutiny. Actually, we feel that that you had enough of the former, so let's have a look at what evidence would be useful.

Dog, the Mind Reader

Picture yourself working in the garden. You were just putting the trash out and on your way back you found yourself trapped outside the fence. The wind slammed the gate and you had left the keys on the bench inside. You looked around helplessly and even laughed at yourself for a moment. But after a while you were showing clear signs of frustration. You started to rattle the handle and push your whole body against the gate as if you were trying to force your way through. Your dog was watching you all the time but left when you started getting irritated. You were just about to try to climb the wire fence when the dog came back and now it is staring at you and waging its tail, your set of keys hanging from its mouth.

A true mind-reader! It seems as if it understood what his owner's thoughts: the owner's intention is the get in, he wants to open the gate and he wishes he had his key. Neither of us two could recall any impressive story like the one above involving his own dog, although we strongly believe that there are smart dogs in the world. In fact, this hypothetical example is based on an actual task invented in the 1970s by David Premack and Guy Woodruff for Sarah, a remarkable chimpanzee. After watching movie clips of men struggling to accomplish different tasks (such as a man trying to free himself from a locked cage), Sarah had no problem whatsoever choosing from among many photographs the one depicting an object that would help the man to succeed (in this case the photo of a key).

Premack and Woodruff famously concluded that the chimpanzee had a theory of mind. However, many thinkers vigorously objected to this interpretation and they had good reason for doing so.

Dog, the Physicist

Let's have another look at the alleged reasoning in the dog-the-mind-reader example. It may look something like this:

> The owner is at the garden gate. He's pushing the handle and pressing the wicket. **So he wants to open it and get in**. But he's not getting in. He has no key in his hands, and neither he is searching thorough his pockets. **So he knows that he does not have the key on him**. It's not possible for him to get through a closed gate without a key. **So he wants the key**.
>
> Therefore I'll bring the key.

This is just one highly speculative example of a string of thoughts that may be happening in the dog's mind. Many of the details are not that relevant. The important part is this: some parts of the reasoning above (in bold) use the concepts of mental representations, while other refer only to physical facts and behaviors. Those that refer to the mental begin with "so . . .," as they are derived from those thoughts that refer to physical facts. That's because we're able to reason about mental states behind physical behaviors only because the former manifest themselves through the latter.

Now, read the same passage but without the sentences in bold. It still sounds like plausible reasoning, doesn't it? The man is at the gate with no key on him, he can't get through without a key, so he'll be given one. This line of reasoning can be pursued with no concepts of mental representations whatsoever. What is needed are concepts pertaining to the physical world (GATE, KEY, BODY) and some naive physical knowledge (for instantce, that the human body cannot make its way through the closed gate and that the gate is opened with the key).

Here's the puzzle: how can we distinguish between these two possible interpretations of the dog's behavior? How can we tell whether the dog is taking our thoughts into consideration or whether all the knowledge it has concerns the physical world?

Dog, the Statistician

We mentioned that not everybody accepts RTM. Some people would prefer to explain the dog's seemingly clever reaction in another way. While living among humans, the pet dog witnessed keys being put into locks on countless occasions. There's nothing that clever in noticing and remembering that keys and doors usually go together, if you experienced them together so many times. From his own experience the dog might have even picked up that particular keys are used on particular doors and gates. On this account you expect the dog to be efficient in *discriminating* different aspects of its environment and in detecting *temporal and spatial regularities* among them. But the dog may possess no understanding of what causes those regularities.

This account becomes even more powerful if it allows for an ability to generalize regularities observed. It should be only a matter of time and frequent exposure for the dog to learn that certain behaviors and expressions of the owner (a sad face, a nervous voice) appear when one of the events that is usually associated with another doesn't happen. First, the dog notices that the owner's nervous behavior occurs when he is at the closed gate with no key in his hand, but also when he is at the stove with an egg in his hand and the burner is on but there is no pan nearby. This may lead the dog to associate the nervous behaviors with the absence of certain elements in the environment, but again: no understanding of the causal link between the fact that there is no pan in view and the human's sad face is required.

Beliefs about False Beliefs

Let's get back to the issue that was bothering many of the readers of Premack and Woodruff: how can we tell whether chimpanzees or dogs are thinking about our thoughts (they use a naive theory of mind) or whether they are thinking only about physical facts and behaviors (they rely on a naive physics)? Is the dog thinking that you're pushing the gate *because it's closed* or is or is he able to conceive that it's because you *think that it's closed?* It seems virtually impossible to tell these two possibilities apart because the thought that the dog is supposed to "put into the human's head" is the thought that the dog itself is likely to have: the belief that the gate is closed. It would be much easier if the human thought something other than what the dog thought. The content of the thought that the dog itself *has* should be different from the content of the thought that the dog is only *thinking about.* A clear way for the two contents to be different is for one being true and the other being false. That's why people who wanted to study 'theory of mind' in subjects like animals or small children invented the so-called *false belief tasks.*

A typical false belief task for children often involves staging a short story about Sally and Ann. Sally has a marble she likes a lot and when she is leaving for a while to play outside she places her marble into a basket. While she is away and can't see what is going on naughty Ann moves Sally's marble from the basket to the box. But here's Sally back again and she wants to play with her marble. Where will she look for her marble—the child is asked—in the basket (where Sally left it) or in the box (where it actually is now)? In order to answer correctly, child has to understand that although the marble is now in the box, so far as Sally knows, it still is in the basket, as she didn't witness it being moved by Ann.

For a long time there seemed to be an almost universal agreement among developmental psychologists that only children aged four or older are capable of such reasoning. A breakthrough study was published in 2005 in the journal *Science*, suggesting that even fifteen-month-old infants may have some understanding of false beliefs in others. Kristine Onishi and Renée Baillargeon managed to show that at this age infants are surprised to see that a person is reaching for some object in the correct location (where the object actually is) even though she wasn't watching when the object was moved from where she had left it.

This study was done with human babies not with dogs, but it's important for the dog case too. It suggests that some understanding of the mind is possible without a developed human language. It makes the claims about the theory of mind in non-verbal animals more plausible. Infants don't talk but they look and they stare. And they stare even more when they see something they like or something that surprises them. This simple fact had an enormous impact on research methods in developmental neuropsychology. Most of what we currently know about the development of infant perception and cognition relies on the times infants spend staring at surprising events. Unfortunately, so far, few researchers have successfully used the same logic and methods to study dogs or other animals.

Pretenders

Dogs do not speak English and we're not sure yet how to interpret their looking-times. Many theorists would advise waiting for the results of the false belief tasks before granting any serious understanding of mental representations to anybody, let alone to dogs. But at the moment we don't really seem to know how to administer a task like this to a dog.

It's even worse. Dogs do not show clear signs of pretense. Why should *this* bother us? The main reason for focusing on anybody's understanding of *false* rather than true belief is this: it is a useful way of demonstrating that the subject is able to reason about the situation not only on the basis of her own mental representation (that the marble is in the box now) but also on the basis of another person's mental representation which is different from her own (that the marble is still in the basket). Arguably, pretense would show the same thing.

When you think that Sally will look for the marble in its *old location*, because she thinks it's still there, you yourself are perfectly aware of the marble *actual location*: if I asked *you* for the marble, you'd reach to the correct box. We're able to use two different representation of the same situation: the true one for ourselves, and the false one for the other person. The first one guides our own actions, but we're able to use the false one as well, just for the purpose of predicting what another person would do.

Children show a similar ability when they pretend for the purpose of play. They'd have a lot of fun pretending that the piece of clay is a cookie and feeding it to a doll but you won't see them trying to eat the make-believe cookie themselves. They'd be surprised if you took a bite! So, although they play as if the piece of clay were edible, at the same time they know it's not. It seems that in both cases (pretend play and false-belief understanding) the same basic mechanism is needed: one's own representation of a real situation has to be kept separate from another representation of the same situation which happens to diverge from reality but is used for particular purposes (playing or predicting somebody's actions). Dogs, like many other animals, certainly do engage in play, but unfortunately at the moment nobody seems to have a slightest idea of what canine behavior could count as pretend play.

Deceivers

It's not that clear whether dogs deceive people, although for our case it would be great if they did. When you deceive somebody, you are actively trying to make her mental representation differ from yours, as well as from reality (to be more exact: from what you think is real—you might be wrong all along). In order to want somebody else to be deceived in this sophisticated manner one has to have a notion of false belief.

But consider this: oftentimes we deceive in order not to allow somebody's mental representation to originate in the first place (a kid would snatch candy off the table only when granny's not watching and many dogs would master this 'technique' as well). But here it seems that the deceiver wants another person just to remain ignorant about something and not necessarily to have a belief with a particular false content. In this case a less advanced ability is required on the part of deceiver. She has to understand that it's possible for another mind *not to have a belief* that she herself has, but she doesn't have to understand that another mind can *have a belief with a content* which is different from the content of her own belief. So, evidence of deception in dogs may not only help to answer the question of whether dogs think about our thinking, but it may also suggest in what ways their theory of the human mind differs from the one that we have.

We went through the laundry list of behaviors which many people would like to see before granting any serious understanding of mental states to non-verbal subjects like dogs or human infants. And it seems that dogs do not show them or, at least, that we cannot spot them in dogs yet. Now what? Is the case for dog the psychologist lost?

The Point of Pointing

There's one spectacular dog ability that may shed new light on our problem: dogs are just amazing at reading human behavior and especially our pointing gestures. A setup for a typical study looks like this: there are two identical opaque containers standing in front of the dog. One of the container has just been baited with a snack or a toy. During the baiting, both containers were hidden behind a short screen so the dog couldn't see where the snack actually went. But now the screen goes down and all the dog is left with are those two identical containers to choose from and the human pointing at one of them with a finger. You really don't have to wait for the dog to make up its mind. Most of the dogs most of the time would go for the one pointed at.

We can almost hear all the dog-lovers shrugging their shoulders and saying "Big deal! My Fido does it all the time." Good for you and good for Fido, too! Stay with us to see why some people think this common behavior might not be trivial at all. We can also hear all the skeptics saying: "Big deal! Wouldn't they use their noses in the first place?" Nice try. Of course only those studies are worth mentioning in which researchers bothered to make the bait undetectable by smell alone and managed to show that dogs do not rely on odor (they do not prefer the baited container when nobody's pointing).

Here's another concern: there's nothing clever about a dog reacting to human behavior; dogs live with humans and they know how to benefit from searching the locations made salient by a stretched human finger (remember the idea of dog the statistician?). Well . . . of course they learn. All minds do. The question is not: 'How come that dogs read human gestures?' but rather: 'How come that they are so efficient and fast at doing this?' There are two important reasons to suspect that dogs do not build up their ability to read human gestures piecemeal by laborious detection of how the sight of a pointing hand occurs together with the appearance of food. First, even dog puppies, with no extensive contact with people, are able to use human communicative gestures in order to find hidden food and a lot of dogs are successful at the very first trial. Second, the range of different human gestures that the dogs successfully rely on is far greater then just a familiar hand with a stretched finger. Much less obvious cues would do as well: bowing, nodding, head-turning, glancing and even placing a piece of plastic in front of the baited container. How many experiences might those dogs have had with humans placing plastic markers at the location of the food?

For us, what make all those different gestures similar is their meaning derived from the intention behind them. You can point for me with your elbow, hip, chin or forehead (especially if there's a good reason for this, such as if your hands are full or busy). I'll get what you mean, if not at the very first time, than soon after. It's my understanding of mental states behind the gesture that makes me so efficient, flexible, and fast in reading the gesture itself.

Unlike false belief tasks (or pretend play or some forms of deception) the pointing studies do not provide clear evidence of thinking about mental *representations*. But they provide evidence for what is a prerequisite of the human-like mental reasoning: dogs find some non-obvious, deeper similarities between human behaviors as superficially diverse as gazing, finger-pointing, and placing a plastic marker. For dogs, human behavior seems to be something more than just a movement of the human body.

What Your Dog Can Tell You about Philosophy

We're eagerly looking forward to new experiments with dog thinking, and we strongly believe that when it comes to the dogs' thinking about our thinking, the last word hasn't yet been said. In fact, this quest for understanding has only just begun. Yet this enterprise, unlike that of Malebranche and Descartes, seems much more focused on learning from dogs about the concepts we may share with them rather than on teaching us why we can't share any. Philosophy can tell you things about your dog, but your dog can also teach you things about himself. And if this happens, your philosophy can only get better. So take you dogs for a walk and pay attention. Walk with them often.[1]

[1] The writing of this chapter was partially supported by a Polish government grant awarded to Hernik, from the State Committee for Scientific Research grant (No. 1 H01F 045 29).

8

The Dog Who Mistook His Leg for a Meal

SARAH JONES

German Shepherds have a long-held reputation for great intelligence. From their heroic service in wars to their remarkable rescues and recoveries, their intelligence is virtually unrivalled. My shepherd, Aristotle, seemed no exception. Indeed so great was his early cleverness that my neighbors nicknamed him Houdini. Then, however, came the harrowing experience that forever shook my confidence in such attributions. I returned home one day to find that my clever canine—face drenched in blood—had eaten his own leg. Fur, skin, and flesh—from shoulder to paw—were gone. All that remained was bone—and the look of proud success on Aristotle's face.

Just weeks before this incident, Aristotle's (now consumed) leg was grossly injured in an accident. In addition to damaging the nerves, a large area of skin was ripped from his upper leg, leaving the muscle exposed. The exposed flesh required daily trips to the vet for cleaning and re-bandaging. And, until he mistook it for a meal, the raw flesh was on the mend; incredibly, there was new skin already forming over the exposed muscle. Apparently, however, the fresh sinewy assortment and newly generated skin proved too tantalizing a temptation to Aristotle. In less than an hour, and in seeming hedonistic delight, he removed—and ate—it all.

Aristotle's act is food for philosophical thought. Surely, eating his leg reveals something fundamental about the nature of Aristotle's mind, but what? Does it reveal that his sense of bodily identity is so limited that he can't recognize his parts as his own? Or, does it reveal that his consciousness is so tied to the present that his behavior is not informed by the consequences it will likely yield? Or, on the contrary, does it show the same sort of sophisticated thinking as that displayed by Aaron Ralston who had the courage and intelligence to cut off his hand to save his life when it became lodged under a boulder?

What Aristotle's act reveals depends, of course, on *why* he ate his leg. If he ate it because, failing to recognize it as his own, he mistook it for a meal, then his act suggests that a dog's sense of self-identity is extremely limited. Yet if he ate it, not for want of recognition, but rather, because he sensed it hindered his survival, then we have a very different story: his act reveals not discontinuity with the human mind, but continuity. But which of these is the better explanation? Which has the weight of reason on its side? Before we begin to judge the alternative explanations themselves, we need to examine more closely Aristotle's apparent act of auto-cannibalism and the events surrounding it. After all, our explanation of any event can be no better than our description of the event itself.

The Accident

It was not a good day. I was feeling ill. So, rather than his usual off-leash run at the beach, I kept Aristotle close to my side, and he was feeling cheated. I felt guilty, but believed his return-from-the-beach treat would make up for it. When we retuned home, I flung open the Jeep door and we both jumped out. I fully expected Aristotle would race to the front door, barge into the kitchen and, drooling with anticipation, park himself at the refrigerator.

Things certainly didn't go as planned. Rather than faithfully racing to the door, Aristotle bolted full-speed into the street and a very large, speeding SUV. In an instant, his head was pulled under the wheel and his body violently twisted as he was dragged down the pavement. Aristotle lay in the road, his cries of agony matched only by mine.

As a consequence of the accident, Aristotle lost all sensation in his left front leg. The nerves that gave his leg sensibility were severed, and thereafter he showed no capacity to use it. "We'll give it a couple of weeks," the vet said. "Sometimes the feeling comes back. If not, we'll have to remove the leg." In the meantime, I was instructed to lift his leg as he walked (without my doing so the leg dragged and became twisted) and tap his now dead paw, so as to "remind" him of its function.

Terrified he might lose his leg and gripped by the guilt that I had facilitated his accident, I did not leave his side for two weeks. I designed a pulley for his insensitive leg and lifted and tapped with each step. Aristotle grew stronger and faster each day. Soon he was running at full speed again. I ran alongside, lifting high the insensitive leg to prevent it from being dragged or twisted. Things were looking up. In the course of two weeks, his superficial wounds had all but healed, his spirit seemed better than ever, and the likelihood that his leg would recover seemed high.

Optimistic and confident, after fourteen days of constant companionship, I left him alone for an hour to attend my daughter's skating exhibition. That was the hour he ate his own leg. It was as if he had been planning it all along, just waiting for the chance. Returning home, I discovered him in a blood-drenched room, his leg bones licked clean and dangling from his body. He showed no shame. He seemed proud and satisfied, as if he had achieved something great. But why did he do this? How should we explain this act of self-mutilation?

Identity and Difference

Could Aristotle have simply mistaken his leg for a meal? As his teeth carved through and removed his muscle, might he have believed he was enjoying a juicy tender steak? As he gnawed away in hedonic delight, was he oblivious to the fact that *this* bone (albeit delicious and satiating) was *his* bone? Could such a flagrant—and gruesome—misidentification be possible? Perhaps the problem is one of identity.

Philosophers have long been concerned with the problem of identity. There are in fact several problems of identity: numeric (what makes one thing one, not two); qualitative (whether two things that are qualitatively identical are in fact one, not two); personal (what makes a person the same person over time). The kind of identity that may prove philosophically important here, however, is the problem of bodily self-identity: the problem of distinguishing what parts of the world belong to one's bodily self and what parts do not.

Ordinarily, identifying which parts belong to one's self at a particular point in time is not problematic: one has no problem recognizing which parts (borderline cases of eyelashes and fingernails aside) are parts of one's bodily self and which are not. I, for example, easily recognize both that these legs are mine and that those (yours, for example) are not. I do not confuse myself with the table, nor do I misattribute the parts that properly belong to me to another. This holds true for dogs and humans alike. Canines do not—any more than humans—ordinarily evidence problems identifying their parts as their own. Yet an identity explanation would have it that the day of the incident Aristotle did mistake a part of himself for something it was not. Apparently, in Aristotle's case something went entirely wrong.

One might be tempted to explain Aristotle's self-mutilation by pointing out that since he could no longer feel his leg, it's not surprising that he ate it. It did look, after all, just like a store-bought meaty treat, and doubtless smelled and tasted like one too. This explanation, however, is incomplete. For Aristotle's absence of sensation, though significant, cannot—in itself—explain how or why he could mistake his leg for a meal. That the mere absence of sensation is not sufficient to explain mistaking one's parts for something they are not is clear from analogous cases in persons where sight, smell, and taste are intact, but tactile awareness is wanting (cases of peripheral neuropathy, for example). In such instances a person does not begin to *gnaw* at or consume her affected digits. Rather, in the absence of neural normalcy, a person continues to recognize her parts as her own; she certainly does not mistake them for a meal.

Even in cases of the most radical sensory deprivation, such as those described by the neurologist Oliver Sacks in his best-selling *The Man Who Mistook His Wife for a Hat* (1985), a person still recognizes her parts as her own and continues to treat them accordingly.[1] Consider Sacks's "Disembodied Lady" Christina. Christina suffered a complete loss of proprioception. Proprioception, a sense we hear little about, is central to our awareness of our parts, their location, and our parts *as parts* of ourselves. It's that sense which makes us aware, for instance, of the position of our parts without the need for looking. As Sacks describes it, "it is only by courtesy of proprioception . . . that we *feel* our bodies as proper to us, as our 'property', as our own" (p. 43). Christina's massive propriocep-

---

[1] Sacks describes a few notable exceptions in both "The Man Who Mistook His Wife For a Hat," and in "The Man Who Fell Out of Bed." Though each of these cases involved a failure to recognize one's parts as one's own, neither involved sensory loss.

tive failure resulted in her inability to feel the location of her arms and legs, for example, and also in an inability to feel her body as her own. As she described it, she felt "disembodied."

Though Christina's complete loss of proprioception left her *feeling* disembodied, incapable of *feeling* her body as her own, she continued, however, to *recognize* her body as her own. Admittedly, her continued sense of her parts as her own was awkward and abstract, requiring strained and continuous attention to nearly every part of herself. Yet, she retained that sense in spite of gross sensory loss.

Why then did Christina, but not Aristotle, continue to recognize her parts as her own? Why, although like Christina, unable to *feel* that his parts where his own, could Aristotle not simply *see* that they were? Aristotle's accident left his leg insensitive; it had not left him blind. Yet, in the absence of sensory stimulation from his leg, Aristotle seemed lost: he seemed not to recognize the belongingness of this limb to himself, even with his other senses fully intact; at least consuming his leg suggests that. That Aristotle *could* mistake his leg for a meal, in spite in particular of the intactness of his visual awareness, suggests that the nature of his sense of bodily identity is vastly different, and comparatively far more limited, than our own.

As Christina's case makes clear, the capacity to recognize one's parts as one's own is not—in persons—tied to any one sense: where one sense fails, other senses (notably sight) take over. In Christina's case sight and cognition took over, compensating for the loss of sensation, and allowing her to retain a sense of her own bodily identity. Aristotle's case, by contrast, if his meal really was a mistake, suggests that a dog's sense of the belongingness of its parts is inextricably tied to the single sense of tactile awareness. Seemingly then, whereas a human's sense of bodily identity is over-determined, governed not merely by tactile awareness, nor proprioception, but also vision and cognition and the organs of balance such as the inner ear, a canine's sense of identity evaporates in the absence of sensory normalcy. Perhaps, then, Aristotle's act does reveal a profound difference between a dog's mind and our own.

Intellectual Acts

It's possible, however, that in spite of the simplicity of this explanation, Aristotle's act was no mistake at all. It's entirely possible that

Aristotle continued to recognize his leg was his own but ate it anyway, deliberately, knowingly. But if he was not suffering a lack of self-identity, if he did recognize that the flesh he ate was his own, what was going on? Perhaps Aristotle, fully in command of his faculties, removed and consumed his own flesh for the sake of his own survival, much like Aaron Ralston. Ralston had been hiking solo in Utah's Blue Canyon when his hand became pinned under a thousand-pound boulder. After five days with no sign of rescue, Ralston recognized that his only chance to survive lay in amputating his hand. Forlorn and desperate, he wrapped a make-shift tourniquet around his arm. Using a pocket-knife, he began cutting: first through his skin, then his muscle, and finally his bone. Bleeding, hungry, and exhausted, he rappelled down the canyon wall.

> "It hurt to break the bone, and it certainly hurt to cut through the nerve. But cutting the muscle was not as bad." (Aaron Ralston, "Climber Who Cut off Hand Looks Back: interview by Michael Benoist," *National Geographic News*, National Geographic.com, August 2004)

Ralston's story received world-wide attention which led to the publication of his book, *Between A Rock and a Hard Place*. His act elicited admiration, and no one questioned his sense of bodily self-identity. No one questioned his capacity to recognize his parts as his own. No one questioned *why* he removed his own hand because the reason was so seemingly obvious: had he not removed his it, he would have died. He removed it to survive. Ralston's act was unquestionably an act of intelligence and will. Might the cause of Aristotle's act be better understood—like Ralston's—as an explicit and conscious act of self-preservation? Might Aristotle's act too be an act of intelligence, foresight, and courage, rather than of impulse, short-sightedness, or limited self-awareness?

Neurotic Attachments

In retrospect, Aristotle's leg—like Ralston's hand—was doubtless only a hindrance to his survival. With both tactile and proprioceptive awareness gone, he could neither feel it nor sense its whereabouts. Even with our pulley system, it was constantly in his way, threatening to trip him and become twisted, and making every motion potentially dangerous. Truly, the leg posed more threat than promise to Aristotle's future. Why then all my efforts to preserve it? Removing it was clearly the better choice. In fact, the vet made it clear from the beginning that there was only a small chance that Aristotle's nerves would ever regenerate, that he would ever regain the use of his leg. From the moment of the accident to the time of lunch, his leg showed *no sign* of improvement. The periodic sensory tests were unambiguous: his nerves simply no longer functioned. His leg was no more felt by him than my shoe is now felt by me. Arguably, it was equally inessential to his identity.

It was not Aristotle, not even his veterinarian, but his owner, that desperately sought to preserve his limb. In retrospect, how ridiculous it must have looked to passers-by, my frantic lifting and tapping, my hyper vigilant watch for any sign of sensory recovery. How intractable the vet must have found my neurotic and guilty attachment to his limb, a connection that led me to insist there was hope even when blood-drawing pins pushed into his paw elicited no response.

Perhaps Aristotle's intelligence took over where mine left off. Maybe—like Ralston—Aristotle realized his limb was useless. Maybe he knew there was no hope for sensory recovery, that the efforts to save his limb were both ridiculous and futile, and so tried to remove it with the courage and foresight I lacked. If Aristotle did gnaw through and consume his leg because—like Ralston—he *knew* that he must, then his act was neither a mistake nor evidence of a limited sense of self-identity. On the contrary, it was an act of foresight, self-awareness, and intelligence. And if it was *that* kind of act, then his act discloses not a fundamentally different sense of identity, but rather, a cognitive sophistication much like our own.

According to Ralston, it was on the basis of his beliefs about the direness of his situation and his reasoning about his chance of surviving that he decided to cut off his hand. If Aristotle's act was *literally* like Ralston's, an act issuing from conscious and deliberate reason, then his act must have involved relevantly similar thoughts and processes. Aristotle must have arrived at the belief that his leg was now useless, for example, by considering he empirical evidence (the leg's continued insensitivity, its impairment of his attempts to walk), just as Ralston must have considered the degree to which he was dehydrated and his inability to move so long as his arm was pinned. To arrive at the further belief that the limb should be removed, Aristotle, again like Ralston, must have believed that the situation was not going to resolve itself, that his mangled insensitive leg was not going to regain sensitivity, for example.

The Problem of Justification

But can we justify such an intellectualized explanation of *Aristotle's* "reason" for acting? Is it reasonable to ascribe such processes (inference, generalization) and types of mental states (beliefs, reasons) to a *dog*? These capacities and types of mental states are necessary for that kind of conscious calculation: without them, one cannot believe, reason, or infer. So if Aristotle's act was truly like Ralston's, we must attribute the same states of mind. It's to the justification of these attributions that we must turn our philosophical attention.

Questions about justification, what it is and what the standards for it should be, belong to a field of philosophy called epistemology. Most epistemologists agree that the degree to which any belief is *justified* depends on the quality and extent of the evidence. In his "The Ethics of Belief," W.K. Clifford expresses a classic view of justification: "It is wrong always, everywhere, to believe anything upon insufficient evidence." Without evidence, there is no justification. In terms of the evidence, however, claiming that Aristotle's act was the intellectual equivalent of Ralston's is highly problematic. In fact, though perhaps more consistent with our common sense about canines, *all* such explanations of canine behavior are deeply troubling.

Unfortunately, to claim that Aristotle reasoned his way to gnawing off his arm seems to require more than the evidence will warrant. For part of that explanation requires that Aristotle had certain beliefs, the belief, for instance, that his insensitive leg would not recover. Therein, however, lies a problem. Beliefs seem to be essentially tied to linguistic structures of a sort that dogs don't understand. The problem isn't that our descriptions of a dog's beliefs are composed of words and sentences. Rather, the problem is that the phrases used to describe the belief's content, for example, "that his leg is insensitive," in the belief ascription, "Aristotle believes that his leg is insensitive," must be understood by Aristotle in order to justify ascribing the belief to him. To believe anything, we must first and necessarily *understand* what we believe. Thus, for Aristotle to believe that 'his insensitive leg would not recover', he would first and necessarily have to *understand* what 'his insensitive leg would not recover' means. And because statements are linguistic structures, he could understand that statement only if he understood both its terms and its structure: in order to *believe* 'insensitive legs should be removed', that is, he must understand the concepts ('insensitive', 'leg', and 'remove') *and* the structural difference between this statement and the statement that 'insensitive legs ought *not* to be removed', for example; otherwise he would have no idea *what* he is believing. To paraphrase the logician Alfred Tarski, it is true that Aristotle *believes* that his leg is insensitive if and only if it is true that he believes *that* his leg is insensitive.

There is, however, no evidence and hence no justification for believing, that dogs—no matter how sweet or how clever—comprehend the language or structures toward which states of belief are directed. Moreover, there's good evidence that they don't. Though Aristotle responds to familiar individual concepts ('sit', 'treat', 'beach', 'walk'), it's obviously a stretch of imagination to think he understands the concepts of 'insensitive' or 'unrecoverable'. "Unrecoverable," for example, implies a kind of judgment about the probable connection between a present condition and time, a leg without feeling, and a future condition and time, a leg more useful, but this seems to require a theoretical explanation that is beyond the canine mind. Moreover, there is good evidence that his mental states—whatever they are—lack the structure essential to belief: whether I say, "It certainly is *not* a good day for a walk," or "Today we will go for a walk," Aristotle's response is the same: Ears pointed and tail wagging with anticipation.

Although it's certainly common enough to describe one's dog as 'wanting to go for a walk' or to say that the dog inferred from the leash in one's hand that 'it's time to go', it is best not to take such casual canine communication too seriously. For, as the preceding shows, to literally want to 'go for a walk' or believe that 'it is time to go', one must understand not merely a term or two, but rather the entire linguistic expression, and that requires mastery of both the particular language in which it is expressed and the capacity to discriminate the particular linguistic structure through which it is expressed. And, though Aristotle is indeed clever, he certainly is not *that* clever.

Therefore, we can't justify the claim that Aristotle's act resulted from the same kind of cognitive deliberation as Ralston's. Lacking the beliefs necessary for such cognitive deliberation, Aristotle could not have acted on their basis. In fact, careful consideration of the kinds of attributions involved in that kind of explanation reveals that explaining Aristotle's act as the result of his *belief* that his leg was insensitive, is not merely epistemologically problematic, it is manifestly absurd.

Intelligence in Action

What then can we say of Aristotle's act? Clearly we cannot justify saying it was the intellectual equivalent of Ralston's. Ralston's act required linguistic sophistication, an understanding of semantics and grammar. But from the fact that Aristotle lacks this type of sophistication, it does not follow that he is entirely unsophisticated. Indeed, though his intelligence cannot be of the same type as Ralston's—linguistic or propositional—it certainly does not follow that he is unintelligent, nor that he blindly mistook his leg for a snack. Indeed, as Gilbert Ryle pointed out in his groundbreaking work *The Concept of Mind*, it's a mistake (what he called the "intellectualist legend") to assume that the only kind of intelligence is linguistic or propositional:

> The general assertion that all intelligent performance requires to be prefaced by the consideration of appropriate propositions rings implausibly, even when it is apologetically conceded that the required consideration is often very swift and may go unmarked by the agent. (*The Concept of Mind*, p. 29)

There are many kinds of intelligence, not just one. To conclude, therefore, that Aristotle unintelligently mistook his leg for a meal because he lacked propositional intelligence no more follows from the evidence than concluding that Ralston's act was a colossal mistake.

Why don't we conclude that Ralston mistook his hand for a rope, for example? Of course, we don't draw that conclusion because Ralston explained his action. But, suppose Ralston had not explained his action, or that we simply did not know his explanation. Suppose that we knew only that Ralston was trapped by a boulder, cut off his hand, and survived. Why, without hesitation, would we still conclude his act was intelligent? Why would we still assume that he acted *for the sake of* his own survival? Our conclusion cannot be based simply on the act of self-amputation. The act, in itself, is silent.

We would reach the conclusion that the act was intelligent only because we assume that this otherwise gruesome act is continuous with Ralston's more pedestrian acts; that is, we unconsciously place Ralston's self-amputation in the context of his other actions, and because so many of these other acts are manifestly intelligent, we infer that here also his act was intelligent. The intelligence revealed in his other actions is not limited to sentential or propositional intelligence: consider, for example, the intelligence required to navigate his way up and down the sides of rocky cliffs or through deep canyons. In the absence of the assumption that the act of cutting off his hand is continuous with his other acts, given only the act itself, we might (of course mistakenly) conclude that Ralston—blood dripping from a self-severed limb—was insane, or suffered from bodily dismorphic disorder; we certainly could not infer on the basis of the act alone that it was rational. It is, then, only in light of our implicit placement of this action in its larger context that we conclude—and are warranted in concluding—that its cause was intelligence, not insanity.

Equally with respect to Aristotle, if we consider his act in isolation we are likely to draw the wrong conclusion. As an isolated act, we are distracted by its gruesomeness and seemingly anomalous nature. But this myopic restriction of our attention to the exceptional features of this singular act ignores much relevant evidence and leads to explanatory error. The correct explanation of Aristotle's act, like Ralston's, is not disclosed in the singularity of the act of self-amputation, but rather, in the context of the rich variety daily actions which consistently amaze me. It is here, in his everyday canine cleverness, that the true nature of his canine mind is revealed. And what's revealed is not an insensitive automaton, but rather, an animal of great sophistication and intelligence. It is that intelligence, consistently evidenced by all of our canine companions, which can direct us to the best explanation of what Aristotle did on that harrowing August afternoon.

Aristotle's intelligence—both before and after the accident—is unmistakable: as a puppy, his canine shenanigans drew continuous admiration, mostly from neighbors, but occasionally also from "animal control." Within moments of being introduced to his rather large and perennial-laden yard, for example, Aristotle learned precisely which paths to take and which to avoid, never once crushing the perennials, never failing to stomp on the weeds. His swiftness in early learning was surpassed only by his ingenuity in escaping the fenced yard and circumventing all efforts to contain him. Indeed, even when left in the "expert" care of a kennel, (the only, and regrettable, time), he learned to undo their "un-undoable" steel latches, and fled.

Now, with only three legs, Aristotle's intelligence in action is only more remarkable. With incredible speed and competence, he mastered the complex balancing acts required to continue his old four-legged habits. The simple act of marking a fire hydrant or tree, for instance, initially posed a most obvious problem, but after a few stumbles, Aristotle's stood proud and balanced. Climbing and descending stairs like a tripod was initially a great challenge, but after plummeting to the bottom just once, he had it licked. Even his old tricks of sneakily scavenging food from garbage cans and unattended tables, in a few short weeks, posed no problem. Shortly, Aristotle's competent and mischievous nature was indistinguishable (excepting, of course, the missing leg) from its old four-legged self.

Such consistent examples of obvious intelligence impressed even the ancient Greeks. As remarked by Sextus Empiricus:

> The dog even shares in the far-famed "dialectic." The dog makes use of the fifth complex indemonstrable syllogism when, on arriving at the spot where three ways meet, after smelling at the two roads by which the quarry did not pass, he rushes off at once to the third without stopping to smell. The dog implicitly reasons thus: The creature either went by this road, or by that, or by the other: but it did not go by this or by that: therefore it went by the other. (Sextus Empiricus, *Outlines of Pyrrhonism*, Harvard University Press, p. 41)[2]

These behaviors, of course, are commonplace for canines. But that's the point. Aristotle's pedestrian acts, like Ralston's, *consistently* evidence intelligence. And though they may not (Sextus notwithstanding)—indeed *cannot*—evidence the kind of intelligence necessary for belief (what Ryle would have called "knowledge that," where the intelligence displayed is of propositions),

---

[2] The "fifth complex indemonstrable syllogism" is reasoning which takes the form, "Either A or B or C is true. Neither A nor B is true. Therefore, C must be true." Although Sextus may go a bit too far here in implying that the dog's reasoning is based on his beliefs, the kind of intelligence that underlies the dog's behavior is what matters. For a fascinating discussion of this example of dog reasoning, see "Logic For Dogs," Chapter 13 in this volume.

they certainly do evidence another kind of intelligence, the intelligence necessary to know *how* to do so many things.

Consistently, like people, dogs display a keen understanding of their environment, their parts, and how to manipulate both to their purposes. They know how to escape from their yards, they know how to sneak food when no one is looking, and they know how to care for their young. Moreover, they seem perfectly competent at recognizing the boundaries of their physical selves, and they do not mistake their parts for meals.

Why should we think Aristotle's singular act of eating his own leg is unlike all these other acts?

In truth we have no more cause to conclude that Aristotle mistook his leg for a meal than we do for concluding Ralston mistook his arm for a rope. On the contrary, we have many reasons for concluding his act—like Ralston's—issued from the same natural intelligence that governs his daily behavior. For, like Ralston, the majority of Aristotle's acts too are the product of intelligence. Arguably, therefore, far from being anomalous, Aristotle's act—like Ralston's—was in fact continuous with the intelligence he manifests daily and elsewhere.

It's only apart from the rich and intelligent context of his other actions, then, that we might mistakenly conclude that Aristotle's act (indeed, Ralston's as well) was not merely grotesque, but irrational and unintelligent. What kind of creature, after all, removes or consumes its own flesh? A broader analysis of Aristotle's action requires that we conclude that his act—though perhaps neither linguistic nor syllogistic—was demonstrably intelligent. In fact, in spite of my piles of propositional states, Aristotle, in the end, on that late August afternoon, proved to possess the intelligence I lacked. The only explanation that respects his intelligence is that he, like Ralston, removed his leg to survive. And this act, no less than Ralston's, is remarkable. Thus, though philosophy may, as Aristotle said, "begin in wonder," wonder begins with Aristotle.[3]

---

[3] Many thanks to my brilliant, always quick-witted and linguistically gifted sister Katharine A. Jones for her generous help with this paper. Who knew philosophy could be so fun? Thanks also to my better philosophical half, James Peter Greene, for his careful and cautious commentary on my ideas.

III

Loving Our Best Friend

9

Our Embodied Friendships with Dogs

GLEN A. MAZIS

It's frustrating to many of us that we can't convince others of the reality of our friendship with dogs.

Some of us have a strong sense that our dogs are truly our friends. We might even be tempted to say that dogs are more reliable in the feelings they have for us than are fickle humans, who are often willing to betray or manipulate us for their selfish interests. We might agree that the familiar epithet, "Man's Best Friend," may be apt, because our dog truly is our fondest friend in all the world.

Upon hearing this kind of claim, many people shake their heads sadly, not merely doubtful that it could possibly be true, but also suspecting that anyone capable of such a belief must be a pitiful human being, unable to engage with other humans in fellow feeling. According to this cynical way of thinking, we emotionally disabled dog lovers desperately create an illusion of shared love with an animal to compensate for our inadequacies.

Among such skeptics are a couple who are also dear friends of mine. They are generally knowledgeable and perceptive people. Yet faced with my assertions of friendship with my dog, Bhakti, they are inclined to smirk. They confidently object that animals can only react to food or to some other stimulus which directly indicates the presence of something the animal needs. They feel impelled to break the news, firmly but gently: dogs, like other animals, have no feelings for any particular human individual—nor can they even register the sense of any person around them as a distinctive individual. Dogs, they say, have no emotional capacity to enter into a relationship with a person based upon affection. To the dog, so my these friends of mine tell me, I'm just the guy with the dog food. They admit that the dog might superficially seem emotionally attached to me, but really, they say, the dog's just conditioned to do what it has to do to get some more chow.

My friends are not atypical in their opinions, especially for non-pet people. Non-pet people are quickly identifiable by their rigid postures when approached by a dog, as they lean away from intimate contact and look about for a human worthy of directing their gaze upon, instead of this annoying beast. If they're forced by the dog to pay it some attention or by the group pressure of other people greeting the dog, they will slightly bend over and wave their arms in a skimming motion near the dog, but never bend their knees to get down to a level on the same plane as the dog's face— a respectful way to engage canine companions. To get down on the dog's level, especially that much lower level of a dog like mine, an apple-headed Chihuahua, would be an absurdity to them, whereas to me it's a gesture of accommodation and recognition, a perceptible invitation to enter into a relationship.

Apple-headed Chihuahuas, by the way, are fuller dogs than regular Chihuahuas, more mellow, with faces that somewhat resemble a seal's, unlike their more emaciated, highly-strung cousins. I grew up with a very large boxer, so I have experienced both ends of the dog stature spectrum.

Do Dogs Have Feelings?

I had been living with my dog Bhakti for seven years, when I became ill. Being a marathon runner, I was more concerned about my damaged cartilage and knee surgery than the painful intestinal difficulties I was experiencing. Once my knee was surgically repaired, I suddenly realized my gut needed attention and was astounded to be told that I had a softball-sized cancerous tumor blocking my bowel. Bhakti was well cared for by a person whom she had known closely for her whole life and certainly fed each day of the ten days I was in the hospital having a bowel resection (and thankfully that's all, despite the more dire predictions about the spread of my cancer).

When I was released from the hospital and we drove home and walked in the door to my house, Bhakti came running out and literally cried and howled, and howled and moaned in a wrenchingly pitched way I have never heard from her before or in the six years since. Not only had she missed me, not only had she sensed that something had been threatening to my well-being, but she obviously had been incredibly anxious and distressed in such a way that all this pent up feeling was being released. She carried on for quite some time and reduced all of us to tears and hugs, trying to console her, all the while that she was also continuously snuggling her little head up to me and stopping her hysterics to lick me gratefully. It seems obvious to me that her actions expressed these emotional experiences, but philosophers often have the task of arguing in favor of what seems to be too obvious to need argument.

Non-pet people are not the only ones who would deny Bhakti's fears for my well-being and fears of losing the object of her love, her anguish, pain, relief, and warmth. The smugness of those who deny animal feelings and their capacity for friendship with humans comes from this belittling view of animals being being backed by the experts. Most philosophers or ethologists (scientists who study animal behavior) would tell me that my claim to be friends with dogs are instances of 'anthropomorphizing'. Anthropomorphizing means attributing human feelings and thoughts to entities which don't really have them. Another term is 'projection': dog-lovers are sometimes accused of projecting their own thoughts and emotions onto dogs.

As I wrote that last sentence, Bhakti was peering up at me intently. I know that she had no idea what I was doing or what I was asserting as I wrote. She was probably hoping that some of the muffin I was absentmindedly munching as I typed at the keyboard would end up as a handout to her—the last thing an elderly diabetic dog needs, but again this fact is not something Bhakti is aware of or factors into her lust for blueberry muffins. There's a lot that I could project onto Bhakti, but don't, and there's a lot of projection going on collectively by people in our culture—toys, clothes, and other treats for dogs have become big business at the same time that our busier, more socially fragmented, and isolated lives have made the need for nonhuman companionship stronger.

Misunderstanding Animals

The charge of "anthropomorphizing" has become as destructive to open dialogue about the nature of animals as the phrase "political correctness" has become to a truly open and meditative exploration of political questions. To anthropomorphize is to be blind to the actual experience of animals by attributing human thinking and feeling to them. In regard to friendship with animals, this would mean that people project feelings of loyalty, affection, respect, and shared commitment onto animals in order to meet our human need to overcome loneliness through bogus friendships with animals. Any report that we have identified feelings in animals can be discounted by the charge of anthropomorphism, no matter how real such a feeling may seem to be, given the way the animal behaves.

Certainly, when we look at "teacup" Yorkies in pink dresses and matching hats, St. Bernards lugging around flasks of Johnnie Walker Red Label, or poodles being laced up in jogging shoes, we can see that humans in the contemporary American culture are doing a lot of projecting their own thoughts and feelings onto dogs. Anthropomorphism can sometimes be a real danger. But this doesn't show that *all* perceptions of canine feelings are a result of projection.

Ethologists all know the story of the counting horse, "Clever Hans." Hans achieved fame a hundred years ago for being able to solve arithmetic problems, whether adding or multiplying the number flashed on cards before him, giving the answers by the number of times he tapped his foot.

This was supposed to prove that animals could have human-like intelligence. What's wrong with this approach is that it assumes that animals need to demonstrate *the same kind of intelligence* as humans in order to be intelligent. Assuming animals should make sense of the world in exactly the same ways that humans do, whether by reasoning out situations, doing some abstract mental operation like arithmetic, using tools, or communicating by language, is to be "anthropocentric," to assume that human ways of understanding, communicating, or creating are the only standard against which any other ways are to be measured. It would mean that for animals to be considered capable of friendship, they must behave just as a human friend might, whether by having shared values, being supportive, or being considerate to their friends.

At first Clever Hans passed impartial tests administered by the famous psychologist Carl Stumpf and a panel of judges at the Berlin Psychological Institute in 1904. They failed to find any trickery in Hans's performance. It began to appear that Hans really could add and multiply numbers. That all changed when Stumpf's student, Oskar Pfungst, discovered what was really going on. Hans was responding to subtle cues given completely unconsciously by

Hans's handlers and by others who tried to test the horse's abilities. The horse was sensitive enough to pick up on their emotional excitement and expectation. Without knowing it, the handlers widened their eyes, flared their nostrils, flushed, or altered their breathing, when the right answer was arrived at. Hans could sense this, and would stop tapping at the right number of taps.

Hans didn't fail to demonstrate intelligence by not being able to do abstract mathematics with flash cards. Instead he showed how sensitive and understanding he was in grasping the barely perceptible signs of the feelings of the humans around him. I retell this famous story because it can be used to promote a shift in how we approach our understanding of animals' abilities. In order to consider our dogs' ability to be friends with humans, we should look at other levels of understanding than the usual abstract, rational cognition that we humans often employ to assess ourselves, others, and our relationships. Rather than looking at the traditional standards for entering into friendship based on the assumed essential human abilities, we should look at differing ways that animals might demonstrate having friendships.

The power of this approach is not only that we will no longer fail to see animal's unique abilities, but also that we will reconsider our own feelings and behavior. If philosophy is to tell us something about dogs, it can approach dogs with an eye to their unique and non-human abilities. Since we too are animals, we may learn more about ourselves by seeing hidden aspects of dogs and finding that there are key elements of human friendships that we have ignored. Animals may have lessons to teach us about the nature of friendship in general.

Some might be tempted to *define* "friendship" as a specifically "human activity" that relies upon specific human capacities and interests, and thus close the question without further inquiry. After all, this definitional approach had been taken for thousands of years in regard to the capacities to use language, to reason, to draw analogies, to count, or to recognize the meaning of death, or in regard to the activities of making art, holding funerals, playing games, giving directions to others, or describing which of many possible enemies are approaching. These are all capacities and activities that ethologists have demonstrated to exist in various animals, despite previously defining them as purely human capacities and activities.

Cormorants won't dive again after diving seven times for Japanese fisherman unless they are given the fish treat they receive every seventh dive; bees describe how far and in what direction and how much honey is to be found through their "waggle dance" to other bees; Irene Pepperberg's parrot performs impressively on analogy tests; prairie dogs communicate to other prairie dogs what sort of predator is approaching by making differing sounds; elephants will not leave a member of their group who has died without covering the body with soil and remaining in an extended vigil over the site; Koko the gorilla learned to communicate through American Sign language and then using a computer keyboard responded to an online question of what is "death" by answering "sleep forever" (in reference to his cat who was killed by a car); and these are just a few of the capacities and activities that have been discovered to be true of animals in recent decades—or at least, so many scientists assert.[1]

Phenomenology to the Rescue

The approach that I follow as a philosopher is phenomenological, which means that what counts for me is not to work within a logical system of defined terms, and construct arguments on that basis, as many philosophers do, generating lovely conceptual systems which miss much of the richness of our experience and of reality. Phenomenologists attempt to discover by observing the world whether they can find new ways to look outside traditional categories, to experience new kinds and levels of meaning that may have been hidden by previous assumptions.

If animals seem to experience fondness for each other, or seem to form bonds of attachment, or seem to prefer companionship while engaging in certain activities, or demonstrate a loyalty to particular other individuals that motivates them even to risk their lives—and some or all of these characteristics define what humans have meant by 'friendship'—then a phenomenologist will look to see if he or she can make sense of an animal's experience as also being shaped by friendship. If the phenomenologist can generate

---

[1] Many books which detail these findings but a few of my favorites as most readable and comprehensive are Gary Kowalski, *The Soul of Animals* (Stillpoint, 1991), Donald R. Griffin, *Animal Minds: Beyond Cognition to Consciousness* (University of Chicago Press, 2001), George Page, *Inside the Animal Mind*, (Broadway, 1999) and Daisie and Michael Radner, *Animal Consciousness* (Prometheus, 1996).

descriptions which put into language aspects of experiences that had not yet been articulated, this will enhance the human capacity for new observations and in turn these observations will add more to the descriptions.

If we're seeking to give a "deeper" or "thicker" description of our experience of the world and of other beings' experience of the world, then emotions, intuitions, imaginings, bodily feelings, perceptual associations, aesthetic recognitions, temporal senses, and other ways to "take in" what is around or within us *may* reveal aspects that either supplement or replace what rational understanding indicates.

Many traditional philosophers assert that we can only understand other people or other creatures by finding rational principles that would underlie and connect the differences among them by seeing how they are instances of these same rational principles. For example, in a famous case in animal science, the fact that wasps repeat the same motion many, many times was judged as "dumb" and proof of the wasps' lack of grasping the situation confronting them because it was so inefficient. But the "utterly mechanical" label given to the wasps' activities reflects more of our own feelings about humans having to perform numerous repetitions. Scientists saw that modifications to the wasp behavior could be made that would be more in line with a rational principle of efficiency and used this principle to compare the activities of humans and wasps in the same situation. However, in the wasp's context, there may be other reasons that make sense for it to repeat actions in a way that would be numbing to a human consciousness. It may be the way the wasp achieves a coherent approach to the totality of tasks in its world.

This "rational yardstick" approach of assessing animal behavior and experience goes hand in hand with the perspective that assumes all sense experience, all emotional experience, all bodily feelings, and all memories, can only be understood by being interpreted according to rational principles. Phenomenologists take experience as their guide and listen to how emotion and imagining, for example, shape our experience as much as rational ideas. The evidence from emotions and from imagination may be an equally valuable input about the nature of existence.

Clever Hans could not do addition or multiplication. He could not reveal the aspect of the world illuminated by arithmetic. But given the horse's emotional sensitivity and perceptual sensitivity to very small details, he could "understand" the emotions of his questioners and attempt to please them. It is an insight of phenomenology that we "take in" and have an immediately felt understanding of certain aspects of the world through emotion, through imagination, and through bodily feelings. This insight has been shared by psychologists who speak of "emotional intelligence," and even by brain scientists who have discovered that the more rational cognitive functions of the brain work inseparably from those processing centers in the brain handling the emotional, the imaginative, and the bodily.

If it were true that humans and dogs had to communicate through rational assertions or could understand each other only through abstract reasoning, then there could be little mutual understanding. If friendship relied on rational insights being communicated and reflected upon by each friend, and not on an emotional immediate communication through embodied perception giving each friend a better sense of shared experience, emotions and feelings, then friendship between humans and dogs would be impossible. However, it might also be impossible between humans.

By "embodied perception" I mean that we take in not just bare sensations, like "red," but apprehend the red as part of a larger web of relationships that are its interwoven context, so that a florid red complexion is immediately seen as a possibly revealing illness, or overheating, or chronic drinking of alcoholic beverages, or as expression of embarrassment. The "red" doesn't stand alone, for the sensations perceived by the body are immediately part of a larger cluster of meanings.

With other humans, I "get" their joy in walking with me, or playing with me, or being together in activities, from their smiles, their laughter, their hugs, their skipping about, their matching their rhythms with mine, and a host of other expressions and apprehensions which occur on an immediate embodied level of "lived understanding," as fitting together to convey this sense. I do not have to think about these things reflectively and rationally to understand the warmth of the shared happiness and fondness. Equally, in the sneer of the lips, in the menacing, rigid posture of the body, in the glare of the eyes, in the attacking tone of the voice, in the wariness of the steps, and so forth, I immediately have a lived, felt embodied understanding of another person's hostility.

Both animals and humans understand the world to a great extent through their bodies kinesthetically, emotionally, perceptually, memorially, viscerally, and imaginatively. Dogs are especially sensitive to tone of voice, to posture, to rhythm, to touch, to entering into shared activity co-operatively and rhythmically, to spontaneously giving themselves over to play and inviting others to join them through gesture (the famous hunched over "v" formed by their front paws, for example) and to a host of perceptual ways of taking in those with them. Yes, they lack the reflective and rational capacities for the kind of communication that adds another dimension to human friendships, but this sort of shared understanding or communication that dogs do employ is important also among humans as another "level" of understanding.

We are not only rational beings, but also feeling creatures as other animals are. If a dog's way of encountering and making sense of the world were exclusive to dogs, we would never know what they comprehend or what their actions mean, but we make similar gestures inviting others to play, for example, or immediately apprehend in another human's guttural response, something very like a "growl" of annoyance. Since a dog's way of understanding the world overlaps with the human way, mutual understanding is possible to some extent, even if it's not perfect. We don't even understand ourselves or other humans perfectly, so that standard is way too high to be interesting or significant. Imperfect understandings can go a long way to opening worlds to each other and to keeping us walking down the difficult path of "knowing thyself" and also knowing other beings, such as our dogs.

Being Caught Up in the World

Maurice Merleau-Ponty was a French philosopher who died in 1961 at the age of fifty-three, but not before turning philosophy on its head by using psychology's observations about the nature of perception to show that as knowers of the world we get our primary sense of time, space, the qualities of things around us, the social sense of situations, and the sense of relations with other people, from a "bodily knowing," through a resonating with our surroundings. Perception not only registers physical characteristics of what is around us, but does so inseparably from also giving us emotional, imaginative, memorial, social, practical, motivational, personal, and symbolic senses of these objects, their relationships, and their context.

When I see Bhakti come running up to me, I have an immediate bodily and perceptual sense of whether she is tired or peppy,
dissatisfied or content, playful or concentrating on getting food. I
have an echoing in my own visceral sense of my body of these
states in her or of the rhythm of her gait, I have implicit intimations
of our long history together in its varied ups and downs, such as
the fearful time when she had a huge liver tumor three years ago,
and her sleek body is only perceived in an implicit comparison
with that bloated version of her, in projections of our walk later
today to be taken in the woods, in the comforting enjoyable snuggling and playing within our shared relationship with Judith, in the
context of knowing her frequent proclivity to sit in the sun on a
dry, sunny day.

However, this sort of sense of perception that contains so many
elements inseparable and without any explicit thought or expression seems also to be experienced to some degree by Bhakti about
me. She may bark and protest if she sees me lacing up my running
shoes or taking the car keys since this is inseparable from the sense
of being left alone without the walk or dinner coming, that the
leash gets a wag of anticipating the walk or this street a protesting
pull in some other direction since it is the veterinarian's, my tears
will prompt a jump on the lap and licking of the face or arms to
cheer me up, or my taking up the stalking posture and moving slyly
towards her will be met with her legs outstretched and the twitch-
ing back and forth of the head in play posture. Neither I nor Bhakti
have to rationally construct these meanings. As a human, I may
reflect and modify my initial "take," as when I realize that she is
late for her insulin shot and maybe that is why she is dragging
along, but often our "initial take' remains as my guide.

Even our sense of location, of direction, and of orientation are
more felt, in emotion, in the visceral depth of the body. This gives
us our sense of "belonging"—an experience vital to both humans
and dogs. When humans feel as if they don't belong, they're anxious, out of sorts, and stressed. Dogs, when they sense they are not
where they feel at home, seem to experience the same feelings, as
they whine or tear things up, or pace nervously.

Being There

Merleau-Ponty offers a story in explaining this more felt and immediate sense of space. He recounts a period of his life when he is

vacationing down in the south of France, but World War Two is still not over. He says that as the weeks go by, his life becomes permeated with the rhythms of the village around him, being concerned about the harvest, the rainfall, and the level of the river, like all the locals. His sense of his body is one that has meshed with the world around it, feeling connected to the fields, in tune with the rhythm of the rising sun, the passing of rain clouds, and the pull of the market. However, as soon as he hears about a bombing in Paris and is overcome with worries about the safety of his family and friends, he is "no longer there" in the village, but instead is riveted to Paris. His body is directed towards it through tension, worry, concern, and feels centered in its pulse. He feels his "belonging" among those people he loves in Paris, not where he is physically located at the moment. He can reason to himself that he knows he's in this physical location, but his experience is dislocated from that logical conclusion. Fortunately, in the flow of everyday life, these two most often coincide: where we are physically located and where our ties of emotion and concern are centered at that moment are the same or at least largely overlap, but having them out of sync shows us that it is the emotional lines, felt through the body, of connection and orientation that give us a primary sense of being located, directed, and belonging within a place.

Merleau-Ponty also looks at indigenous peoples' description of home: it is not a spot on a geometrically laid out grid, or at a certain distance from topographical landmarks, but is rather "the place of *peace* and *warmth*," the site of "*belonging* and *security*." This is expressed in their languages. "Home" is an important matter to both humans and dogs, and is established first by a felt understanding of the body whose perception is woven with memory and emotion, not by rational judgment. This is important for the possibility of friendships between humans and dogs, because it's an example that points to a level of common understanding of their respective realms of experience, that might serve as a basis for communication and shared "understanding" in friendship, since all definitions of friendship require some sort of shared understanding and communication.

By showing that we're first and foremost feeling, perceiving, expressing bodies caught up immediately with whatever is around us, Merleau-Ponty's account also makes humans into more relational beings, inseparable from their environment. Since we can reflect and detach from our more immediate experience, we have more leeway that animals do in seeing ourselves apart from our environment, but they also may gain an acuity of being aware of their environment we lack.

My favorite example of this immersion and acuity with the environment is the bird, the Clark's nutcracker, which inhabits the mountain pine forests of the Southwest. During a few weeks in the late summer and fall, the nutcracker hides caches of two to five seeds in up to two thousand locations. Each bird needs to retrieve at least three thousand of these stored seeds to make it through the harsh alpine winter. Experiments have shown that they they can return to their caches as reliably after 285 days as after 11 days. The bodily sense of these places in the surroundings is one that has been "mapped" into the bird's immediate perception, just as we find in hummingbirds who have a sense of which flowers they have visited, as bees finding their way back to the hive given the angle of the sun on their flight back, as East African elephants having a sense of where the water hole is to be reached forty miles into the desert and several feet underground, and so on with many animals. These animals do not have to reflectively ponder where to find these things in their environment, but rather they are drawn by felt bodily pulls and pushes, as if the perception of the world in its shapes, colors, and outlines were a kind of intuitable map. Brain science verifies Merleau-Ponty's suggestion that these cognitions do not rely upon parts of the brain involved in abstract reasoning or explicit memory.

What We Share with Dogs

If we look at our dogs with this idea of gaining a sense of who we are only from the relationship with what surrounds us, we can see that we may have grown into *shared understandings* of the home we share with them that are vital to both human and dog in their sense of self. Perhaps, for our dog, the den is the place for resting in the cold winter and feeling contentedly warm in front of the fire and for watching for birds outside the back window in summer when they come to the bird-feeder, the forest across the street is the area for trying to catch rabbits, the park is the place to rush other dogs in confrontation and to get a sense of exhilaration by running or catching a frisbee, that this neighboring house is one to be wary of given the vicious and larger dog who used to live there, that this hole is a possible comfort for the groundhog who lives there but is a galling nuisance in giving him somewhere to escape to, those steps are to be avoided so as not to slip and fall as happened a few times before, the refrigerator is the source of interesting items to be devoured, that cupboard is dangerous as the place of medication syringes, the bed is to be jumped on at night for the chewing of bones, and so forth. It's obvious, however, that if these are the dog's felt sense of things, the partnered person may share many of these feelings and senses of the environment, such as the contentedness emanating from the den of being in front of the fire in the winter, or the thrill of the woods in hunting for rabbits, or being scared of that house and its monstrous hound, or being frustrated by the hole of the groundhogs, or being habitually drawn to the refrigerator.

For my friends, who think of animals as biological machines, pushed and pulled by "drives," they would never realize that Bhakti has a good sense of the world around her without abstract reasoning, since for them as for Descartes, all meaning comes from thought of some sort. Yet, Bhakti's immediately felt sense of things is a similar to the same sense I have of many shared aspects of our home and its environs. Our shared sense is not only about objects, but about daily rhythms of time and space within which we live together: in the late afternoon, it's that time to start circling the food dish, to keep an eye out for what might be for dinner on Bhakti's part, and on mine to start getting the ingredients of our dinners assembled; at late night, it's the time for Bhakti to cock an ear for strange intruders like mice in the pantry or burglars in the yard, and I do so to a lesser extent; the morning is the time for Bhakti to wait by the door for the mad dash to the grass for ablutions, and I do so in another location; or the row of suitcases is the cue for Bhakti to get ready for a ride and stay in obvious sight and whine so as to not to be left behind, and for me to not forget to get Bhakti and install her in the back seat; or the putting on of coats is the immediate down-looking, slinking, and perhaps crying lament of being abandoned again and of Glen to feel a little sad to live a world where Bhakti can't come and to feel a little guilty about leaving her. These meanings are not pondered reflectively, but are the attractions and repulsions, traps and siren songs, delights and securities, registered in the perceiving canine body as it runs or walks or shuffles through the house and neighborhood and echoed in differing but often similar ways by the dog's human companion.

Dogs and humans are more similar beings than we might have thought. Much of our immediate grasp of the world and home in which we live with them over a period of years becomes very similar or at least analogous, and in many ways shared. Understandings, concerns, delights, anticipations, memories, expressions, fears, rhythms and many dimensions of the daily activities are grasped, reacted to, and responded to in ways that overlap. Both dog and human are also caught up in many of the same relationships, living within the matrix of the same environment, events and people. Looking at this felt, embodied level of life, we might be able to meet our dogs in avenues of mutual or at least partially mutual understanding of the kind that makes for friends. We might have to rethink the nature of friendship and care outside the rational and reflective grasp of things.

Reconsidering the Nature of Friendship

About ten years ago, I vacationed with three good friends in the area above Arroyo Seco, New Mexico, in the vicinity of the Sangre de Christo Mountains, for a month of enjoyable reading, relaxing, and hiking. The hiking was exhilarating, following trails through deep forests and up the sides of peaks, crisscrossing numerous mountain streams. Bhakti was only about three years old then and loved to hike.

As my human friends and I struggled across the streams, teetering on slender log bridges or hopping from stone to log, Bhakti would race across the top of the log and wait for us on the other side. I wanted to get to the top of Lobo Peak (12,115 feet) during our stay in the area. It was a bit daunting that early in our stay a hiker had been trapped on the peak during a late afternoon thunderstorm, struck by lightning, and killed. At least once a week my friends—humans and dogs—and I would start out on the hike to the peak. After the fourth time that we turned back somewhere along the trail, because one or more of my friends got too tired or too fearful of the impending afternoon thunderstorms, or were too distracted or indifferent to the project, I formulated a plan for the next to last day of my month's stay at the cabin that exchanged my human friends for a more trustworthy and well-matched partner for the climb, Bhakti.

I got up at 5:30 a.m. when all my human friends were still sleeping and took only Bhakti with me. What followed was a glorious day on the trail while Bhakti and I scrambled across creeks, through forest and alpine meadows, up steep rock climbs, until we reached this heavenly perch in the sky at the peak. I took a picture of Bhakti with all the surrounding peaks about her as she stood on the sky. It is a moment I will always remember, but it is far more than that. It became one of those memorable shared experiences with Bhakti, a shared significant effort, rhythms of hiking matched to one another, and also shared communicated feelings along the trail of happiness in the trek together and affection mutually expressed at breaks when Bhakti would curl up in my lap and give me a little lick on the ankle or hand as I would pet her or cradle her.

Without a Friend . . .

However, it was more than just a memorable experience as it became a symbolic touchstone of having a bond of friendship between us. It involved perseverance, strength, joy in physical exertion, an ability to pick up the rhythms required by this partic- ular trail and mountain, a watching out for the partner in climbing (as Bhakti does every twenty paces or so—runs ahead and turns around to watch me and make sure I catch up to her and then con- tinue, as I also do fro her at times), a shared sense of being tem- perate enough to rest at certain intervals and to pace oneself, an attentiveness to the environment, and other "excellences" of char- acter and behavior in a specific situation, which is precisely Aristotle's idea of virtue. He does not mean "virtue" in a moralistic sense of meeting a standard of morally correct behavior, but rather virtue is the actualization of potential excellences of the organism by using its powers well to augment the well-being of the organ- ism and its situation.

I mention Aristotle in looking at classic Western philosophical ideas of friendship, because his ideas about the role of shared "virtues" in friendship are relevant to the embodied approach to friendship, unlike many other ideas which tend to emphasize the importance of the mind over the body. Aristotle's *Nicomachean Ethics* is probably the most famous statement in Western philo- sophical history on the nature of friendship, as well as the most powerful cultural validation of the importance of friendship, with its statement, "For without a friend who would choose to live?"[2]

---

[2] Aristotle, *Nicomachean Ethics*, Book VIII, section 1.

I admire Aristotle for giving us reasons to question many kinds of friendships that people in our culture embrace: those relationships based on providing us pleasure or those that help us with practical aspects of our lives. This gives us a chance to be more critical about our friendships.

For Aristotle, even if the pleasure is continuous and ongoing in the other person's company or even if the utility the person provides to our existence is of vital and continued importance, these are not really friendships. They are superficial substitute measures for the real thing and will end with the cessation of pleasure or practical need. It's easy to see how we are thrown together with people for periods of our lives out of some shared usefulness or some ongoing pleasure, say in boating together or in going out to delectable dinners, but that we know that Aristotle is right, that the depth of a true friend is lacking. One "friend" loses interest in boating or changes eating habits, and there goes the supposed friendship! By contrast, Aristotle's true friendship is determined by sharing key virtues, working on developing these virtues together, a shared commitment to these virtues and a mutual concern for the other's well-being. Friends help each other to become better people in working together to realize these shared moral capacities, and this is their focus in the relationship.

If Aristotle's ideas of friendship were to apply to my relationship with Bhakti, then Bhakti would have to be more than a mere object or occasion of pleasure for me and offer me something besides being the provider of usefulness in chasing away possible burglars (doubtful for a Chihuahua) or making sure I got exercise by walking her (doubtful for a seven-time marathoner) or meeting some other practical need. The nature of my interaction with Bhakti would have to help me work on developing my virtues in the shared activity of her developing her virtues.

. . . Who Would Choose to Live?

Like other significant principles in the history of Western philosophy, Aristotle's ideas on friendship have often been interpreted in a very rationalistic way that has put a primacy on our rational abilities to be a true friend and therefore would rule out friendships with dogs and other animals. Aristotle's idea of "mutual goodwill" has often been understood as being able to rationally and reflectively envision a friend's possibilities and project a path of how this person could realize these character excellences, such as kindness, honesty or temperance, and then deliberatively commit to helping the friend pursue these virtues. This sort of regard for the other would require reflective capacities that dogs don't seem to possess. Moreover, some, like my skeptical friends, would claim that dogs are only interested in what Aristotle deemed superficial alliances with their humans of practical usefulness and perhaps some shared pleasures, like going for a walk or romp together, not to mention frisbee tosses or mountain hikes. On the human side, we might only care for dogs for enjoyment of these same activities and their usefulness in scaring away burglars or foxes. That would also make these not true friendships, according to Aristotle.

These objections could be carried further by thinking about friendships along the lines of eighteenth-century German philosopher Immanuel Kant. For Kant, what is worthy of respect for myself or for others, is the rational ability to see what is morally right in a universal way (as a law) and to mold our actions to their dictates, no matter what our urges and feelings are. For Kant, this sort of respect has to underlie affection for a friend or else it is just a feeling, nothing more. The affection for another might help me gain a specific focus for my rational abilities in assessing my friend and our relationship, but without that rational intervention there is no real friendship. Needless to say, neither Bhakti nor any other dog shows any evidence of having the ability or interest in making these sort of rational assessments and commitments, nor would I or other humans find any way to apply them to the canine world. Thus, for Kant, as for Aristotle, no true friendships are possible between members of our separate species.

Yet if we consider Aristotle's emphasis on the immediate emotional, imaginative, visceral responsiveness of organisms to their situations, there are senses of friendship that could open an avenue between Bhakti and me, humans and dogs, as friends. Aristotle was one of the few philosophers in the Western tradition until the nineteenth century, to have understood virtues not as rationally articulated values, but as "dispositions" of the entire person to act spontaneously in a certain situation. He was not interested in ethics as a set of rules, but as self-transformation into a different sort of person. According to Aristotle we are like a work of art that we can keep shaping by developing different habits, so that we will then respond spontaneously with a developing excellence of virtues.

I may at a certain age have been a boorish and unhelpful participant in discussions, insensitive to the other person's point of view, but in working at learning how to listen, maybe at first literally biting my tongue and forcing myself to follow other people's words, making myself ask five questions per meeting about their point of view, I would gradually train myself to be a person who will *spontaneously* be disposed to listen to other people's stories, concerns, and ideas. This idea of developing practical wisdom is a holistic response of emotional being, feeling, intuition, bodily remembering, imagination, and vitality, analogous to what I have called "embodied understanding," which may be vital to both humans and dogs (as well as other animals) in understanding and responding with excellence to the world. Dogs are able to lick the faces of their upset human companions, move their puppies away from danger, or protect another pack member from a predator, at this level of spontaneous acting upon immediate feelings called forth by the situation.

Virtue in Humans and Dogs

In my description of a few experiences with Bhakti, I have tried to articulate instances of shared actions that brought out virtues in each of us, but also if we consider the long-term effect of living with our dogs, we might add to this account, since the development of virtue and the friendships that promote this take a rather long time. Not only may many humans and dogs become better attuned through their own efforts to virtuous action in their environments, but they might develop through being and working together the dispositions to perform these actions that Aristotle thought were the virtues.

Prisoners in jail for serious offenses, who seem to lack sensitivity to other people's needs, may be given dogs to raise. In teaching these dogs how to behave and in caring for their needs, the prisoners learn to become more caring people. In sensing the dog's gratitude and affection, they find an affirmation that allows them to care in return. Another example might be a distracted philosophy professor who learns to curb his frustrations and become more patient when his dog won't eat its normal food, needing special accommodations. He also becomes more reliable and responsible when his dog needs insulin shots every twelve hours, and in many ways learns to respond to his dog's nonverbal claims upon him, to mold himself into a more patient, caring and responsbible person. Of course, this second case is mine. It is not a one-way interaction: Bhakti might not be so lean and fit at thirteen, if she had not responded to my urge for a walk when she was feeling lazy, nor as continually affectionate and expressive if she had not been raised by someone who constantly offered affection, interaction, and gentle play. Living together, dogs and people form a bond on this non-rational, fully felt level of disposition, in which they help each other become better people, the power that Aristotle believes friends can share.

This is not to say that the all-night talks with good human friends, or the debates over what actions are ethical or not, or the sharing of the myriad of exclusively human experiences don't provide a dimension of heartfelt friendships and excellence to our lives that can't be provided by a dog. However, there are aspects of friendships with dogs that are equally powerful. One of these is the dog's large nonverbal set of expressions of affections, such as nuzzling, licking, or resting against one's legs while sleeping. These spontaneous, direct expressions of affection build another sort of bond over time.

With dogs humans have to learn to bridge a gap, to try to sense the world of a being that experiences things so differently. This capacity and intention is itself a virtue of friendship—to reach deeply in one's sensibility and sensitivity. This psychic stretching adds something to humans' abilities that many of our human friendships lack, that nevertheless we should cultivate in order to increase our sensitivities to those who are very different from us among the human community, too.

Aristotle is right. Who would want to live without friends? I know that I can't conceive of life without my human friends, but I also can't imagine how much poorer my life would have been with my dog friend, Bhakti—named for the Hindu path of enlightenment through love.

10

Why Is It Easier to Love Rex and Fiffi than Our Teenage Children?

CHRISTIAN MAURER and KAMILA PACOVSKÁ

At least for some of us, coming home after a long and exhausting workday means being welcomed by a dog. And everyone who's ever had a dog knows what that means: trying to cope with a being that cannot stop expressing the sheer joy of seeing you by barking in excitement, jumping around you, and knocking over your partner's grandmother's Chinese vases with its tail. And these beings, Rex and Fiffi, show exactly the same reaction if we've been away for a ten-minute chat with the next-door neighbor.

Some of us also have adolescent children, who most of the time don't even bother showing up when we come home. Sure, we fully respect Jim and Jane's desire for privacy. But, well, there is a certain difference between Rex's and Fiffi's way to say "hello" and saying it with shut doors.

A very similar difference in behavior appears when it comes to another dimension of everyday life: feeding. Rex and Fiffi perform a dance duet around our feet minutes before we have even opened the can. And when the food is in their bowls, they devour it as gratefully as ever. The food is more or less the same as it's always been. Jim and Jane, however, would not set foot in the kitchen before having been called at least three times. And their response to the brand-new recipe on which we've expended hours of creative and dedicated toil: "Not again!" This before going to the fridge for the ketchup.

Is it this difference that makes loving our dogs Rex and Fiffi sometimes easier than loving our adolescent children Jim and Jane? Is it that Rex and Fiffi would never dye their hair green or buy themselves T-Shirts with rude expressions the editor of this book would not allow to be printed? This isn't the whole story.

Which Kind of Love?

Let's think about love. If you listen to the radio, you'll find quite a lot of musical evidence for the fact that love is something beautiful. At the same time, it's also commonly acknowledged that love can be a pretty difficult thing—just turn on the radio five minutes later! But note that most of the songs you'll hear are about romantic love. They are about: Me falling in love with you, me trying to convince you to fall in love with me, me shedding tears about the fact that you don't.

The ancient Greeks called this kind of love *eros*. It's a consuming passion of great intensity and strength, which usually turns the afflicted upside down and inside out. According to the Greeks, we're literally possessed by it, and this can usually be well observed since *eros* often brings about the need to express itself. It is therefore no miracle that an experience of such intensity and dramatic force attracts the Muses not only in music, but also in literature, film or the fine arts.

Nevertheless, there's another kind of love, which is more moderate and less expressive. It's often seen as so natural that we don't feel much need to speak about it, much less compose songs or poems about it. This affection is the basis of close relationships, as we experience them in our families, with friends, children and, last but not least, with our dogs.

To distinguish it from *eros*, the Greeks called this kind of love *philia*. Though not as violent as *eros*, it is more than just a *liking*. It's possible to *like* someone without being as deeply concerned about her as when we *love* her. Many of us would not say that we merely *like* their children or their dogs. We say that we love them. An investigation of *philia* will give us an answer to our initial question: *Why is it sometimes easier to love Rex and Fiffi than to love our adolescent children?*

What Do Philosophers Make of Love?

Before exploring the main characteristics of *philia*, let's make a short detour. How can we characterize the *philosophical* approach to love? That's not too easy. In a sense it's something everyone knows. Imagine a difficult personal situation, like a break-up. It's characteristic of such moments that we somehow suspend the usual course of our lives; we stop planning, deliberating, endeavoring, and we try to make sense of what has happened. We start reflecting on things, the world, us, our life, our relationships, and we want to understand. For some, the typical place for this is at the table with a friend and a glass of beer, or on a long walk with their dog.

Philosophers do the same thing. The basic difference is that normal people eventually stop these reflections and return to practical life, whereas philosophers don't. One might say that philosophers live in a constant sense of break-up. Attempting to profit from this mind-set, they work to further the common understanding of the world. Of course, they try to be a bit more systematic than the friends with the beer. But the main goal is the same: to understand, to explain and to make sense of things that are important for us.

In contrast to scientists, philosophers don't focus on empirical facts, experiments, or surveys. They work with concepts, reasons, and justifications. They try to develop classifications, distinctions, and definitions. When philosophers think about love, whether it is *eros* or *philia*, they're not really interested in questions like: What are the chemical changes in a human body that can be correlated with the fact that the subject loves someone? Or: What is the biological function of the thing called love? Or: What do people in a given society approve and disapprove of when it comes to love?

Philosophers are interested in questions such as: What is love? Is it an emotion like joy, anger, jealousy? If yes, which are the features that distinguish it from other emotions? Can love be influenced by reason? Can we be mistaken in our love? Does our love for a person change our view of her? Are there right and wrong forms of love? Does love create any special obligations? Is love altruistic or, at the end, selfish? Can love exist without relationship? And, more directed to the point of this chapter: Given some obvious differences in the objects of our love, how does our love for our dogs differ from our love for our children?

Loving Children, Dogs, and Friends

Let's think about love, and not just about thinking about love. *Philia* is the kind of love we have for our children, dogs, and friends. Here are three fundamental features of *philia*:

• *We enjoy being with the ones we love.*

We want to spend time with them, and we miss them when they're gone. This holds for close friends, children, and dogs. We want to be with our son Jim, in spite of telling him that we don't want to see him anymore, because we're extremely angry about his latest "achievements" in high school. When the fury passes, we'll enjoy his presence again.

But we're not only interested in gaining pleasure from the company of our beloved ones. If we really love someone,

• *The beloved individual as such is important to us.*

This is a second fundamental feature of love. It's not just *a* child we care for; it's *Jane, our Jane*. We're worried about *Rex* because he ran away to chase the neighbor's cat. Never mind the cat, but if Rex doesn't return, no other dog can simply take his place, because we love *him*, the one and only *Rex*. Since we love Jane and Rex, we see them both as individual creatures, and not just as substitutable members of a group or a species. We care about *them*, and to lose them would cause us a lot of grief.

As beloved individuals, they become irreplaceable and special for us. Maybe we would have come to love two other puppies of the same brood we got Rex and Fiffi from, had we chosen them instead of these two dear friends eight years ago. But as a matter of fact, Rex and Fiffi are now the objects of our love, and our relationship with them is unique.

A third essential feature of love is somehow connected to the previous one: To care about an individual also means that:

• *We care about the loved individual's well-being.*

We're prepared to do things for those we love without first asking whether there will be an appropriate payback. When love is in the air, altruism isn't far away. We're willing to drop an important meeting to drive Jim to the doctor or Fiffi to the vet, because they are suffering again from having eaten *we-don't-know-what*. We're also interested in the feelings of the ones we love, and we are likely to suffer with them when they suffer, we are likely to be happy with them when they are happy, and we are likely to do our best to make them happy.

Though seeing them happy makes us happy too, this fact is not our *motive* for doing things for their benefit. We would want the best for them even if we knew, sadly, that we would never see them again. We act for them because we love them, and the fact that we love them makes us likely to promote their interests without thinking first of our interests. We don't drive Jim to the doctor or Fiffi to the vet because we want to get rid of the uneasy feeling we have when we see them suffering. We do it because we want them to become healthy and happy again.

Nevertheless, the story isn't so straightforward. How can we know what promotes the well-being or the good of the ones we love? Very often we have problems with knowing this for ourselves. Our close friends can sometimes help us by giving advice or by setting an example, but too much help seems overprotective and disrespectful. As adults, we're supposed to know best what is in our interest. This is different with our children, whose well-being is very much in our hands. And then again, my child's good is not the same as my own good.

Love versus Business

These three features make the relationships we have to those we love different from relationships that are formed for a specific purpose. Take the example of someone we want to collaborate with in our business: a potential partner. We maintain our relationship with this person, not always exclusively but mainly, to have the business benefit from our collaboration. Looked at in this way, *any suitable individual will do.*

It doesn't matter to the business *as such* whether the partner is Smith or Jones. As long as doing business is the principal reason we meet them, and as long as one of them doesn't smell worse than Rex after his run-in with the skunk, we won't care too much about which one will become our partner. It's not ruled out that we may eventually become friends, but in their role as business partners they are replaceable. We don't necessarily enjoy being with our business partners unless we really like them. We may enjoy doing business with them, but if making money is the goal, we don't act for their sake. We meet them for the sake of the business and to further our own interest (unless we're economic madmen or experimental psychologists). This attitude, which would seem very strange in our relationships with our friends and family members, is acceptable in a business relationship. Unless we inhumanly exploit them, there's no problem with the fact that we care about our business partners mainly as a means for benefiting our company or ourselves.

Love and Dependence

We said that we care about the happiness and well-being of those we love. We care about Jim's, Jane's, Rex's, and Fiffi's happiness, and we care about our friends' happiness. But what exactly does this mean? On the one hand it involves a certain *attitude*: We're not indifferent about things that influence the happiness of those we love, and we tend to be worried, to hope, expect, fear, be proud and have many other emotional responses. But on the other hand, caring about the happiness of our beloved can also require *doing* something for them, to *take care* of them, and thus actively promoting their well-being.

This will differ considerably from one type of relationship to another. First, *what* constitutes the good for our dogs obviously differs from what constitutes the good for our friends and again from what constitutes the good for our children. Second, the suitable *ways* to help, give advice, lead and take care in our relationships with our friends, children, and dogs are very different.

Caring about a friend or a spouse usually doesn't involve feeding, walking, and washing them. But if we don't do that with a small child or with a dog, then there's something wrong with our relationship to them, and maybe even with our feelings towards them. And whereas *we* have to take care of Jim, Jane, Rex, and Fiffi, *they* don't have to take care of us—at least not in the same way we have to take care of them when they're small. And considering the food preferences of all four of them, we'd rather take care of ourselves. This rather trivial observation about who has to take care of whom reveals an important aspect of the kind of love we have both for our children and for our pets: it is love that involves *dependence*.

Our adult friends' well-being is not dependent on us in the same way and to the same degree as Rex's and Fiffi's, Jim's and Jane's. This holds even if our teenage children should reasonably be expected to gain at least a certain degree of adult independence without succumbing to their self-destructive tendencies. A big part, if not most, of the life, health, and comfort of our children as well as of our dogs is in our hands. Just think of all the feeding, pooing, peeing, cleaning, warming, paying attention, playing, and entertaining that a parent and a dog-owner has to do. For a notable time of their life, we are their most important plea-sure-providers. The difference between a child and a dog in this respect is only a matter of degree: Rex and Fiffi eat once a day (unless given the opportunity to eat more often), Jim and Jane eat five or more times (unless being forced to eat something whole-some and healthy). From this point of view, it simply costs much more effort and energy to be a pleasure-provider for a child than for a dog.

Dogs, Children, and Morality

It's not only the satisfaction of their needs that is in our hands. Unlike our potted plants, dogs and children can lack manners. If Rex tries to impose his royalist instincts on others with aggressive behavior, it's partly us who didn't properly fulfill our job as dog-owners. People will not only have a queer look at Jim if he tries to impress the neighbors' girls by beating up the neighbors' boys again—in the end, people will also think of us as bad parents. Both as masters and parents we're *responsible* for the development of some basic social skills in our children and our dogs. It's our task to educate them so that they acquire some elementary notions of what they are and are not allowed to do. As their most important pleasure-providers we are in a very advantageous position to achieve that: by pleasant rewards and disagreeable punishments.

However, even if both dogs and children have to acquire some manners, there starts to appear an important difference between them, namely, only children have to acquire a sense of fair and unfair, right and wrong, moral or immoral. We won't think of Rex as acting *unfairly* if he chases the neighbor's old cat. But we will think of Jim as being unfair if he ridicules the clothes of his poorer companion, and we think of Jane as unfair if she beats up a weaker boy. In contrast to animals, we consider human beings capable of judgment in general, and of moral judgment in particular. That's why we call people without moral restraints "beasts."

How do we teach morality as parents? At first we influence young children's behavior by rewarding them for the right actions and by punishing them for the wrong ones. In that respect, our treatment of Jim and Jane used to be similar to the way we still treat

Rex and Fiffi. But older children should become capable of judging and acting by themselves. We can help them to think about moral values by explaining specific examples and by showing analogies. At the same time we know that it would be a vain eneavor to try to *explain* manners to a dog. Admittedly, Rex's and Fiffi's expressive behavior patterns can be very sophisticated. But we wouldn't suppose Rex capable of *understanding* us, if we tried to convince him that it is morally wrong to chase the old cat—not only because his linguistic capacities are insufficient for understanding an argument from Kant or Aristotle, but also because we don't assume that he can really think in moral categories.

Conflicts with Our Beloved

We said above that to a large extent we're responsible for our children's actions and character, and for their education. Now, if we say that we are responsible for their education, this means that we also have to be able to influence our children to a certain extent, somehow making them *do* what we want, maybe even *want* what we want. But here comes the main stumbling block: it is an essential feature of children that they don't obey. So, do we have to force them to do what we want?

Compare the following cases: A perfectly well-mannered Rex that obeys his master with pleasure in whatever order he gets, and a perfectly well-mannered Jim who obeys his parent with pleasure in whatever order he gets. (We don't know of either of these cases in reality. But standard philosophical procedure allows us to analyze nonexistent, even totally improbable, situations.) There's something particularly wrong about the second case. If we give it some thought, we realize that we don't really want our children to obey and follow our decisions in everything they *do*, and we don't want them to *want* precisely what we want.

If we want our children to be happy, we can't even want them to obey totally. And as we've seen, it is an essential feature of our love for our children that we want them to be happy. For a human being, it's far from happiness to obey someone else all the time and to always surrender or adapt one's wishes to those of another person. A human being, to be really happy, has to develop its individuality. If the child's wants and desires are systematically suppressed or reshaped, it's very improbable that this child will become a happy adult.

An important aspect of human well-being is to develop one's natural talents and inclinations and tastes, likes and dislikes. Morality and manners form a rather general framework in which such individuality can flourish. But there is no individuality without individuality in desires, decisions, and actions. At the same time there are no individual decisions and actions without the capacity to judge and without the capacity to assume responsibility for one's own judgments. When Jim and Jane become adults, the burden of responsibility passes slowly from us to them. We let them off the leash, or rather they take it off themselves. They become autonomous and responsible individuals.

Why It Can Be Easier to Love Our Dogs

We said that in order for our children to be happy, we want them to become individual human beings as we are. But this doesn't mean that they have to become similar to us in everything! If they are to be different, they are to be different in what they want as well. And that's the crux of the matter. Rex and Fiffi either do what we want, or we order them to do it. But what Jim and Jane want can conflict with what we want, and it's not always a good solution to impose our will from the position of authority. If our child is to become an adult human being, we have to respect its decisions within certain bounds.

If there are two wills, they can clash. The point of adolescent revolt is to develop one's own personality. Unfortunately nature couldn't find a different way from constant disagreement and negation of the former supreme authority. Yet if we want our children to be happy in their life, we have to partly accept the role of the one who is always wrong, whom they don't listen to—and this makes our love for Jim and Jane sometimes very difficult. What causes most of the uneasiness in our loving relationship with our children comes from the fact that they are to become humans, and therefore individual and autonomous.

Here lies the main difference between children and dogs. Even if there's some sense in saying that Rex and Fiffi have their individual personality, this rather refers to their habits, and their likes and dislikes. Nevertheless, there is no individual judgment and decision to be respected, because there is no true autonomy to be developed as in the case of Jim and Jane. Autonomy is not a substantial part of a dog's well-being (in spite of the meaning of Rex's

Latin name), and therefore it's not harmed by having to obey. Caring for the well-being of a dog doesn't involve the difficulty of dealing with conflicts and phases of total revolt in view of their becoming happy adults.

Unlike Jim and Jane, it's very easy to make Rex and Fiffi happy. What often makes our love for them easier is the fact that they never grow up.[1]

---

[1] The writing of this chapter was partly supported by the doctoral research grant #401/03/H047 from the Czech Science Foundation.

11

What I Learned from My Dogs about Being an Animal

HEATHER DOUGLAS

We humans are rational animals. Although both the rational and the animal parts of this ancient view of humans are intriguing, philosophers spend most of their efforts attempting to understand the rational part. This isn't surprising. Philosophy is about using reason to grapple with some of the most difficult aspects of being human. Given the centrality of reason in this effort, it's little wonder that the rational aspect of humanity is the centerpiece of philosophical effort.

Yet what happens when we focus on the animal part? We can't ask this question, or even begin to answer it, without relying heavily upon our reason, which can then interfere with the pursuit of understanding our animal nature. This is where dogs, our best friends of the animal kingdom, are invaluable to us. Dogs, even if shaped by human hands over years of breeding to become ideal companions, are still very much animals. That is part of the joy of having dogs. In thinking about dogs and our relationship with dogs, we can come to understand our own animal nature more deeply.

I think that dogs have a lot to tell us about being animals. This is not because I think dogs are or are not rational. I will make no attempt to decide that issue here. (Other chapters in this book do investigate this.) Instead, it is because dogs are different from us, "more animal," if you will, that we can learn so much from them about being animals. Indeed, the help dogs can provide in bringing us understanding about our animal nature may be their most important gift to us.

Dogs in the Present

Every dog owner knows the joys of coming home to their dogs. Our dogs *always* seem happy to see us, and that is a reaction we can rarely get from our fellow humans. Our dogs wag their tails, occasionally jump up, attempting to lick our faces, and sometimes fetch toys to present to us. Even if we know that the jumping up is a potential attempt to dominate us, and the licking and tail wagging is just a show of our importance in the dog pack, it is a wonderful way to be greeted.

Every dog owner also knows the despondency dogs can exhibit when they know we're leaving. My dogs are never happy when the suitcase comes out, and when I begin the ritual of packing for a trip to a conference. Ears go down and tails get tucked. They also know that which clothes I put on in the morning is an indication of what the day will be like. Gardening pants and a T-shirt indicate good times ahead in the yard. They run around me with tails wagging and bright eyes, encouraging our upcoming outside time. If I don the usual teaching clothes, they simply watch, or give up and go lie down where they will sleep the morning away. I will be no fun for the next few hours at least.

Even if I promise, "I'll be home later and we will play outside," or "We'll go for a walk in the woods this afternoon," or "This evening we will go to the park" (always sure to get an excited reaction), the dogs don't understand the promise of "later" or even "soon." We're doing it now, or we're not. There's no placating dogs with promises of the future. We humans can take future promises seriously, and while that may not be as good as something now, it can be nearly as good, and sometimes, if now is not convenient for us, even better. Every dog owner wishes at some point in time that their dogs could grasp the future promise, could hold in their heads the idea of later in the day or week. When I leave our dogs for a three-day trip, I tell them I'll be home soon, but that doesn't make any difference to them. They hate the suitcase, they hate the packing, and they think "I'll be home soon" is no promise of anything but my certain absence in the immediate future. If I promise my dogs a biscuit, and it doesn't materialize in the minute or two after it is promised, they quite forget about the promise and proceed with business as usual. Our dogs are in the present, always the present.

Some might object that I am shortchanging my dogs' abilities here. After all, how could they develop patterns of recognition if they are always in the present? Mustn't they remember that in the past, when I promised them a biscuit, I gave them one? And isn't that what training is all about? Surely I'm not suggesting that dogs can't be trained! And indeed I am not. Understanding what happens when we train our dogs is part of the project of understanding the animality in dogs, and in us. How is it that dogs can be such creatures of the present and, at the same time, in some sense remember that suitcases are bad news, and gardening pants good news? Why do our dogs get all excited at the mention of "park" or "biscuit"? To understand this, we need to look at the emotions of dogs.

Dogs and Emotions

Philosophers, while largely focused on human reason, have also often turned their attentions to human emotions. These efforts, however, have not been as sustained as their efforts in examining reason, and the focus of recent work on emotion has centered on the rationality of emotions. Such efforts will not avail us much here. But our dogs can tell us much about the nature of our emotions, particularly if we consider the role emotions play in the continuity of dog behavior.

So why do my dogs get excited when I mention the park? The park is certainly a great place to be for dogs, and they have a fabulous time running around the open spaces with other dogs and pursuing the innumerable scents. I also usually tell my dogs that we are going to the park before we go. Once in the car (which the dogs excitedly bound into), they settle down until we get close to the park, and then the whining to be let out begins. They are utterly inconsolable until running over the grass. I have not "trained" them to do any of this. How do they remember the park and respond in this way if they are such creatures of the present?

The answer lies in the emotions of dogs. One need not have a conscious memory to have an emotional response to something. There need be no recollection like "I remember what it was like to be here last week." The words "park" or "biscuit" invoke the emotional response to those things in the past, the excitement and pleasure of biscuits and parks, and not a temporal memory. As dogs can quickly learn, there's a course of actions that usually follows the particular use of these words, especially the way I tend to emphasize the words to my dogs. In the case of "biscuit," once I say "Is it time for a biscuit?" their routine is to go over where the biscuits are, sit attentively for my next command, and get a biscuit. In the case of "park," if I say "Do you want to go to the park?" their routine is to get into the car, go to someplace really fun, and run around a lot.

It helps that the key word in these cases comes at the end of my sentence, where my dogs can readily pick it out. They can then associate the word with a set of events, events that invoke a certain emotional response in them. This response becomes an emotional pattern, forming rather quickly for strongly good or bad experiences. Like tracks laid down over a rough surface, the routine becomes the pattern of expectation that the emotions follow, even if the dog does not remember or think about the last time, or the next time, like we do. Emotions can provide the source of continuity over time, without the presence of conscious memory.

Even though we do have conscious memory, we have these emotional routines too. Some are important rituals, embedded in key social practices. Things like the annual putting up of the Christmas Tree, trick-or-treating at Halloween, or fireworks on the Fourth of July are part of many people's annual traditions. If they are part of a person's traditions, the day just won't feel right without them. And if we have any of these traditions, we are loath to change them. A Halloween without pumpkins and kids in costumes asking for candy is a day missing something. We *feel* the absence.

Some routines are even more mundane, daily rituals that if not followed make us feel out of balance. If I usually wake up in the morning to a certain radio program, and then can't because the power is out, or I have slept too long, the day begins out of kilter, a tangible off-ness that cannot be readily fixed. It's part of the joy of a vacation to break with these patterns, forcing us into the present experience, away from our habits. But once back from such breaks, we rely upon these habits to give us a sense of stability and continuity over time. Breakfast with the morning paper, a cup of tea midafternoon, a daily program we always try to hear—all these become patterns we barely think about, until they get disrupted. This is also partly why catastrophic news is so upsetting, aside from the news itself. Our routine is thwarted, even if we didn't realize we had one.

Our dogs have these mundane routines, as any owner knows. If you feed your dogs at a certain time every day, and then try to change it (maybe because of daylight savings), the dogs get quite distressed. The routine has changed. The emotional track is disrupted. The expectation of when this happens, then this happens, is thwarted. Neither human nor dog need be consciously aware of the pattern or expectation for its alteration to be disturbing. We can even employ these routines to help us get through the day, using our dogs' expectations as an alarm clock or an encouragement to exercise. There's nothing like an expectant pooch at the side of the bed to get you up in the morning, whether from doggie breath, a wet lick, or the thumping tail against the bed. What produces such excitement in our dogs, and gets us up, are emotional patterns that can operate beneath conscious awareness and rational reflection.

Once these emotional courses get laid down, they are hard to change, much harder than changing one's mind rationally. If you learn some new fact, and it alters the way you think about something, that change can happen very quickly. If I learn, for example, that a kind of bird that I thought was one kind, is really two (there is a distinguishing throat marking I missed), I can quickly change my way of seeing and identifying the birds. It's rather easy to add that information into one's knowledge, even if doing so corrects older information. The rational aspects of our minds can be quick to change.

The emotional aspects are much harder to change. Like a long train on a track, with lots of momentum behind it, getting it to stop or even shift direction is difficult. We experience this regularly. Suppose you associate a certain place, like a charming café, with a former love, a relationship that ended painfully. One of your first nice afternoons together was spent at this café. You know, on the rational level, that the place is simply a place, that it bodes you no ill, and that it is a really nice place, objectively speaking. Nevertheless, every time you pass by, it pangs you with a sense of loss or anger. It takes months of effort, of redirecting the emotional track with persistent nudges, to change this feeling. For many, it is simply too much work and we give up, opting for avoidance over the work of change. We find a different café to frequent, a different street to travel down.

Retraining our dogs out of bad habits can be extremely difficult, and so can changing our own bad habits. Our dogs' habits are emotional habits, not rational knowledge. We have to change the emotional track laid down, shifting the pattern of response. All dogs have these tracks, and they can be shaped in all kinds of ways, especially when they're puppies. Once they're worked and grooved, changing them takes persistent and consistent attention, which is a lot of work. The good news is that it can be done, even with adult dogs (and adult humans). And if we can lay down the right patterns early, we can enjoy the fruits of our labor for the rest of the dog's life (with gentle reinforcement).

So this is how dogs can be creatures of the present and still be trainable. Consciously, they are just in the here and now. But they have learned habits, ingrained patterns of response, emotional pathways that give them continuity over time. This continuity can be so persuasive we might think our dogs can project themselves into the future or remember the past the way we can. It would be a mistake to do so. Dogs are thinking only about the here and now, but they think about it with the emotional patterns they have developed. And these emotional patterns are an essential part of being an animal.

Symbols and Continuity

Part of being able to develop these complex sets of emotional responses is being able to respond to symbols. As well as words, humans have enormously complex sets of symbols to which we are responsive. From music to art to religious and political symbols, our culture is full of symbols that give structure to our lives. We're not alone in responding to symbols. Dogs have symbols too. Granted they are not nearly as complex as ours. But they have a rich body language with which they communicate among themselves, and, if we pay attention, with us.

One of the most common sources of symbolism in the dog world is the tail. We know that a dog tail that is straight up and down as it wags is from a dog that is giving everyone a warning, whereas the side-to-side wag is an open invitation to greeting or play. Lots of animals have body language that serves as warnings or invitations. Dogs, by virtue of being pack animals, have more complex symbolism as well.

In my family, we have two large dogs, and while the older and larger male is the dominant of the two, the younger female is faster and generally more aggressive. She's constantly challenging our older male for dominance. In response, he takes plenty of opportunity to assert that he is, and will remain, dominant over her. Commonly, this takes the form of passing his head over the back of her neck. Or, he will mount her (a reproductively futile act as they are both fixed). He had never mounted any dog before we adopted her from the pound, when he was a mature three years old. But once there was another dog in the house, and a young bitch who wanted to be dominant, he rather quickly took to this behavior.

Worse for us, he started attempting to mount any other new dog he met, but only when our younger dog was present. So, if we take just the male dog to the park, he is happy to play with all the other dogs, with no sign of mounting behavior. But if we take both dogs, our older male mounts every dog he can, much to the consternation of both us and the other dog owners. (The behavior is so impolite for human company.) Because he only does this when our other dog is there to see it, it is clearly just a show for our younger female dog, to impress her that he really is top dog.

Now, this complex set of behaviors cannot just be about physical strength and ability. Dogs don't do dominance displays just because they can, and many dominance displays occur with smaller dogs dominating larger, stronger ones. Dogs do them to show certain things about their place in the pack. Our older male is performing for the younger female, showing her certain things about her place in the pack (that she is beneath him, both literally and symbolically). I don't think he has rationally decided to do this. He seems to go into an oddly focused zone in the midst of these encounters, and it is hard to get his attention. Rather, there are certain symbolic gestures dogs have, with important emotional content, that get invoked by a specific context. Dominance behaviors are central in this repertoire.

Many of our own symbolic gestures, while far more complex, have the same structure. Our wedding and funeral ceremonies have a certain structure, and thus evoke a certain emotional content. If key aspects are out of place, the emotional resonance gets lost. The emotional resonances vary with culture, so it's not surprising that really different wedding or funeral ceremonies don't strike us with the same force. It's also difficult to construct new symbolic actions that carry the emotional impact of the traditional ones. Symbols are tied closely to our emotional aspects, not just our rational aspects.

Our Animal Natures

In reflecting on the animal aspects of dogs, we can see both why they can be so wonderful to be around and what they can teach us about ourselves. Dogs live in the present. Although how they respond to the signs and stimuli of the present is shaped by their emotional structure, they are nevertheless only concerned with the here and now. Being with our dogs, paying attention to our dogs, requires of us that we focus on where we are, and what we are doing, while we are doing it. There's no yesterday or next week to think about for our dogs, just right now, and if we are to spend quality time with them, we must be in the right now too.

Dogs thus bring us to the immediacy of our current experience. This is one of their great gifts to us. With the incessant chattering of our rational brains, we are often anywhere but the present. We are thinking about what happened yesterday at work, or worried about next week, or daydreaming about that upcoming vacation— sometime, someplace else. Some people meditate to achieve this immediacy. Some play competitive sports. Dog owners need only interact with their dogs. They help provide relief from the concerns and endless workings of our rational minds, to focus on the joy of the moment, to appreciate the space of the present.

An animal that can help us do this tells us much about both animals and ourselves. It reminds us that we are not merely cerebral rational actors, but embodied animals as well. With the perpetual overlay of the rational on the animal in our minds, we sometimes have a difficult time getting a clear view on the animal aspect. We can use dogs to think about our animal selves, and in doing so, gain a clearer understanding of the nature of our emotions.

Thinking about the nature of our dogs is an opportunity to reflect on our own natures. But it can be a distressing thing to realize that we have these powerful emotional undercurrents as part of our human nature. These emotions are tied to some of the darkest aspects of humanity, such as our racist tendencies, our fear of the unknown, our willingness to be led to kill and destroy when afraid. Thinking about the challenges of retraining bad dog habits enables us to see what we are up against when tackling bad habits of mind or action in ourselves. Mere rational reflection, though essential, is not enough. Persistent and consistent effort directed by rational reflection is needed.

Our emotions are not just tied to these darker aspects, however. Our emotions also create the basis for the greatest joys of being a human. Joys of deep love, or the quiet comfort of long-standing friendships, the joys of our attachment to our dogs, are made possible by having strong emotional patterns laid down. Having these emotional patterns can bring out the best in us, not just the worst, and not just in our treatment of those closest to us. These emotional patterns spur the impulses to empathize with others, to help others, to give to others.

Finally, understanding the strength of these emotional patterns can also help us see how important the rational aspect of humanity is. Certainly my dogs don't like to get their rabies vaccine from the vet. They get nervous when the needle comes out. Their emotional response is not what guides the decision of whether or not to vaccinate them, however. Instead, it's my rational decision that this really is the best thing for them (especially because we live in the woods with lots of other critters), and I can reflect on past knowledge and make future predictions in their best interest. Usually, for these kinds of decisions, the rational part of us is better than our animal, emotional part. It's good for both our dogs and us that we exercise this part. As dogs constantly remind us, our humanity is both rational and animal. Understanding both is essential for the well-being of humans *and* dogs.

12

Would You Clone Your Friend?

MICKEY GJERRIS

This chapter is about why you shouldn't clone your dog.

You might think this will be like reading an essay explaining at great length why you shouldn't put your bare hands on a hot stove. But the point is not simply that you should not clone your dog. The point is *why* you should not do it—a point that mostly has to do with the idea of friendship and a sad story from my own life about how I totally failed to behave decently towards a dog. Hoping to make some sense of this by the end, I'll begin with my own guilt-ridden conscience.

A Sad Story . . .

When I was eleven years old my father died. This was a tragedy. Time, though, has a way of slowly weaving the unacceptable into the background fabric of reality. Tragedies somehow become basic conditions in the shadows of which you have to live your life.

Tragedies sometimes also entail opportunities, although we're often blind to them and, if we do see them, we often close our eyes to them because we feel guilty about exploiting the tragic situation. But that was what I did. I begged and crawled and became a general nuisance until my mother gave in and bought me a dog. A large, friendly, hairy, golden carpet of a retriever. He became my buddy and with him the next few years went by somehow, and he was always there for comfort, playing, cuddling, and plain companionship.

This dog, in other words, became my friend. It was an unequal relationship, I know. I was a human and he was a dog. The power

155

relations between us were all skewed. Yet this happens between humans too and it doesn't always mean the end of a friendship or the foreclosure of starting one. Friendships are, in my experience, not so much about equality as about acceptance.

With a friend you find yourself accepted as who you are. No pretense needed. Dogs know when you pretend. They are smart animals. All the running after their own tails, having to walk in circles before sleep, willingness to run after sticks, drooling, yapping and goofiness—that's just a facade. It's just dogs saying to us: "I'll be your friend and if you can accept me with all this goofiness of the heart then I'll love you forever."

So, we became friends and trusted each other's motives and this dog became the therapeutic tool of my childhood. I owed my dog a lot, as we usually do with friends. Not that we're always aware of it. Friendships depend on the fact that friends don't go around counting the favours each owes to the other. As soon as you do that, you know the friendship has gone. I would love to continue here by saying that our friendship never died. Unfortunately this story has a sad ending. Before getting to that, though, I'd like to say a bit about the idea of friendship.

What Is a Friendship . . .?

Friendship can be seen as an example of the concept of *natural love*. Friendships and thus natural love lie in between two other kinds of human relationships. The first I will label *enlightened egoism*. Here you only treat other people decently to assure that they will treat you the same way. It's the selfish interpretation of the *Golden Rule* from the Bible (Always do unto others . . .). This relationship was addressed by the philosopher Thomas Hobbes (1588–1679). Hobbes (in his book *Leviathan*) suggested that this was the basic relationship between people.

The other end of the spectrum of human relationships I will label *sacrificial unselfishness*. These are the relationships where we give up totally on our own interests, well knowing that is what we do, and act in the sole interest of another person. We sacrifice ourselves to benefit the other. The modern version of this is the cultural image of the Catholic nun Mother Teresa who devoted her own life to helping children living in the streets of India.

Friendship lies in between these two radical extremes. It is a relationship where there is no exploitation and no sacrifice—or at least the acts we act within friendships are not interpreted like that by any of the humans involved. Friendships are relationships based on *natural love*. This concept has been discussed throughout the western tradition of religious and philosophical thinking. Relationships based on natural love are relationships that can be understood as win-win situations. When my friend's doing well, I'm doing well, just as in romantic relationships between spouses (and yes, I realize I am talking in a somewhat idealized fashion here). When we give something to a friend, it isn't a sacrifice, but a way of making both our lives better. The deeper motivation of this can of course always be questioned, whether our friendships are at bottom just well-concealed egoism. But in friendships, we do act as if there's no difference between our own good fortune and that of our friend.

As with Humans, so with Dogs . . .

Some important characteristics pop up when we seek to understand friendships between humans, and these can also be seen in our relationship to dogs. When my dog wants to take a walk and it's raining hard (though never cats and dogs), I can either act out of *enlightened egoism* and take him for a walk in the belief that I will have a more quiet evening than if I do not, or I can do so out of *sacrificial unselfishness*, feeling sorry for myself while at the same praising myself for being such a good and responsible dog owner. Or I can act out of natural love and just walk the dog, not reflecting too much about it, but experiencing the happiness of the dog as part of my own happiness.

When I experience the joy of meeting friends who welcome me and invite me into their lives and homes not because of what I do for them, but simply because I am me, it resembles the joy of coming home and being welcomed by a mass of yapping and jumping hairs that simply exults in the sheer joy of seeing me. In both cases we experience our selves as accepted as persons in a way that we seldom experience in other settings where we constantly get evaluated on our abilities instead of just our existence.

A Sad Story Continued

A boy and his dog. It's no surprise that this is one of the strong images of bonding in our culture. It's hard to find anything other than a dog that more closely resembles the general clumsiness, joyousness, and spontaneity of ten to fifteen year old boys. A certain heart-melting silliness seem to cling to both of them—at least in their good moments.

They can also be aggressive, noisy, smelly, and a general nuisance, I know. But I am seeking a point here, so allow me some space to idealize reality. A boy and his dog. Two friends bound together by the needs they have. One of figuring out how to continue without a father, the other mostly in need of a good meal, a warm bed and someone who likes playing ball for hours and hours. But what happens when the needs change? In this case I simply got rid of my best friend, since I was suddenly occupied by growing up, chasing girls, going to parties, being irresponsible. I took my friend, who had seen me through the difficult years after my father's death, and gave him up for adoption. I took him to the vet, who had found a new home for him, and then went home. At that point he was five years old and I never saw him again.

That's no way to treat a friend. Friendships should be treated with reverence and humbleness. A friendship is something we enter carefully and leave reluctantly, if at all. We don't just give up on friends when we find that our needs change. We take our friends with us on the journey. But not in this case. As you might guess this still makes me feel pangs of guilt whenever I think about it, although it happened twenty years ago and the dog is now playing an eternal game of fetch where he is the one throwing the stick and a cat is chasing it. That is however not the point here. The point here is to say that there was a history between me and the dog, a history that involved a friendship. The history turned out sad, but in many other case histories between boys and dogs or other kinds of humans and dogs have turned out happily. And yet they all seem to be sad in the end, because in most cases the dog dies—or we die. We lose our friend one way or the other.

Although many beautiful things have been said about the interconnectedness of deep meaningful experiences and their finitude and the necessary relation between love and loss, saying these things only creates an excuse for our harsh and painful existence. Everything must end and everything must die. This can be interpreted in meaningful ways and we can teach each other to carry our sorrows with grace and dignity, but nobody who has lost a love has not hankered for the blind hope of the prophet Isaiah: a new heaven and a new earth where death no longer rules (Isaiah 65:17–25).

Saying "Oh, it's just a dog" when somebody loses a beloved dog is simply the most stupid thing anyone can say. If you talk to people who have lost a dog, it is clearly "not just a dog" that has died. It is a friend, and shame on any person who does not grieve the loss of a friend. So what do we do when life gets sad, meaning is lost, the sky turns grey, and we're reminded of the shortness of life, or, as Albert Camus put it, we observe the dark cloud that blows from our future? What do we do when we lose our friends?

The Age of Cloning

In February 1997 the British researcher Ian Wilmut and his team from Roslin Institute in Edinburgh presented the world with the first mammal cloned from a cell taken from an adult animal. That was the Dorset ewe Dolly, the only sheep to make the cover of *Time* magazine.

To be cloned from an adult animal means that you are produced in a very special way compared to the more conventional sexual creation of a new life. Let's imagine that I were to make a clone of the dog that was my friend when I was a kid. I would begin be getting an egg cell from a dog of the same breed—in this case a Golden Retriever. I would then suck out the genetic material residing in the middle of the egg cell leaving a genetically almost blank egg cell. There would be a few genes (twenty to thirty, out of ten to twenty thousand) left in the egg cell that I couldn't remove. But still, it would be an egg cell devoid of almost all genetic material. I would then take a cell from a skin sample from my old dog that I had frozen. I would carefully place this cell, containing all the genetic material of my old dog, in the almost empty egg cell. I would then fuse the two and, if all went well, the egg cell would begin developing and splitting like a normally fertilized egg cell. I could then place it in the womb of another Golden Retriever and a clone of my old dog would be born when the foster mother came to term. The clone will be *almost* genetically identical to my old dog. Only the few genes from the almost empty cell would make a difference.

This isn't science fiction. Dogs have been cloned already. The success rates are very low (between zero and one percent), but they're likely to improve as researchers and companies understand the technology better. A couple of years ago a company that sought to commercialize the cloning of cats and dogs was opened. The company, called *Genetic Savings and Clone*, only succeded in cloning a few cats, before the plug was pulled and the company no longer exists. But it's only a question of time before the price of fifty thousand dollars will drop to more acceptable levels and a new company will appear, offering to produce an almost identical copy of your dog at an affordable cost.

So What's the Problem?

Why isn't this the perfect way to get rid of my feelings of guilt? I could make a copy of my dog and this time around treat him as friends should be treated. Why should not dog owners who have had a happier story with their friend until he or she died, have a copy made and thus be able to continue the relationship? The answer to this is either extremely complicated, relying on a lot of science, or extremely simple, even too obvious, resting on the very common-sense notion of friendship discussed earlier.

The Science of It All

The complicated scientific explanation basically says that it won't work. Even if you succeed in having a viable clone born, it will in all likelihood only resemble the dog it is cloned from in a way that you might as well obtain by training another dog the same way. It all comes down to genetics. The genes from the mitochondria of the almost empty cell, although they are very few, seem to play an important regulatory role in the development of the early fetus. So as the original dog and the clone do not share the mitochondrial genes, they will differ, perhaps not so much genetically, but certainly in their appearance and probably also in temper and other more complex traits.

At the same time more and more research suggests that the environment plays a much more important role in the development of an animal than was previously thought. Factors such as the chemical environment the fertilized egg is placed in, the diet of the foster mother, and various other uncountable influences on the developing foetus, all seem to influence what genes will be switched on and what genes will lie dormant. These 'epigenetic' factors are still only poorly understood, but they are obviously there. Clones do not necessarily resemble the original, either physically or psychologically.

Cloning my dog will therefore in all likelihood not produce a copy that I can use to get rid of my guilt. Rather, I will have another dog, a new dog that I will have to build a new friendship with—a dog with whom I have no previous history—and a dog that I run the risk of being very disappointed in, because it does not resemble what I had hoped for. Hardly the best way to begin a beautiful friendship. Just as cloning a dead child will not bring back the original child, so cloning of a dog does not bring back the original dog. Our stories from the past cannot be retold. We have to carry them with us and, if we are the sole survivors of them, continue the tale on the conditions that we are the only ones left.

It all boils down to identity. We are who we are because of the relationships we have been in and continue to live in. We cannot begin again, imagining that nothing has happened since birth and everything important is somehow isolated in an untouchable place in our minds or hearts, there from birth to death. We are not isolated atoms that occasionally react with other atoms, like the famous billiard balls of David Hume (1711–1776). We're more like knots of relationships. We are the place where our relationships meet. And this is where science and ethics meet—and where the scientific arguments against cloning and the sheer impossibility of it all becomes irrelevant, because the ethical implications of seeking to recreate a meaningful relationship through technological fixes just seems wrong.

The Ethics of It All

So what if? What if science—which has made such impressive leaps forward in understanding and controlling the world for the past hundred years—what if science overcame these obstacles and was actually able to produce a genetic copy of my childhood dog that looked and behaved in much the same way. Could I not seek to make up for past wrongs by being a decent friend? Or could others, who have more happy tales to tell about their departed dogs, not have copies made and thus continue the happy stories?

I don't think so. I actually think we would do great harm to dogs that way. And being a person who has already once failed miserably in a friendship with a dog, I become very emotional when people begin speculating about these things.

What's left out of the whole cloning equation, the idea of repeating the biological patterns, is that we, humans and dogs, are not just biological entities, based on carbon and organized through complex molecular processes in genes. We're also, and first and foremost, historical beings. We are the histories of our lives. I am not just biology, but biology that has experienced this planet for thirty-seven years and even learned a lesson or two. I am who I am primarily because of my history. And cloning is basically an attempt to get around that basic condition of our existence. It is an attempt to bring back the past. But we cannot do that because the past is made up of history.

Imagine meeting a clone of one of your friends, and having to begin all over again becoming friends with the clone. The clone does not carry the experiences that you had with your friend. He will not be the same dog that ran after cars as a puppy and ate your favourite sneaker and slept in sunbeams on the patio. The new dog will probably do much the same stuff, but you will experience it in the light of your existence now, not as you did then. We cannot bring back the past. It just lies there, deciding who we are, helping us to interpret today and shaping our ideas of the future. Sometimes things happen that make us re-evaluate what happened in the past, but we cannot make it happen again.

To clone a departed friend like trying to swim in the same river twice—it can't be done, as Heraclitus (540–480 B.C.E.) pointed out. Our failures and successes are ours to live with—not to change. That does not stop us becoming wiser from our experiences. I believe to this day that to the extent I am able to see the vulnerability of other living beings, it is to a large extent because of my experiences with my friend from childhood that I failed so utterly to take care of. I would not wish to seek to repair that or turn it into something else by cloning him. And I don't believe that many dog owners will want to have a copy (if such a thing were possible) of their old departed friend to run around.

Life goes on and we may make new friends who will eat our shoes and dig up our lawns. And we will treat them with respect and love as the friends they are, because we know from our history with dogs that that is the right thing to do. And by doing it we might imagine that our lost friends are somehow honored and their lives remembered in a respectful way. This might not seem like much, when we carry around on our shoulders the burden of a mistreated friend. We are creatures of the age of fixing and repairing. Cloning of dogs is a shining example of this. Yet some pains are not here to be fixed or mended. They are here to talk with us, reminding us what and who we are. Creatures of utter vulnerability in need of friendships to survive.

This is what dogs can teach us about philosophy—or perhaps what philosophy can teach us about dogs. At least this is what I have learned from once having a friend that was a dog. So here's to you, Mikkel, a great big bowl of your favourite snacks.

IV

My Dog Ate My Dogma

13

Logic for Dogs

ANDREW ABERDEIN

I own it was a dangerous project,
And you have proved it by *dog-logic.*

—JONATHAN SWIFT

In March 1615, His Majesty King James the VI of Scotland and I of England participated in a debate concerning the use of logic by dogs.

The debate was one of several entertainments provided for the King during a visit to the University of Cambridge. At first glance, this event might seem wholly frivolous. Certainly the King's enthusiasm for hunting played a part in the choice of topic. But King James was no idle, anti-intellectual prince. He had assembled a hothouse of Protestant theologians to produce the English Bible that still bears his name, and his own collected works were to appear the following year. Moreover, the arguments rehearsed before King James echo down the history of logic, from antiquity to the twenty-first century.

The Dog Has His Day

The specific proposition which the Cambridge scholars disputed was "Whether dogs could make syllogisms." A syllogism is a piece of logical reasoning like this:

- **All pointers are gun dogs.**

- **All Weimaraners are pointers.**

- **Therefore, all Weimaraners are gun dogs.**

A syllogism is a derivation of one statement, the *conclusion*, from two others, the *premisses*. The *major* premiss, which makes the more general claim, is conventionally given first; the other is termed the *minor* premiss. Logicians are particularly concerned with *valid* syllogisms, in which the truth of the premisses guarantees the truth of the conclusion.

The theory of the syllogism is only a small fragment of modern logic, but until the nineteenth century, it comprised the principal subject matter of the discipline. Most attention was paid to *categorical* syllogisms, in which each of the statements of which the syllogism is comprised expresses a relationship between a pair of categories, or sets. For example, our syllogism proving that all Weimaraners are gun dogs.

This is the simplest sort of valid syllogism, sometimes known, in accordance with a medieval mnemonic, as *Barbara*. In a valid syllogism, the conclusion *must* be true, if the premisses are. *If* it's true that all pointers are gun dogs and *if* it's true that all Weimaraners are pointers, then *it must be true* that all Weimaraners are gun dogs. You don't have to know anything about gun dogs to be sure of this: the conclusion follows from the argument.

Categorical syllogisms were invented by Aristotle (384–322 B.C.E.), the first logician. Other varieties of syllogism were devised by later logicians, such as Chrysippus (280–204 B.C.E.), who was ultimately responsible for the principal exhibit laid before King James.

At Cambridge in 1615, the claim that dogs use logic was defended by John Preston (1587–1628) of Queens' College:

> He instanced in a hound who hath the major proposition in his mind, namely, *The hare is gone either this way or that way*; smells out the minor with his nose, namely, *She is not gone this way*; and follows the conclusion, *Ergo this way*, with open mouth. (Thomas Ball, *Life of Preston*, 1628)[1]

The inference which the dog is supposed to have followed is *disjunctive syllogism*, which we might abbreviate as:

---

[1] Quoted in John Mayor, 1898, "King James I on the Reasoning Faculty in Dogs," *The Classical Review* 12, p. 94. Emphasis in the original.

- *P* or *Q*.

- Not-*P*.

- **Therefore, *Q*.**

—where P means "The hare has gone this way" and Q means "The hare has gone that way."

Preston was answered by Matthew Wren (1585–1667) of Pembroke College, for whom dogs were distinguished by the excellence of their noses, not their reasoning: surely the dog determined the quarry's path by scent. While the moderator, Simon Reade of Christ's College, agreed with Wren, the King took Preston's side, gave an example of a reasoning dog from his own experience, and suggested that Reade should "thinke better of his dogs or not so highly of himselfe." Reade successfully mollified his sovereign with the suggestion that dogs that hunt by royal prerogative must be exceptions to laws governing common hounds, and the debate concluded in good spirits.

The Dog's Tale

Preston's dog story was not a new one. As John Mayor observes, the King and the other disputants could have known it from multiple sources. For example, they might have been reading Edward Topsell's (1572–1625) recently published *Historie of Foure-footed Beasts*, wherein we learn that

> Ælianus thinkes that Dogges have reason, & vse logick in their hunting, for they will cast about for the game, as a disputant doth for the truth, as if they should say either the Hare is gone on the left hand, or on the right hand, or straight forward, but not on the left or right hand and therefore straight forward. Whereupon he runneth foorth right after the true and infallible footesteps of the Hare. (Edward Topsell, *The Historie of Foure-footed Beasts*, 1607)[2]

Or they may have seen the 1600 play *Summer's Last Will and Testament* by Thomas Nash (1567–1601), in which they would have heard (lines 698–708) that

---

[2] Quoted in K.J. Höltgen, 1998, "Clever Dogs and Nimble Spaniels: On the Iconography of Logic, Invention, and Imagination," *Explorations in Renaissance Culture* 24.

Chrisippus holds dogs are Logicians,
In that, by study and by canvassing,
They can distinguish twixt three several things:
As when he cometh where three broad ways meet,
And of those three hath stayed at two of them,
By which he guesseth that the game went not,
Without more pause he runneth on the third;
Which, as Chrisippus saith, insinuates
As if he reasoned thus within himself:
Either he went this, that, or yonder way,
But neither that, nor yonder, therefore this.

But they most likely encountered the anecdote in the longest of the essays of the influential Renaissance philosopher Michel de Montaigne (1533–1592). First published in 1580, this appeared in English translation in 1603. Here we may read that

> *Chrysippus*, albeit in other things as disdainfull a judge of the condition of beasts as any other Philosopher, considering the earliest movings of the dog, who comming into a path that led three severall wayes in search or quest of his Master, whom he had lost, or in pursuit of some prey that hath escaped him, goeth senting first one way and then another, and having assured himself of two, because he findeth not the tracke of what he hunteth for, without more adoe furiously betakes himselfe to the third; he is enforced to confesse that such a dog must necessarily discourse thus with himselfe, '*I have followed my Masters footing hitherto, hee must of necessity pass by one of these three wayes; it is neither this nor that, then consequently hee is gone this other.*' And by this conclusion or discourse assuring him selfe, comming to the third path, hee useth his sense no more, nor sounds it any longer, but by the power of reason suffers himselfe violently to be carried through it. This meere logicall tricke, and this use of divided and conjoyned propositions, and of the sufficient numbring of parts: is it not as good that the dog know it by him selfe, as by *Trapezuntius* his logicke?"[3]

Trapezuntius, otherwise known as George of Trebizond (1395–1484), was the author of a popular logic textbook.

Montaigne's version closely follows the accounts in Sextus Empiricus (who was active in 190 C.E.), and in Plutarch (46–120

---

[3] *Essays* II.12, "An Apology for Raymond Sebond," John Florio's translation, 1603. Emphasis in the original.

C.E.), the acknowledged inspiration for Montaigne's revival of the literary essay. Other ancient versions have survived in the works of Philo of Alexandria (active in 39 C.E.), Claudius Aelianus (170–235 C.E.), Porphyry (233–301 C.E.), St. Basil (330–379 C.E.), and St. Ambrose (340–397 C.E.).[4] These multiple versions of the tale differ in minor details—whether the dog faces two or three possible exits, whether he is chasing a hare or tracking his master—but coincide at least in crediting the story to Chrysippus. Unfortunately, Chrysippus's own account is lost. Sextus follows Chrysippus's arguments closely, but only in order to rebut them, so reconstructing exactly what Chrysippus meant is a delicate task.

An Old Dog Taught New Tricks

The tale has been retold by many different authors, in much the same way, but to very different ends. Two questions posed during the Cambridge debate may help us understand how these different contexts are related: "Are dogs logical?" and, as King James demanded of Dr. Reade, "Should we think better of dogs or not so highly of ourselves?" Since each question has two possible answers, that makes for four positions, each of which has been defended by somebody:

1. We could say that dogs are logical, and so we should acknowledge that they are almost as clever as we are.

2. We could say that dogs are logical, but that shows that we are no cleverer than dogs.

3. We could say that dogs are illogical, but praise them for accomplishing so much without logic.

4. We could say that dogs are illogical, which only goes to show the worthlessness of logic, and the superiority of thinking like a dog.

Option #1: Dogs Are as Clever as Humans

On the first position, the dog story is accepted at face value. This is the perspective of Aelianus, and his medieval followers, such as

---

[4] The relevant passages in Latin or Greek may be found in Mayor's article, pp. 94–96.

the anonymous author of the twelfth-century *Roxburghe Bestiary.*
Here the story culminates with the moral: "And so, by rejecting
error, Dog finds the truth."[5]

Topsell agrees, as does the Enlightenment polemicist Jean-
Baptiste de Boyer, Marquis d'Argens (1704–1771), for whom "this
behaviour of the dog is an evident proof that his mind is capable
of the three operations of logic, and I do not see why a Shock Dog
and a Mastiff may not carry their reasoning as far as a Regent of
Philosophy in the College of the Four Nations."[6]

This interpretation of the story helped to establish a curious
career for the dog as emblem of logic. Beginning with the *Hortus
deliciarum* (*Pleasure Garden*) of Herrad of Landsberg (died 1195),
numerous emblem books, iconologies, and systems of visual
mnemonics employ dogs to symbolize logic.

Perhaps the most successful example is the woodcut representing logic in the 1503 liberal arts textbook *Margarita Philosophica*
(*Pearl of Wisdom*) by Gregor Reisch (1467–1525). Here, amongst
many other mnemonic images, Dame Logic hunts the hare
Problem, armed with the sword Syllogism, and accompanied by the
dogs Truth, which is hot on Problem's heels, and Falsity, which is
sniffing an unlabeled tree stump.

This image was plagiarized by Thomas Murner (1475–1537) as
the frontispiece to his 1508 *Logica memorativa vel Chartiludium
logice* (*Logic Remembered, or the Logical Card Game*). This work,
which sought to popularize the teaching of logic by means of elab-
orately illustrated playing cards, is sometimes credited with inadvertently inspiring tarot card reading.

Option #2: Humans Are as Stupid as Dogs

For those in the second camp, the dog's logical acuity serves the
very different purpose of undermining what these skeptical authors
perceive as an exaggerated reverence for human reason. This take
on the story is Sextus's contribution. His broader goal was to sug-

---

[5] T.H. White, *The Bestiary: A Book of Beasts* (London, 1954), p. 64.

[6] Quoted in Luciano Floridi, 1997, "Scepticism and Animal Rationality: The
Fortune of Chrysippus' Dog in the History of Western Thought," *Archiv für
Geschichte der Philosophie* 79. The three operations of logic are generally taken as
apprehension, judgment, and reasoning; a Shock Dog is somewhat like a Poodle;
a regent is a professor; and the College of the Four Nations was a pre-Revolutionary
college of the University of Paris.

gest that the trust we have in our senses is misplaced: many species of animals have superior, or at least different, sense organs, and so ours is merely one way of perceiving the world.

Sextus unleashes his dog in anticipation of the response that human perceptions of the world must be the correct ones, because of our superior intellects. If dogs can work out syllogisms, he suggests, we might not be so superior, and so we must concede that ours is merely one way of seeing the world. Porphyry and Montaigne set their dogs to similar skeptical work.

Option #3: Dogs Are Clever Yet Illogical

Proponents of the third and fourth positions seek to debunk the dog story. How do they do this? Wren's suggestion that the dog merely followed its nose is the most obvious strategy. As Samuel Taylor Coleridge (1772–1834) asks, "Why does this story excite either wonder or incredulity? . . . the Breeze brought his Master's scent down the fourth Road to the Dog's nose, and . . . *therefore* he did not put it down to the Road, as in the two former instances."[7]

Paradoxically, it's in the earliest surviving version of the story, that of Philo (and in Aelianus), that we find the most direct counterargument. For Philo's dog the trail runs cold at a deep shaft beside two tracks, which the dog inspects, and then "with no further scenting it jumped into the shaft to track down hastily," whereas Aelianus's "dog came upon a ditch and was puzzled as to whether it had better follow to the left or to the right. And when it had weighed the matter sufficiently, it leapt straight across."[8] In both cases an obstacle has been interposed, seemingly to require the dog to employ disjunctive syllogism, rather than its nose. However, this underestimates the extraordinary canine sense of smell: contrary to popular myth, crossing a stream does nothing to put a scent hound off one's track.[9]

---

[7] *The Friend*, No. 5, 1809. Emphasis in the original.

[8] Philo: *De Animalibus adversus Alexandrum*, 45; Aelianus: *De Natura Animalium*, VI.59, both quoted by Floridi. Philo's original Greek survives only in an Armenian translation, which Floridi read in French, and Mayor quotes in Latin. Mayor's version of Philo resembles Aelianus's account.

[9] See, for example, *MythBusters*, Season 4, Episode 5: "Dog Myths." Original air date: 14th March, 2007.

Moreover, Wren's sensible suggestion misses the point. Dismissing the specific story as implausible does not answer the real questions about the intellectual capabilities of dogs which the story raises. Notice that in almost every version of the story the dog is credited with an internal reasoning process, whereby he summarizes his predicament in statements which may serve as the premisses for his argument. For critics of canine cognition this is where the problem starts: do dogs really "say things to themselves" as the story apparently requires? If it is granted that they do, even non-linguistically, they have come close enough to human cognition that whether they also perform syllogisms seems a minor detail. And so, philosophers who deny dogs access to logic proceed by denying that they can form premisses.

The rejection of canine belief formation goes back to Aristotle. Unlike his teacher Plato (427–348 B.C.), who distinguished only between the perceptions derived from our senses and the beliefs founded upon them, Aristotle introduced a third sort of mental content, that of appearances, which mediates between the two.[10] Hence Aristotle could deny, as Plato could not, that animals were rational. Seemingly rational behavior by animals could now be explained away as the product of some process at the appearance level.

Animals, for Aristotle, do not have beliefs, but they do have appearances upon which rudimentary internal reasoning processes can operate. The crucial difference is that animals are not aware of their own reasoning process. For an appearance to qualify as a belief one must be convinced of it, that is persuade oneself that it is true. Hence, not just reasoning, but self-aware reasoning is required, if one is to have beliefs, and thereby qualify as rational.

Philo makes use of this strategy in his critique of the dog story. The dog has an appearance of no scent from two of the trails, and by an instinctive natural capacity proceeds in the direction of his quarry. We might interpret his behavior in accordance with the disjunctive syllogism, but that no more means that he is explicitly employing it than it would if we made similar observations of a human being eliminating false leads. People look for things all the time; they seldom think of syllogisms while doing so. Hence Philo

---

[10] See Richard Sorabji, "Rationality," in Michael Frede and Gisela Striker, eds, *Rationality in Greek Thought* (Oxford, 1996), pp. 311–334.

is in the third position outlined above: the dog is not logical, but does not need to be.

St. Thomas Aquinas (1225–1274) also seems to interpret the story this way. On his version, "the dog, chasing the stag, reached a crossroads, and having smelled the first and the second path, missing any information, ran with all certainty in the third direction, without further investigation, *as if* he had used a syllogism."[11] Indeed, Chrysippus himself may have held this view: Sextus only has him say that "the dog *in effect* reasons."[12] So the whole point of his story could have been not to suggest that dogs are really logical, but to illustrate the way that their natural intellect of appearances might be mistaken for reason.

Option #4: Dogs Are Clever Because They Are Illogical

Finally, for those who retell the story from the fourth position, this natural intellect seems rather more attractive and useful than the much vaunted logic which the dog lacks. This suggestion is found in Plutarch, and reinforced by the church fathers Basil and Ambrose. St. Basil observes approvingly that "Whereas the wise of our world may spend a life-time of laborious meditation on the combinations of syllogisms, dogs manage to clear up such problems naturally."[13] This perspective was especially influential among the empiricist philosophers of the early modern period, who trusted in experience and mistrusted what they saw as a bankrupt tradition of logical obfuscation perpetrated by mediaeval obscurantists. Thus Pierre Gassendi (1592–1655) asks "what olfactory sense is logic endowed with that it sniffs out and runs to ground the hidden nature of things?"[14] This trend culminates with David Hume (1711–1776), for whom "the whole conduct of life depends" not on logic, but on "experimental reasoning . . . which we possess in common with beasts"[15] This "is nothing but a species of

---

[11] *Summa Theologica*, Prima Secundae, Quaest. XIII, Art. II.3, quoted by Floridi. My emphasis.

[12] *Pyrrhoniae Hypotyposes*, A 69, in Benson Mates *The Skeptic Way: Sextus Empiricus's Outlines of Pyrrhonism* (Oxford, 1997), p. 98. My emphasis.

[13] *Homelia* n. IX.4, cited by Floridi.

[14] *The Selected Works of Pierre Gassendi*, edited and translated by Craig B. Brush (New York, 1972), p. 63, cited by Floridi.

[15] David Hume, 1748, *An Enquiry concerning Human Understanding*, Section 9, p. 108.

instinct or mechanical power, that acts in us unknown to ourselves; and in its chief operations, is not directed by any such relations or comparisons of ideas, as are the proper objects of our intellectual faculties."

Empiricism, which privileges experience over reason, is invariably contrasted with rationalism, which reverses these priorities. However, the deprecation of logic by empiricist philosophers coincided with a deprecation of dogs, or rather of the intellectual capabilities of animals in general, by their rationalist rivals.

The chief rationalist René Descartes (1596–1650) is well-known for his contention that non-human animals are unthinking automata. He left no explicit comment on Chrysippus's dog; the closest he comes is a remark in a letter that, "as for what concerns the capacity of understanding and thinking that Montaigne and some others attribute to brutes, I cannot be of the same opinion"[16] Under this dual assault the dog began to lose his status as patron beast of logic. For Thomas Hobbes, writing his *Leviathan* in 1651, the imagination works "as a spaniel ranges the field, till he finds the scent." Although the dog still represents a thought process, canine logical inference has given way to mere dogged persistence. By 1711, the date of its earliest citation in the *Oxford English Dictionary*, "dog('s) logic" is a term of abuse: "bad, spurious, bastard, mongrel" logic, according to the lexicographers.[17] The once celebrated logical dog was now in full retreat.

The Dog Returns to His Syllogism

In recent decades the dog has made an unexpected reappearance in works of logical scholarship. To understand why, let us look more closely at what we know of his first appearance. Sextus tells us that

---

[16] Letter to William Cavendish, Marquess (later Duke) of Newcastle, 23rd November 1646, quoted by Floridi.

[17] The OED cites *The Examiner*, No. 50, attributing it, wrongly, to Jonathan Swift (1677–1745). Swift did use the phrase, to comparable purpose, in 1723: see the epigraph at the beginning of this chapter, taken from "Upon the horrid plot discovered by Harlequin, the Bishop of Rochester's French dog," in R. Maynard Leonard, ed., 1893, *The Dog in British Poetry*, p. 229. The OED traces "dog-rimes" back to 1611, and the usage of "dog" within plant names, "frequently denoting an inferior or worthless sort," to 1548.

According to Chrysippus, who was certainly no friend of non-rational animals, the dog even shares in the celebrated dialectic. In fact, the author says that the dog uses repeated applications of the fifth indemonstrable argument-schema when, arriving at a juncture of three paths, after sniffing at the two down which the quarry did not go, he rushes off on the third without stopping to sniff. For, says this ancient authority, the dog in effect reasons as follows: the animal either went this way or that way or the other; he did not go this way and he did not go that; therefore, he went the other." (*Pyrrhoniae Hypotyposes*, A 69)

The aside in the first sentence, subsequently echoed by Montaigne, flags up what Sextus takes to be self-contradiction in Chrysippus: denying that animals can be rational and then attributing a syllogism to a dog. As we saw above, this may be a misreading: Chrysippus might have shared Aristotle's view that primitive inferring could take place without rationality. Sextus uses "dialectic" to refer to the process of logical argument, and the "fifth indemonstrable argument-schema" is Chrysippus's name for disjunctive syllogism, that is "*P* or *Q*, not-*P*, therefore *Q*." It is indemonstrable because he takes it as axiomatic: something just so obviously correct that no further justification is required, or, indeed, possible. This view is not universally endorsed.

Indeed, some twentieth-century logicians have sought to banish disjunctive syllogism. Their concern is that its presence in a system of logic validates what they call *irrelevant* inferences. These are arguments held to be valid by mainstream logicians, but in which the conclusion is seemingly unrelated to the premises. Consider the following case. Suppose your neighbor owns a small yappy dog, which you have heard from a usually reliable source to be a Pomeranian. You might harmlessly conclude that the dog was either a Pomeranian or a Rottweiler. This might seem an odd conclusion to draw, but it is a secure one: if one of the components of an "or"-statement is true then the "or"-statement must be true, even if the other component is obviously false. But if you were now to learn that the dog was not really a Pomeranian (perhaps it was a Shock Dog), you might apply disjunctive syllogism as follows: the dog is either a Pomeranian or a Rottweiler; it is not a Pomeranian; so it must be a Rottweiler. Something has definitely gone wrong. Proponents of *relevance logic* would place the blame with disjunctive syllogism.

This diagnosis might seem to ignore a more obvious problem: the conclusion that the dog is a Rottweiler turns on two contradictory pieces of information, that it's a Pomeranian and that it's not. Surely these can't both be right, and that is where the problem really lies? Certainly no dog is both a Pomeranian and not a Pomeranian. But you would not need to believe this of the dog in question in order to follow the above argument. Having inferred that the dog was a Pomeranian or a Rottweiler, you might have forgotten everything else about it. When subsequently, perhaps years later, you learn that it is not a Pomeranian, this does not contradict anything you by now believe, although it supports the erroneous inference that the dog is a Rottweiler. So, while it is reasonable to stipulate that holding contradictory beliefs is irrational (if all too common), and that arguments that depend on our doing so are unsound, *this* argument would be unaffected. You could impose an even higher standard of rationality—perhaps that whenever you stopped believing something you should also stop believing everything that depends essentially upon your discarded belief. But this would be very hard to do: who keeps track of where every belief comes from? Moreover, is it never rational to hold on to beliefs that you only have because you previously believed something false? Arguably much scientific progress has required such behavior.[18]

Of course relevance logic has its complications too, but they are not necessarily any worse than those besetting accounts of rationality which retain disjunctive syllogism. More to the point, the relevance logic side of the debate has tossed a bone to Chrysippus's dog. The new problem which the dog now poses is that, although his behavior still seems rational, the principle of logic by which it has been explained for over two thousand years is, according to the relevance logician, not a principle of logic after all. How is this to be resolved? The answer lies in exposing a fundamental ambiguity in the understanding of "or."[19]

---

[18] Jay Garfield, "The Dog: Relevance and Rationality," in J.M. Dunn and A. Gupta, eds., *Truth or Consequences: Essays in Honor of Nuel D. Belnap, Jr.* (Dordrecht, 1990), p. 104.

[19] What follows is inspired by Stephen Read, "In Defence of the Dog: Response to Restall," in S. Rahman *et al.*, eds., *Logic, Epistemology, and the Unity of Science* (Dordrecht, 2004), pp. 175–180. The dog's relevance logic début was in Alan Ross Anderson and Nuel D. Belnap, Jr., *Entailment: The Logic of Relevance and Necessity* (Princeton, 1975), Volume I, Section 25.1.

Logicians typically interpret "or"-statements as statements about the truth of the components. Hence "The hare is gone either this way or that way" is understood as saying that one of the following statements is true: "The hare is gone this way"; "The hare is gone that way." (Whether it says that *exactly* one of them is true, or that *at least* one of them is true, is an important debate in its own right, but of no significance here, since it is obvious that in this case only one of them can be true: the hare has not gone both ways.) This interpretation is called the *extensional* or *truth functional* sense of "or," since it makes the truth of an "or"-statement a function of the truth (or falsity) of its components.

Somewhat counter-intuitively, mainstream logicians also define "if" truth functionally, such that "if P then Q" is equivalent to "not-P or Q." Hence, "if"-statements may be seen as disguised "or"-statements. Relevance logicians deny that "if" can be captured in this fashion, offering an alternative definition, the details of which need not detain us. It's still possible to define a truth-functional "if" in their systems, but relevance logicians do not accept that this translates our everyday understanding of "if." However, they do accept that "if" and "or" can be defined in terms of each other. So systems of relevance logic characteristically contain two "or"s: an extensional "or," the same as that in mainstream logic, and an *intensional* "or," defined in terms of the relevance logicians' non-truth-functional "if." But the two sets of connectives are distinct: there is no way of defining an intensional connective in terms of an extensional one, or *vice versa*. Indeed, the distinction between extensional and intensional "or" will collapse if only the truth-functional sense of "if" is available. A central motivation of relevance logic is its more attractive treatment of "if": not the least of its attractions is that it sustains this distinction.

On the intensional reading, "or"-statements are disguised "if"-statements: such an "or"-statement says of each of its components that, if that component is false, then (one of) the other(s) must be true. Hence "The hare is gone either this way or that way" becomes "If the hare is not gone this way then it is gone that way, and if not that way then this." This interpretation captures the assumption credited to the dog at least as well as the more familiar statement. However, the dog's syllogism would no longer be disjunctive syllogism, "P or Q, not-P, therefore Q," but rather "If not-P then Q, not-P, therefore Q."

This syllogism is accepted as valid by virtually all logicians, and certainly by relevance logicians, whose grasp of the dog's logical acumen is thus vindicated. But note that this trick cannot be performed on every instance of "or." Your belief that your neighbor's dog was a Pomeranian would not support the belief that if it wasn't a Pomeranian then it was a Rottweiler. You could still believe of the dog that it was either a Pomeranian or a Rottweiler, but only in the extensional sense of "or," which, for the relevance logician would not support the application of disjunctive syllogism. Hence the troublesome inference that a small yappy dog might somehow be concealing an extra hundred pounds of muscle is safely neutered.

Of course, you might have an independent reason for believing the intensional form of this "or"-statement: that, if your neighbor's dog is not a Pomeranian, then it is a Rottweiler. Perhaps you have seen your neighbor and his girlfriend walking one of each, and you couldn't be sure whose dog was which. Or perhaps you hear that he has recently acquired a dog, and he has said that he could own no other breeds. But if, in one of these rather contrived situations, you were to learn that he doesn't have a Pomeranian, then your inference that he must have a Rottweiler would be entirely sound.

There are many irrelevant inferences which mainstream logicians accept, but disjunctive syllogism is the most conspicuous. Hence the dog story posed a very pertinent challenge: its apparent rationality, for humans at least, seemed to be at odds with the relevance logicians insistence that the move was unsound. However, not only have relevance logicians answered this criticism, in doing so they have explained what mainstream logic does not: why some instances of disjunctive syllogism appear more persuasive than others—these are the cases which also instantiate a relevant inference. Thus the ostensible criticism has been turned to the advantage of relevance logic.

The dog has an impressive pedigree. From his beginnings with Chrysippus, after Aristotle the foremost logician of antiquity, he has kept company with many of the most eminent thinkers of subsequent centuries: poets and scholars, saints and kings. Along the way he has made himself useful in a diverse, if not always mutually consistent, collection of arguments: critiquing the reliability of the human senses, defending the rationality of animals, and arguing for the superiority of experience over reason. In his heyday his image came to be emblematic of logic itself, and most recently he has emerged from a long retirement to resolve a dispute over the future of that discipline.

As this account suggests, a simple tale can have great philosophical value. In each of his incarnations the dog has helped us to see what it means to attribute logical reasoning, not just to dogs, but to ourselves. Time and time again the faithful creature has proved himself the logician's best friend.

14

How to Prove that a Chihuahua Is a Saint Bernard

JIRI BENOVSKY

Hollywood producers have decided to create another sequel to *Beethoven*, the successful movie starring a Saint Bernard, and they're looking for a suitable candidate to play Beethoven's part. Such a dog is rare since it has to be trained very well in order to be able to perform as an actor. As it happens, a certain Mr. Arnold Schwarzenegger does have such a Saint Bernard and suggests to the producers that it would suit the part perfectly well.

His neighbor, Mr. Sylvester Stallone, is furious—again, he would have to suffer that his competitive neighbor would beat him and show off with his dog's success. But he becomes really furious when he learns that Arnold has called his dog "Sylvester." Mr. Stallone picks up the phone, calls a dog vendor, and without even bothering to come and look at it, orders that a Saint Bernard must be delivered to his house immediately. Already, he enjoys the idea that it's *his* Saint Bernard that will get the part (he'd make sure of that!) . . . and of course, he'll call it "Arnold."

Mr. Stallone doesn't know much about dogs. In fact, he doesn't even like dogs. But even though he is well aware of his total ignorance on the subject, he feels that something isn't as it should be.

"Isn't it supposed to be . . . hum . . . *bigger?*" he asks the delivery man who's just arrived at his house with a small basket containing a wonderful dog. "I did tell your boss that I need an *adult* Saint Bernard!"

"Oh, but this is an adult", replies the delivery man "and look! It seems he already likes you!"

"Yeah, yeah, . . . whatever . . . well, leave it there, I'll see what I can do with it."

Mr. Stallone scratches his head. He didn't see the movie, and he has no idea what a Saint Bernard really is, but he does know that his neighbor's dog is *much* bigger than that. Being a man of action, he picks up the phone again, and calls his lawyer who, he knows, owns a dog and should be able to help. Then, things go fast: the lawyer first bursts out laughing when he sees that Sylvester has purchased a Chihuahua instead of a Saint Bernard without even knowing what happened, then he forces himself to calm down when he notices Sylvester's furious expression, and decides in favor of a lawsuit against the vendor.

The judge has never seen a lawsuit like this. On one side, Mr. Stallone, stone-faced, holding a Chihuahua in his arms, and on the other the vendor claiming that, of course, the dog Mr. Stallone has been given *is* a Saint Bernard. Furthermore, he adds, he can prove it, if only everybody would come tomorrow to his ranch outside the city. Full of curiosity, the judge agrees to this, and so the following day the judge, the vendor, and a whole bunch of lawyers accompany Mr. Stallone and his dog to the ranch.

The spectacle is impressive: a long line formed by dogs that starts at the ranch and seems to go further and further for miles. The vendor then starts his argument. He points to the very first dog in this long line, obviously a shaggy and robust Saint Bernard, and asks:

"You agree that this is a Saint Bernard, right?"

"Yes, of course it is," Mr. Stallone says "so give it to me and let's go home!"

"Not so fast, not so fast", the vendor smiles. "Let's have a look at the second dog in the line. As you can see, the second dog is very, *very* similar to the first one, there is only a very slight difference between them in color and size, the second being just a very tiny bit smaller than the first. But of course such a really small difference can't be important enough in order to claim that it is not a Saint Bernard anymore, you agree on that don't you?" When both the judge and Mr. Stallone agree they do, the vendor goes on. "You see," he says, and starts to walk along the enormous line of dogs "this line is formed in such a way that each dog has as its successor a *very slightly* different dog, just a tenth of a millimeter smaller, with some very minor differences in color and shape. So it's true at each step we take that if one dog is a Saint Bernard then its successor is also a Saint Bernard, since clearly a tiny difference such as there is between each one and its neighbor can't be enough to make it a different breed."

The vendor starts walking faster and faster while he speaks, and after some time, they all arrive, almost running, at the opposite end of the line. And all the way long the vendor has been pointing out that there never is any big or significant difference between any dog and its neighbor in the line, and everybody just has to agree to that. At the end of the line, the vendor stops, takes the last dog that clearly is a Chihuahua in his arms and says: "See, this dog *is* a Saint Bernard, exactly like the one I sold you. We started with a dog that you all clearly identified as a Saint Bernard, and we all agreed that any successor of a Saint Bernard in this line is a Saint Bernard, so this little guy, *just has to be* a Saint Bernard too, no matter how small he is and how different he is from the first member of the line."

"But that's a dirty trick!" poor Sylvester exclaims. "Your so-called 'proof' is just complete nonsense!"

"Well then," the vendor smiles. "It shouldn't be difficult for you to show what's wrong with it."

Philosophy often starts with such completely counter-intuitive but seemingly true (or hard-to-disprove) claims, not (only) because it's fun, but because identifying what exactly it is that makes them look like true helps us to learn something about the world — in this case about dog breeds in particular and about certain features of the nature of material entities in general, as we will see. So, apart from the fun, philosophers are serious people and have designed over time conceptual and logical tools in order to evaluate arguments and see whether they are good or bad. Before we go on with our story, let's then talk about some of these tools.

What Is an Argument?

What actually *is* an argument? Surely, a fully loaded Kalashnikov can sometimes seem like one, but you'll probably agree with me that this is not the kind we're looking for. An argument, as simple as it is, is just *a series of statements* (a series of affirmative sentences, if you like). This series has to be ordered in a certain way and most importantly it is composed of *premises* and *conclusions*. Premises are the statements that you take to be true by hypothesis, and conclusions are those statements that *logically follow* from premises.

What does it mean that a statement logically follows from some other statement? Well, simply that *if* the premises are true *then* the conclusion *must* be true. If an argument satisfies this condition, we can say that it's logically valid (or just valid). There's something very important about this: logical validity of an argument is independent of the truth or falsity of the premises. This probably sounds strange, so let's take an example:

1. If pigs have wings, then they can fly.

2. Pigs have wings.

3. Therefore: pigs can fly.

This argument is unlikely to convince anybody—yet it is logically valid, for it is correct that *if* the premises (1 and 2) were true, then the conclusion (3) would have to be true. Try to imagine a world where, first, it's true that pigs have wings and, second, it's true that if pigs have wings then they can fly. In this world, it would just have to be true that pigs can fly! And this is what it takes for the argument to be logically valid.

The reason we have to reject this particular argument is not its logical structure, since this is perfectly okay, but simply the fact that at least one of its premises (here, the premise 2) is false. And of course, it's enough to find out that one premise of an argument is false to be able to reject it. So the recipe to reject an argument has two independent parts: either show that there is a problem with its structure, or show that at least one of its premises is false. (Remember this recipe the next time you face an argument, you'll see how easier things are—once you've been able to identify what the premises and what the conclusions are, of course, it's not always that easy!)

Let's get back to Mr. Stallone. His lawyers having been totally inept at finding out how to deal with the vendor's argument, he hired three philosophers instead. But as things are, he was at first very disappointed, since they all told him that yes, of course, the argument is logically valid. (Mr. Stallone had no idea what 'logically valid' means, but it seemed to be something important.) Indeed, the vendor's argument has almost exactly the same *logical form* as the argument about flying pigs, once we put it this way:

1. The *first* dog in the line is a Saint Bernard.

2. If the *first* dog in the line is a Saint Bernard, then the *second* dog in the line is a Saint Bernard. (This is what Sylvester himself had to accept since he accepted that a really tiny difference, like being a tenth of a millimeter smaller and very slightly different in shape and color, cannot make a Saint Bernard to be something else.)

3. If the *second* dog in the line is a Saint Bernard, then the *third* dog in the line is a Saint Bernard.

4. If the *third* dog in the line is a Saint Bernard, then the *fourth* dog in the line is a Saint Bernard. . . .

5. If the *billionth* dog in the line is a Saint Bernard, then the *last* (billion-plus-oneth) dog in the line is a Saint Bernard.

6. Therefore: the last dog in the line is a Saint Bernard.

But, of course, the last dog is a Chihuahua. The argument is logically valid, since its logical form is:

1. A

2. If A then B.

3. If B then C.

4. If C then D. . . .

5. If Y then Z.

6. Therefore: Z.

—almost like the argument about pigs, except that it has more conditional steps. *Any* argument of this logical form is logically valid. So it's clear, the three philosophers say to Mr. Stallone, that it's not the logical validity of the argument that one can attack, but rather try to show that one among the premises is false. But which one?— there are actually *a lot* of them (as many as there are dogs in the line). The first premise has a special status, because it's the only one that is not a conditional: it simply says that the first dog in the line is a Saint Bernard. And it is just totally obvious to everybody: even Mr. Stallone, who is just starting to learn something about dogs, sees that it is impossible to deny this. So we have to consider the very many conditional premises (ii, iii, iv, . . .). The trouble is, they all seem to be true too!

Remember what the vendor said and what the judge and Mr. Stallone both (rightly) accepted: being a tenth of a millimeter smaller and of a *very* slightly different shape and color cannot make a Saint Bernard be something else (after all, many Saint Bernards are a bit different from each other, and some are smaller than others). A very tiny difference such as this one cannot make a difference between dog breeds. But wait! We've just seen that the argument is logically valid, *and* now it also seems that all premises are true. Since the conclusion follows from the premises, it just has to be accepted as true! (The vendor smiles.) But it just isn't acceptable; it flies in the face of common sense to accept that a Chihuahua is a Saint Bernard.

We will now hear what the three philosophers have to say, but before we do that, I dare suggest to you, Dear Reader, to take about ten minutes and try to figure out by yourself what to do (say, put yourself in the position of the judge). That's what doing philosophy is all about—*and* it's fun, as you'll see.

The First Philosopher's Anwer:
The World Is Vague

"Did you know," the first philosopher says to Mr. Stallone, "that the vendor's argument is actually very famous in the history of philosophy? It's been around for more than two thousand years. And it shows us something very important about the nature of dogs' breeds and the nature of the world in general: dogs' breeds and many other aspects of the world are *vague*.

"The phenomenon of vagueness arises whenever we face *borderline cases*. When walking along the line of dogs, nothing really interesting happens at the beginning, since everybody will happily accept that the first dog is a wonderful Saint Bernard and that its successors are Saint Bernards too, but sooner or later we'll get to a point where we'll start wondering whether the dog we are passing by is a Saint Bernard or not. By very small steps, it will become to us *indeterminate* whether 'being a Saint Bernard' is applicable to the dog in front of us or not, and if the statement 'This is a Saint Bernard' is true or false—it's in this case that we can say that the dog is a borderline case of a Saint Bernard. And the reason for our hesitation and of the indeterminacy is that the property of being a Saint Bernard is vague. When considering the line of dogs, there are some determinate and clear cases at the beginning and at the end, but there's a whole zone somewhere in between the ends where it is indeterminate whether the dogs are Saint Bernards or not."

"All right," the judge interjects, "but when we start to walk along the line, and at each step we point at the dog in front of us and say 'This is a Saint Bernard' there must be a first (and so a precise) moment when the statement ceases to be true and becomes false!"

"Not at all!" the philosopher answers. "You see, what I'm suggesting is precisely to reject the following principle that your honor has implicitly appealed to:

The Bivalence Principle: Any statement is either true or false.

Indeed, because of the vague zone where it is unclear whether 'being a Saint Bernard' applies to the dog in front of us or not, the statement 'This is a Saint Bernard' is, at this stage, *neither true nor false*; we can say that it just *lacks* a truth-value. The vendor's argument is then easy to reject, since certain of the premises (the ones in the vague zone) simply are not true. Granted, they are not false either, but to reject an argument it is not required that the premises must be false, it is enough that they are not true."

"Oh, I get it!" Mr. Stallone interrupts. "We can divide the line of dogs into three zones: one where it is true that the dogs are Saint Bernards, one where it is indeterminate (neither true nor false) whether they are Saint Bernards, and finally one where it's false that they are Saint Bernards."

"But wait," the judge intervenes again. "When we start walking along the line and point to each dog in turn and say 'This is a Saint Bernard', when does exactly the indeterminate zone start? If your way of rejecting the vendor's argument is that there's an indeterminate zone, you should be able to say where exactly it is."

"Yes, you're right, it's not so simple" the first philosopher replies. "Because not only is it vague whether some dogs in the line are Saint Bernards or not, but it's also vague when exactly the line starts to be vague. Thus, there is a zone where it is indeterminate whether it is indeterminate whether a given dog is a Saint Bernard. This phenomenon is called *higher-order vagueness* and it goes on much further: there will also be a zone where it's indeterminate whether it's indeterminate whether it's indeterminate whether a given dog is a Saint Bernard, and so on. Consequently, it will be impossible to say with precision at which moment the statement 'This is a Saint Bernard' when walking along the line will lose its truth-value (when it will cease to be true and will become neither true nor false).

But there's worse, the philosopher goes on, for the problem is much more important than just to find out how to reject the vendor's argument, since the only thing the vendor did was to exploit a very general feature of the world—that is, that many properties are vague. Think of the following: being a Saint Bernard, being a Chihuahua (by the way, did you realize that you can also formulate the vendor's argument in the reverse order and construct a proof that the *first* dog in the line is a *Chihuahua*?), being red, being big, being a child, being drunk, . . . All of these properties are vague. And not only that: ordinary material objects are also vague."

"What!?" Mr. Stallone exclaims, "You mean to say that this table over here outside the entrance of the ranch is vague? It seems perfectly all right and non-vague to me! Perhaps you philosophy guys need a thicker pair of glasses!"

"Before talking about the table, let me take another example— a cloud. When the sky is blue and there is only one isolated and well delimited cloud, it seems to be a precise object, but if we took a plane and approached it, it would become very hard to say where exactly it begins and where it ends. It would be very hard to say if such and such a droplet is still part of the cloud or if it is part of the surrounding atmosphere. And the closer one gets, the more one realizes that the cloud just does not have precise spatial boundaries, its boundaries are *spatially indeterminate*. You see here easily the parallel with the case of the line of dogs: just as it is indeterminate if a certain dog is still a Saint Bernard, it's indeterminate if a certain droplet is still part of the cloud, in both cases there's nothing that would allow us to decide the matter. So we just have to accept that properties and objects *are* vague. This is, of course, also true about the table over there, since it would be enough to take a microscope and look at it very closely in order to realize that it is indeterminate whether such and such a molecule is still part of the table or if it is already part of the surrounding environment. In this way, even you people are vague: examine your hand with a powerful microscope and consider the atoms and molecules at the 'edge' of you, or even consider what happens when you eat—at which moment precisely the food you swallow becomes a part of you? Of course, all this is genuinely vague."

"All right, let me see whether I have got you right," Mr. Stallone says. "In the vendor's argument, a number of premises are in the vague zone and so they don't have a truth-value—they're neither true nor false. And what's important about this is that they are not true, which is then enough to reject the argument. But, as much as I would like to accept your view, since it would allow me to win against the vendor, there is something that deeply troubles me about it . . . I can't say really what it is . . . it's all vague in my head . . ."

"What troubles you," the second philosopher says, "is that . . ."

The Second Philosopher's Answer: The World Is Precise but We Don't Know Where the Boundaries Are

"What troubles you," the second philosopher says, "is that even if this alleged solution to the problem seems to work, it's based on a central assumption which is intuitively totally unacceptable—as unacceptable as the counter-intuitive claim that your Chihuahua is a Saint Bernard, and so the cure is no better than the disease. Of course, I am speaking about the claim that objects and properties are vague.

This claim, I say, is just complete nonsense. Try to *imagine* a spatially vague object, like the table. As the philosopher David Lewis has suggested, you have three possibilities there: either you can imagine *several superimposed* objects that overlap (the table that contains molecule m1 and molecule m2, the table that contains molecule m1 but not molecule m2, the table that contains molecule m2 but not molecule m1, and so on), or you can imagine that the table *does* have a precise spatial boundary but that you *don't know* where it is, or you can imagine that the table is like a circle of light cast by a spotlight that is very bright in the center and less and less bright towards its edges.

"But in none of these cases have you succeeded in imagining a *vague* object: in the first case, the so-called vague object is nothing more than a set of precise objects, in the second case the phenomenon of vagueness is replaced by the phenomenon of ignorance (we'll get back to this one), and in the third case, it's always *precise* as to which degree of 'brightness' is present at each point. So It's never vague whether an object exists in one place or not, and the fact that we can't imagine a vague object shows us that we just have no clear idea of what such an object is supposed to be. And of course, we cannot accept a theory that uses as a central notion something that we cannot even intuitively grasp.

Besides, this metaphysical theory of vagueness—metaphysics is, roughly, the subdivision of philosophy that studies the nature of the world, and so that's why this view is called 'metaphysical', since it claims that vagueness is a real phenomenon out there in the world—also has some serious problems with logic. As we've seen it rejects the principle of bivalence (that is that any statement is either true or false) which is a much less innocent move than it may seem, because it forces us to abandon classical logic.

"In classical logic, it's important that any statement of the form 'A *or* non-A' is always *true* (which is the intuitive thing to say, isn't it?), but the metaphysical theory of vagueness, because it rejects the principle of bivalence, just can't go along with this. Suppose that we're walking along the line of dogs and that we are in the 'vague zone', that is, we are facing a dog about which it is indeterminate whether it is a Saint Bernard or not. The statement 'This is a Saint Bernard' is then, according to the metaphysical theory, neither true nor false—it has an indeterminate truth-value. Then of course, the negation of this statement ('This is *not* a Saint Bernard') is also indeterminate. But now, take the statement: 'This is a Saint Bernard *or* this is not a Saint Bernard' that has the form 'A or non-A'— according to our intuitions, and according to classical logic, such a statement is always *true*, but not according to the metaphysical theory of vagueness, which has to claim that the statement is indeterminate (and so, is *not true*) which is in conflict with both common sense and classical logic.

"Of course, philosophers who defend this view propose solutions, such as new logics that work differently from classical logic, so I'm not saying that I have refuted their view completely, but I *am* saying that their view is much more complicated than needed (for technical reasons arising from logic) and very much against common sense (remember that on top of what we have just seen, we do not even have a clear intuitive conception of what a vague object is supposed to be). So I suggest we simply say good-bye to this unappealing theory."

Mr. Stallone and his lawyers are not very happy. The metaphysical theory of vagueness would allow them to reject the vendor's argument and win, but now, since it seems that the theory does not work, they're back to square one.

"I hope you have something better to suggest, 'cause otherwise I'm stuck with this!" Mr. Stallone says, pointing to his Chihuahua, and imagining the whole neighborhood making fun of him.

"Oh, but it wouldn't be so bad, would it? He's so cute!" the second philosopher replies petting the Chihuahua. "But of course, not only I have another theory to propose to you, but as you will see it is beautifully elegant and simple. In fact, I already mentioned this theory above: it says, very simply, that there are no vague objects and that properties are not vague, and that the world is completely precise (including dogs, clouds, tables, and so on), it's just that *we don't know where the precise boundaries are*, and that's really all there is to it. My theory is simply a theory of our ignorance of certain facts about the world (this is why it's called 'the epistemic theory of vagueness', since epistemology is the field of philosophy that studies the nature of knowledge). In short, my theory is a theory of ignorance of the boundaries, rather than of a non-existence of these boundaries, as the metaphysical theory would have it.

"Consider again what happens when we walk along the line of dogs. As we have noticed, there is a point where we don't know what to say—is the dog in front of us a Saint Bernard or not? I suggest we take this literally: we *don't know* what to say, because we *don't know* the precise boundaries to dog's breeds—*we* are ignorant, our knowledge is vague, not the actual world. Dogs, clouds, and tables have precise spatial boundaries, but we don't know where they are—when we walk along the line, there *is* a *precise* moment where the dogs we are passing by cease to be Saint Bernards, but we ignore it. This provides an even easier solution to the vendor's argument than before: we can simply say here that *one* of the premises is false. For instance, we can suppose that even if it's true that

If the *102,289th* dog in the line is a Saint Bernard, then the *102,290th* dog in the line is a Saint Bernard.

it is *false* that

If the *102,290th* dog in the line is a Saint Bernard, then the *102,291st* dog in the line is a Saint Bernard.

—because there's a sharp (non-vague) boundary between the 102,290th and 102,291st dog that *does* make the difference between a Saint Bernard and a non-Saint Bernard. Of course, this is just an example of how my theory works, since we don't know *which* of the premises is the false one, but it's enough to know that there is one premise that's false in order to reject the argument. And there are two big advantages to my view over the metaphysical theory.

"First, I don't reject the principle of bivalence, since all statements are always true or false, and so I'm not forced to abandon classical logic. Just for this reason, my view is probably to be accepted, since this is not only a question of a technical kind that interests only logicians, but this is the only way to preserve our common sense intuitions that are in conflict with the rejection of classical logic. Besides, my view does not yield the problem of higher-order vagueness, as the metaphysical theory did.

"Second, my theory is conceptually much more satisfying, since we don't have to embrace a counter-intuitive and under-explained notion of vague objects—my theory does not rest on any such mysterious assumption."

"Not so fast," the third philosopher interrupts . . .

The Third Philosopher's Answer: The Problem Comes from Our Language

"Not so fast," the third philosopher interrupts. "I really cannot, Mr. Stallone, encourage you to accept this epistemic theory of vagueness, for two reasons. First of all, this theory also contains a central thesis that is very mysterious and under-explained. The theory claims that there are sharp boundaries in the world but that we ignore them. But does this mean that these boundaries are *unknown* to us or that they are *unknowable?* If we had more information about the world, could we discover exactly where the boundaries are?

"Of course not! Because we already know all that we need! When we walk along the line of dogs, we know exactly which dog is in front of us, and we see exactly how big he is, his color, his shape, and so on. We could even stop and measure him if we wanted more details. So, we know (or we could easily know) *everything that is relevant* about the dog in order to determine what breed it is, but according to the epistemic theory of vagueness, we still *ignore* whether it is a Saint Bernard or not. But then, it is really unclear where this alleged ignorance comes from, and we were given no good explanation of that! This phenomenon of ignorance is then also a very mysterious assumption.

On top of that, there's a second reason why this epistemic theory is simply incredible: it says that there's a sharp boundary to all objects, and means to take it seriously. But this is just crazy: there is no way that we can intuitively accept that a single molecule or a single subatomic particle will make a difference between a Saint Bernard and a non-Saint Bernard, this just flies in the face of common sense. From the start, when we were first considering the vendor's argument, we all accepted that such a tiny difference cannot be enough, and of course we should stick to that, since it *is* the reasonable thing to say. A theory of vagueness must do justice to our common-sense intuitions, not reject them, and this is why the epistemic theory of vagueness simply fails in its task."

"I'm getting sick and tired of all you philosophy guys," protests Mr. Stallone. "Whenever it seems that there's a way I can win against the vendor, you come up with reasons that help him to make a fool out of me! You're not seriously telling me that I should accept that this thing (he points to his Chihuahua) really is a Saint Bernard!"

"All right, all right, let me give you my theory on this, and see whether you're satisfied" the third philosopher replies. "See, my view has something in common with the epistemic theory of vagueness: I agree that the world is precise (that the notion of a vague object is incoherent) and that the appearance of vagueness comes from *us*, not from the world. But it doesn't come because of our ignorance of something in the world, but because of our *language*. Let's put it very simply: 'being a Saint Bernard' is vague simply because nobody has ever given a precise enough definition of the term 'Saint Bernard' such that it would allow us to decide exactly which dog in the line is a Saint Bernard and which one is not. And that's all. Our words are not well enough defined. Nobody ever defined 'cloud' precisely enough to be able to say whether such and such a droplet is part of it or not. And with good reason: in most practical cases, we just don't care, and this creates no problem. But if we wanted, we could define our words in a much more precise way. For instance, instead of having the linguistically vague term 'Saint Bernard' we could have many precise terms like 'Saint Bernard-1', 'Saint Bernard-2', 'Saint Bernard-3', and so on, that would all be very precisely defined in such a way that it would be made clear, for instance, whether such and such a dog in the line is a Saint Bernard-2 or not. And each of these words being precise (very precisely defined), it makes reference to precisely some dogs (or perhaps to just one dog) in the line, and the phenomenon of vagueness disappears—all we had to do was to be more accurate about how we define our words."

"Hmm . . . I understand that if we use more precise words, the problem disappears, and that's nice," says the judge. "Indeed, if we use words like 'Saint Bernard-2' but we don't use words like 'Saint Bernard', the vendor will not be able to go through with his argument. But what if I point to a dog in the line and say, as we usually do in everyday life, 'This is a Saint Bernard' without saying anything more precise like 'Saint Bernard-2'—am I saying something true or false? I mean, we don't usually go around and say things like 'Look at this puppy ! What a wonderful collie-149,582!' You propose to use a very specialized language, and granted, this language is precise, but what happens to our ordinary language? You objected to the former theories that they cannot accommodate common sense, and yet you seem to suggest that we should abandon our language, isn't that as bad as what you criticized?"

"Good point!" the philosopher agrees. "So let me show you how my view is compatible with assertions of our ordinary language. We have seen that the words 'Saint Bernard-1', 'Saint Bernard-2', and so on, are precise. All these precise words are in fact different ways to make precise the word 'Saint Bernard', and we call them *precisifications* of 'Saint Bernard'. And as far as the word 'Saint Bernard' is concerned, it is vague, and I say that its being vague just means that it is indetermined whether it says 'Saint Bernard-1' or 'Saint Bernard-2' or something else. We can simply say that the word 'Saint Bernard' is ambiguous between all of the precisifications."

"Okay, I get that," the judge says. "But is the statement 'This is a Saint Bernard' true or false about a particular dog in the vague zone of the line?"

"Here's the recipe for that," the philosopher answers. "There are three possible cases:

1. If the dog in front of us is the first dog in the line, then according to *all* sensible precisifications of the word 'Saint Bernard' it will turn out to be a Saint Bernard, and so the statement 'This is a Saint Bernard' is *true*.

2. If the dog in front of us is the last dog in the line, then according to *all* sensible precisifications of the word 'Saint Bernard' it will turn out *not* to be a Saint Bernard, and so the statement 'This is a Saint Bernard' is *false*.

3. If the dog in front of us is the a dog in the vague zone of the line, then *according to some precisifications* of the word Saint Bernard it will turn out to be a Saint Bernard and *according to some other precisifications* it will turn out *not* to be a Saint Bernard, and so the statement 'This is a Saint Bernard' is *neither true nor false*.

"In short, what's required for statements of ordinary language to be true or false is that they must turn out to be true or false under *all* admissible precisifications of the vague words they contain."

"But then you're also rejecting this principle of bivalence like the metaphysical theory of vagueness, which was, if I recall correctly, a bad thing" the judge objects.

"Yes, you're perfectly right. My view does reject the principle of bivalence since some statements turn out to be truth-valueless, but it is more sophisticated than the metaphysical view because it allows for statements like 'This is a Saint Bernard or this is not a Saint Bernard (of the form 'A and non-A') to be *true*, accordingly with classical logic and common sense—this is easy to see, since whatever precise word you take to be the precisification of 'Saint Bernard' it will turn out to be true that the dog in front of us is a Saint Bernard or not. So my rejection of the principle of bivalence is less troubling.

"So, as we have just seen, we can say that the phenomenon of vagueness is nothing more than our language being not precisely defined, which is in no way in conflict with common sense. The vendor's argument is thus easily rejected: a number of premises in his argument will turn out to be neither true nor false, and so his argument will not go through."

The Vendor's Reaction

"How simple and ingenious! But how completely false!" the vendor exclaims. "Look, you said yourself when you were criticizing the epistemic theory that a statement like

There is a very precise boundary to being a Saint Bernard (precise to a molecule or a subatomic particle).

is false. You said it was absurd to claim that a molecule or a very tiny difference could matter. But actually it turns out to be *true* according to your own view! For however you *precisify* (as you call it) the term 'Saint Bernard', the statement above will turn out to be true—so, the statement being true under all precisifications, it is true according to your view. And you said yourself that this is unacceptable. Add to this the fact you do indeed have to reject the principle of bivalence (even if perhaps you might be able to save some pieces), and it seems to me that your view is as bad as the others."

What Now?

What can we do? If the vendor's right, then it seems that we have no good theory of the phenomenon of vagueness, which *is* troubling since as we have seen almost everything is vague (dog breeds, clouds, tables, people, . . .). It would be nice to have a good—and precise—answer.

What we've seen above is not the end of the story. Defenders of the epistemic view will try to explain in what exactly consists our ignorance of the sharp boundaries, and defenders of the linguistic view will try to show that contrary to what the vendor says their view does *not* force them to embrace such sharp boundaries. A few others will try to make the metaphysical theory less counter-intuitive and more appealing.

But the fact is that the problem of vagueness is among the most resilient in philosophy and that no consensus has been reached. Well, actually this is true of almost all areas of philosophy, and this is probably what philosophy is all about: looking for solutions and never resting until everything has been carefully examined. Until then, I'm afraid that Mr. Stallone will just have to go home and find out how nice a companion a Chihuahua can be.

15

Do I Walk with My Dog?

BERNHARD WEISS

Each morning finds me hauling myself from my bed, sleepily stumbling a couple of steps and crouching down to wish my dog, Pepper, a good morning. Almost invariably he responds warmly, clearly enjoying the pats I lavish on him; though, on colder mornings he certainly seems a little less than pleased about being unfurled from his cosy curl in the centre of his bed. A few minutes later, having thrown some clothes over my frame, I offer him a walk. His enthusiasm for the idea is patent: he immediately whines in excitement, prances jauntily round the room, rubs himself appreciatively on my legs and sets off for the front door. I grab the lead to yet more howls of excitement as the imminence of the outing is thereby confirmed, and we set off.

As I stroll along enjoying the surrounding hills, chatting to an occasional neighbour or lost in thoughts about work, philosophy, family, or food, he investigates a myriad of smells, is suddenly stilled by a barely audible warning bleep as a truck reverses or notices the appearance of another dog and is caught up in the elaborate business of attempting safely to make contact with it.

Some while later we are to be found sitting in the garden; I'm clutching a cup of coffee and he is vacuuming up his morning snack. Nothing could be clearer than that we've just enjoyed a walk together. Obviously we have both been tracing a similar trajectory at roughly the same time. But Pepper shared that much with the dreaded tick fixed to his withers; our togetherness was more than that. Rather we've been *together* since after all we've reacted emotionally to one another, have been aware of what the other was doing or even was intending to do and have noticed many of the same things—such as the group of hadedas (dirty-grey coloured ibises that are common where we live) which, oddly, allow us a to approach them extremely closely.

And yet the worlds of each of our experiences seem so utterly removed from one another. My experience is overwhelmingly visual, includes distant objects—the hills, the valley, the sun emerging through a patch of cloud—and is conditioned heavily by what I know; in a sense, I see the sun *as* a heavenly body, see that house *as* Rob and Sue's. His experience is . . . well that's just the point I don't seem to be able to say very much about his experience except to say that most of the time it is dominated by his nose and ears, and appears to be very short range—try as I might, he fails even to notice, never mind appreciate, the most extravagant of sunsets—and, in an odd way, seems to be an accumulation of the place as its been over the last few hours—the smells of a place's recent occupants—rather than purely the way it is now.

Not only is he aware of sounds and smells that make no impact on me but, even when we detect the same features, they have very little common salience for each of us. The smells he finds fascinating I find repulsive; the views I am captivated by don't give him any pause at all. It doesn't seem daft to say that my world is different from his; each of our worlds is conditioned by very different sensory apparatus, by different intellectual abilities, and by different registers of saliencies in our environments. But if we walk in such very different worlds, in what sense do we really walk together?

Our Different Worlds

Take a mundane object—the desk on which I'm working will do as well as any other. The desk is part of my world—and potentially is part of yours: just pop across to my place to make it so—but seemingly it is not part of Pepper's world. To see something as a desk is to see it as having been constructed with certain aims in mind and as fulfilling certain purposes. Pepper has no inkling of these processes of construction nor the aims and purposes which they serve. He may well choose to lie under the desk but the *desk*—as opposed perhaps to a thing providing a cosy overhang—is not part of his world. And now we can conclude that since something—the desk—is part of my world but not part of his, his world is distinct from mine. Provocatively we might say that we inhabit different worlds.

Let's react immediately to this provocation. We might dismiss it in either of the following ways. We might grant that there are differences between our worlds but these differences, first, need not militate against the idea that there are large overlaps between our worlds and, second, need not sink the idea that there is a single objective world (which we both inhabit) and which gives rise to our different experiences by interacting with very different sensibilities.

Let's take each of these thoughts in turn. I guess when we take the first thought back to our problem with the desk what we are going to be told is something like this. Let's let the desk drop out of contention for being in both our worlds still there are certain basic experiences, let's call them 'sensations', that Pepper and I share which happen to be sensations of the desk. So at the level of sensation our worlds are the same. The trouble with the thought is that it seems simply to be false (despite its having been a powerful thought in empiricist philosophy). Pepper and I have very different sensory apparatuses so our sensations are likely to be very different too. Moreover the thought hinges on the idea that one can extract the sensation from 'higher' level functions such as knowing things about the world, being in command of certain concepts and having certain registers of saliency. This idea of sensation is a myth—the myth of the given as the American philosopher Wilfrid Sellars[1] argued. What I see when I come into my study is the desk, not an indeterminate brown coloured object of such-and-such a shape from which I then infer that there is a desk.

What of the second thought? This thought avoids conjuring up the myth of the given by locating the common objective world outside of what is given either to Pepper or to me. It is a world that Immanuel Kant talked of as the world as it is in itself.

Kant and the World as It Is in Itself

According to Kant[2], the ordinary everyday world of middle sized objects, of houses to walk around and ships traveling past us downstream—the empirical world—is the world of *appearances*. So for Kant, the world we inhabit just is a world conditioned by the

---

[1] *Empiricism and the Philosophy of Mind* (Harvard University Press, 1997).

[2] See his *Critique of Pure Reason* and his *Prolegomena to any Future Metaphysics*.

nature of our sensibility; just as I urged that my world and Pepper's world are different, each conditioned by the character of our different sensibilities.

Kant has an ingenious and very special reason for thinking this. According to him our sensibility has a certain form that in turn imposes a form on the world. The form of our sensibility is spatial and temporal and thus we *impose* the form of space and time on a world that is neither spatial nor temporal. He argued for this view in two ways. On the one hand he notes that the truths of mathematics are knowable independently of experience—they are a priori—but are not empty: 'The black dog is black' is empty because the predicate concept 'black' merely unpacks what is already there in the subject concept 'the black dog' but '7 + 3 = 10' does not appear to be a mere unpacking of concepts.[3] To explain these twin features of mathematics Kant said that the truths of mathematics are grounded in the form—specifically the spatio-temporal form (the spatial form gives rise to geometry and the temporal form gives rise to arithmetic)—of our sensibility; thus they are neither empty conceptual truths nor are they products of experience, they are products of the *way* we experience. He also argues more directly that experience comes to us as a confusion with no inherent ordering of its own—one experience can be followed by any other (imagine an utterly chaotic dream) so there's nothing about the experiences themselves which makes them cohere. So there must be something in us that imposes a unity on the contents of experience. This unity cannot itself be part of experience; it is the form of our experience.

So on the Kantian account we realize that the nature of our world—the way things appear to us—is dependent on the form of our sensibility and that is something that cannot be guaranteed to be other than a feature of the way we *happen* to be. Other creatures, Pepper, for instance, may well have different forms of sensibility and thus will inhabit different empirical worlds.

Let's move a step away from the details of the Kantian account and suppose that we are justified by the sorts of thoughts about difference between myself and Pepper to suppose that we do not share the same worlds. What Kant would say is that the empirical

---

[3] Gottlob Frege famously disputed this contention in his *Foundations of Arithmetic* of 1892. The issue remains controversial.

dog is part of my world but the dog that is the subject of its experiences is not part of my world and vice versa for the dog with respect to my experience. In each case there is an empirical subject and, what he calls, a transcendent subject; the latter has experiences and the former is capable of being experienced. The transcendent subject organises or unifies experience in its own characteristic way and as such Pepper's transcendent subject is not part of my or any empirical reality—it unifies and so brings about a certain empirical reality. Moreover I can form the idea that my empirical reality and Pepper's empirical reality may be different just because I am aware that *his* empirical reality depends on *him* and *mine* on *me*.

Kant allowed—and indeed insisted on—the idea that there is a world distinct from these separate empirical realities. There is a world as it is in itself, which gives rise to possibly different worlds of appearance, different empirical realities. In part he seems to have thought that the very need to think of the empirical world as an *appearance* required that we form some conception of the thing that appears, that is, of the world as it is independently of experience, though he also thought that the world as it is in itself cannot be known; it is, by definition, unexperiencable and thus unknowable.

This is a heady metaphysical brew. I'm not going to defend it here—nor even explain it more fully. What I want to do is to use some of these Kantian notions to think about Pepper and me. So let's go back to the two of us contentedly sitting in the garden having shared a walk—a time before philosophical reflection started to unsettle things. Though we have looked at some reasons why one's mundane view of things might be disrupted, we should spend a little more time getting clear about just why this might be.

An Objective World?

A natural thought—perhaps one underlying the usual view—is this. There is a world that is independent of how it's experienced, how it's thought about or talked about and how it's known. Experience is accurate and thought and talk are truthful just when they represent the world as it is independently of experience, thought, and talk. Pepper and I experience this objective world in our different ways but we are both inhabitants of this, the only world. So quite evidently we walk with one another because we each, as objects in the world, are together, in a variety of senses, on the walk.

So if we have a conception of an objective reality then we can rescue our mundane thought easily enough. However there's something suspicious about this objective reality. The suspicion is brought out by many philosophers in many different ways. One way of focusing it is this. The notion of an objective reality is the notion of a world independent of a perspective on it, the world from a God's-eye-view—God being omnipresent and omniscient has no particular perspective on the world or has *the* all encompassing completely accurate perspective.

And now it can easily seem very hard for such a notion not to become completely empty. As we hinted at before, if there is such a world, it is what our experience and thought is responsible to; it is what experience is experience of, it is what thought is thought about. Can it be any more than that? Well, to be sure it can, but, if it can, then it becomes Kant's world as it is in itself and it can have no impact on us. For to describe how, as such, it can have an impact on us is surely to describe how thought and experience relate to such an objective world. So what this suggests is that the objective word is what experience, thought, and talk are responsible to, insofar as it is more than this, it is nothing *to us*.

Let me take a liberty here and let me suppose that we've suggested something rather stronger, namely, that a world that transcends what experience, thought and talk are responsible to is not just nothing *to us* but is nothing *in itself*. I'll come back in a moment to attempt to placate any misgiving caused by my liberty. But, if we suppose the stronger thing, then reality is what we hold our thought and experience responsible to. Now just what do we mean by talking of holding thought and belief responsible to the way the world is? It's an undeniable, though perhaps unfortunate, fact about us that we make mistakes: we are subject to illusions in experience and to faults in the formation of belief such as wishful thinking.

It's hard to think of there being a thinking or experiencing subject which doesn't in some way monitor its beliefs and experiences for their accuracy. *We* do so in countless ways—checking that our beliefs are justified, using measuring devices to confirm or refute experiences—and Pepper does so too: at one point he thought his reflection in the French doors was another dog in the garden but he soon learnt not to react to this impression, another time he launched himself from a low wall into a pond covered in bright green scum, which he took for a lawn—he never did that again.

What counts as real is what isn't (or, better, couldn't be) weeded out by the mechanisms that pick out mistakes; the notion of reality is coordinate with the notion of a mistake: the one is the flip side of the other. And now the crunch comes because what we now have to realize is that picking out mistakes is what you do from *within* a perspective. So reality isn't an *external* measure of accuracy of belief or experience; rather it's how we constrain what counts as a good belief or an accurate experience from within a perspective. Instead of saying that reality gives a measure of accuracy in belief and experience we should say our measures of accuracy of experience and belief give us reality. Thus when we think in a slightly more considered way about things in the wake of our stroll we might well come to wonder whether we can say that we were together because we were both with one another in the absolutely objective world—according to the last couple of paragraphs there simply is no such world.

It may seem that I've begged the question against the objectivist in moving from reality being nothing *to us* to its simply being nothing. It would in general be a fallacy to move from our being unable to mark a difference to there being no difference at all and, in addition, question-begging when the view we are probing is that there is a character to the world independently of the way it seems to us.

However, I think, that we need to think a little carefully about the context here. We were supposed to be given a conception of a world independent of experience and thought. We surely can't say that we can have such a conception simply by mouthing off the right mantra; that is not enough for us to have a *genuine* conception, that is, for us to be given a useful way of organizing our experience of the world. Let me borrow and adapt an example of Jerry Fodor's.[4] There's a coin sitting on my desk. When it is heads facing up let's say that every object in the world is headish, when not then they're not. So I can alter every object in the world from being headish to being not headish and vice versa simply by turning the coin over. Now it surely seems that the concept of something's being headish is empty: it enables us to explain nothing about its behaviour or our experience of it, or, at least, the concept adds

---

[4] *Psychosemantics* (MIT Press, 1988), p. 33.

nothing to our concept of the coin being heads or tails up. Whatever could be explained by the headishness of an object could be explained by the coin's being head face-up. So headishness isn't a genuine concept. Here our question is not so much about there being a difference independently of our thought but is about whether a conception earns its keep in our conceptual repertoire. The challenge is thus to explain how a notion of reality that is utterly independent of us plays any role in the way we organise our experience and negotiate our way in the world. How would a conception of a world thoroughly independent of my thought and experience help me to understand or explain anything?

Having issued the challenge we invite the following riposte. A concept, we've agreed, has to earn its keep by enabling us to do something with it: it must help organise our experience of the world. Well, we had noted that the notion of an objective reality was useful precisely because it grounded the idea that both Pepper and I have different perspectives on the *same* world. This is a powerful thing to say. It is a deeply seated part of our understanding of the world that there are different perspectives on it. If the notion of an objective reality is required for this notion of perspectives then we'd better admit that it earns its keep. But note that the riposte only works if we *need* to use the notion of an objective reality to make sense of perspectives. So the question for the rest of this essay is: can we make sense of perspectives *without* appeal to an objective reality?

Our problem is this. Once we give up on the idea of a perspective-free world we only have perspectives with which to work but then each perspective constructs a world for its subject and, with no common world, the notion of perspective evaporates: each subject is the focal point of its own world. So how do we resist this fracturing in our picture of things without helping ourselves to an idea of the world as it is in itself?

Different Perspectives Without an Objective World

Let's go back to Kant and then back to Pepper. The thoughts we've just rehearsed are redolent of Kant and, arguably, account for his dogged insistence on maintaining a notion of an unknowable world independent of experience. The Kantian idea was that we discover, by rooting around our ways of thinking, that the world of appearance owes part of its character, not to an objective world, but to our natures—the form of our sensibility. Though I cannot conceive clearly what an alternative sensibility would be like, I cannot deny the possibility of such a thing since I have no reason to think that the form of my sensibility is the only one it is possible for a creature to have: Pepper's hearing and smell dominated sensibility might be such an alternative. Thus, because there may be other ways of perceiving the world that are incomprehensible to me, I have to admit a world that it is independent of all perception. There's no other way for me to think of these very different creatures as each representing *the same thing* to themselves: each represents the objective world in its own way.

Let's grant this argument's force and ask ourselves where it derives that force from. What seems a crux of the argument is the twin consideration that we both cannot conceive of alternative forms of sensibility and must concede their possibility. For it is this consideration that forces us to have a very thin notion of perspective; all we can say, for instance, is that Pepper and I represent the world completely differently. So the argument holds out a certain hope. The hope is that we can escape the Kantian predicament by thinking about how we make sense of different perspectives, by thinking about how we go about understanding Pepper and his like, despite our undoubted differences. So these different perspectives aren't, as Kant thought, mere possibilities that we cannot flesh out.

What is it to make sense of different viewpoints on the world? Do you have a different perspective from mine simply because you have different beliefs? I might, on the basis of what you say or what you do, ascribe to you the belief that Pepper is thirsty—a belief I know to be false—and that ascription may be useful. It would, for instance, help me to explain why you are heading toward his bowl with a jug of water. Though it sounds pompous (we shall see why soon) I might choose to say that from your perspective things appear as if Pepper is thirsty. I understand something of your perspective by attributing certain beliefs to you and can appreciate samenesses and differences between our perspectives.

But you might well think that this doesn't get to the heart of things; this isn't the philosophical profundity we were after. Ascribing beliefs to others is, of course, a mundane enough activity and not one that was being questioned. What we are concerned with is the idea of a *perspective*, something much more fundamental and encompassing than simply that of having or lacking a certain belief.

We might bring out the contrast in a number of ways. First, we might point out that changing your belief about, for instance, whether or not Pepper is thirsty is not to change your perspective; you have the same perspective but just come to have a different belief. Having a perspective is thus not a matter of having or lacking a certain belief it is much more a matter of the *sorts* of beliefs one can have. The point about the difference between Pepper and me isn't just that he doesn't have the belief that that is Rob and Sue's house, it is that he *cannot* have that belief—it is unavailable to him—and vice versa there are beliefs, which obviously I cannot cite, that Pepper has that I cannot.

Second, you might think that having certain beliefs available to you is a matter of having certain other very special beliefs. I can have the belief about Rob and Sue's house only because I have a range of other more basic beliefs about two friends of mine, about people and the sorts of relationships they have and about constructions erected to shelter one from the elements and from unwelcome invasions of man and beast. The belief about Pepper being thirsty, though important to him and to me, doesn't have the right sort of basic importance to make it special. It is only differences in the special, basic beliefs that count as differences in perspective.

Third, we might say that the thing about a perspective is that it is, to speak somewhat metaphorically, a way of viewing the world. It is—again I'm gesturing—a first-personal take on things, a lived way of negotiating the world. If you think this way then it is tempting to suppose that the first personal aspect of a perspective is crucial: you don't understand a perspective, have not made sense of it if you do not know *what it is like* to possess it. The radical difference in what it is like to be Pepper and what it is like to be me accounts for our difference of perspective. So to understand Pepper's perspective I'd need to know what it would be like to be him.

I don't think that there is anything that it is like to have a certain perspective. I can make sense of questions of what it is like to sample a raspberry ice-cream and fish-paste sandwich on Rye bread, of what it is like to deliver a lecture to four hundred restless students at 5:00 p.m. on Friday afternoon, of what it is like to climb Alp d'Huez, or of what it is like to believe in an after-life. But I can make no sense of what it is like to have a certain perspective—of what it is like to be Pepper or even of what it is like to be me—or, at least, I can make no sense of this question if it is divorced from questions of the previous sort. So it cannot be the case that because individuals have perspectives one needs to know what it would be like to be that individual in order to understand the perspective. And there's no reason to think that making sense of having the particular experiences or beliefs involves knowing what it is like to have them. To be frank, I had no idea what it would be like to be married but I could still make sense of what it is to be married. Similarly, I might have no idea what it is like not to find Beethoven's Third immensely moving yet I can make sense of what it is not to find it moving.

Now let us turn to the first two points. These points are, I think, allied. They both insist that the idea of a perspective has to do with the *content* of the beliefs that are available from within a perspective—recall: Pepper cannot have a belief that *has the content* that that is Rob and Sue's house—rather than the beliefs one may or may not have. The second point simply concedes that for one to have a belief with a certain content available to one consists or, at least, entails having certain, special beliefs. Some philosophers argue that, when we construe perspectives this way, there can be no making sense of alternative perspectives since we can only make sense of the alternative perspective from within our own perspective. If the alternative perspective is alternative precisely because it incorporates contents or meanings unavailable from within my perspective then obviously it cannot be made sense of from within my perspective, since to do the latter is to represent the meanings available in the alternative perspective by deploying meanings available from within my perspective. And that, absurdly, makes those unavailable meanings available to me. So the whole notion of an *alternative* perspective collapses. The late Berkeley philosopher Donald Davidson[5] has a famous attack on the notion of alternative conceptual schemes and because the notion of a conceptual scheme is linked to the idea of there being alternative such schemes the notion of a conceptual scheme is accordingly itself undermined.

An Argument Against Perspectives

Davidson's basic thought is this. The notion of a conceptual scheme is the notion of something that fits or can be applied to

---

[5] "On the Very Idea of a Conceptual Scheme," in his *Truth and Interpretation* (Clarendon: 1984).

reality; we use concepts to categorise objects in the world. This is the idea we've been working with of perspectives; it is the Kantian idea that, at its thinnest, a perspective is a take on reality. Now for Davidson the notion of fit is far too metaphorical to have clear content: we need to give the metaphor a clear content and here the notion of truth comes in. A conceptual scheme enables the formation of beliefs and beliefs precisely are the kinds of thing that are capable of being either true or false of the world. The notion of fit essentially amounts to the notion of being apt to be true or false. So being able to make sense of the notion of a conceptual scheme is to make sense of something that delivers entities—naturally called beliefs—that are apt to be true or false.

How then do we make sense of the notion of truth here? Davidson's thought is, at base, this. Suppose we want to say that Pepper had a 'belief' when he was confronted by a plump Egyptian goose during his afternoon walk. Now if the 'belief' is a genuine belief then it is apt to be true or false. In other words there must be some conditions in which the belief is true and some conditions in which it fails to be true. Thus something of the following form must hold:

The belief Pepper had when confronted by the goose is true if and only if ?

—where there is some appropriate filling in of the question mark. And now Davidson's point is this: to fill in the spot marked '?' is to interpret the belief in your own language.

Why? Well, say I told you that the following is true (who knows how I would know),

The belief Pepper had when confronted by the goose is true if and only if the goose is good to eat.

Now ask yourself if you are in any doubt about what belief Pepper had. Surely you aren't: Pepper believed that the goose is good to eat.

Thus, in general, when we fill in for the question mark we interpret the sentence or belief in our own language. But to be able to interpret the scheme in our own language is to show that the scheme is not genuinely *alternative*. So Davidson's point is that in order to understand how truth relates to the belief—that is, in order to think of it as a genuine belief—we need to interpret it. And so he concludes that, since we need to make sense of how truth applies to the 'alternative' conceptual scheme we have to be able to interpret it. But that shows that the scheme isn't really alternative. Thus we can't make sense of the notion of an alternative conceptual scheme (or of an alternative perspective) and so the notions of a conceptual scheme and of a perspective themselves make no sense.

I think that Davidson's view shares a fault with the first personal conception of perspectives. Both insist that there is no making sense of a perspective 'from the outside'; in the one case we need to know what it is like to adopt the perspective, in the other we need to be able to interpret it from within our own perspective. Both reject the idea that we make sense of a perspective from the outside. Arguably Kant gives us too thin a notion of perspective— a notion born simply from the inability to demonstrate the necessity of our own perspective—and Davidson seems to insist on too rich a notion—perspectives wind up needing to be mutually interpretable, which means they cannot be genuinely alternative. Can we find a middle ground here?

Alternative Perspectives that We Cannot Interpret

Ludwig Wittgenstein makes some remarks that hint towards the sort of position we're searching for:

> If a lion could talk we could not understand him. (*Philosophical Investigations, section* 223)

So were Pepper able to express his beliefs I would have no way of interpreting them. In contrast to Davidson, Wittgenstein appears to be saying that we do have a notion of beliefs that we cannot interpret, yet nowhere does he suggest that we need a Kantian objective reality to make sense of this. Elsewhere he is less, though only slightly less, enigmatic:

> Suppose . . . there were a tribe whose people apparently had an understanding of a kind which I do not grasp. That is, they would have learning and instruction, quite analogous [to that in which we teach simple rules]. If one watches them one would say that they follow rules, learn to follow rules. The instruction effects, e.g., agreement in

actions on the part of the pupil and teacher. But if we look at one of
their series of figures we can see no regularity of any kind. (*Remarks
on the Foundations of Mathematics*, section 348)

Here he suggests that there is a kind of behavior, a set of external
signs that indicate the following of rules—he is thinking of understanding a concept as being able to follow a rule—but that we cannot make any sense of the rules themselves. (I just imagine myself
in university physics lectures to make this thought experiment real
to myself!) But as soon as we think we have a clear statement from
him, Wittgenstein equivocates:

> What should we say now? We *might* say: "They appear to be following
> a rule which escapes us," but also "Here we have a phenomenon of
> behaviour on the part of human beings, which we don't understand."

So we might either shrug our shoulders, with Davidson, in incom-
prehension or we might think that we have discerned creatures
who operate with an alternative conceptual scheme or different
perspective. Though Wittgenstein doesn't say that we *must* say the
latter, it is important that he allows that we *can* say it since
Davidson precisely denies this possibility. My guess is that
Wittgenstein says that we *might* say either of these two things
because he thinks that there is no definite set of criteria that determine which we ought to say; rather there will be a somewhat indeterminate set of considerations that push us one way or another.
For our purposes we need to get some clarity on what these considerations might be.

To do this let us finally return to Pepper. Wittgenstein asks us
to imagine a set of externally observable behaviours that betoken
rule following or understanding, even when we cannot make sense
of the rules themselves or interpret the understanding. (Just imagine a couple of characters observing one another's practice attentively, one showing an obvious deference to the other, who
reprimands, coaxes or approves of her doings, but to us there is no
system to what provokes the different reactions.) One way of thinking of Pepper as having a perspective, that is, to make sense of his
having a perspective, without understanding the perspective itself,
is to think of him as exhibiting behaviour that indicates his possession of beliefs which we cannot interpret. I shall end by being
somewhat dogmatic—but I don't mind being so, since I am only
aiming to establish a possibility.

My dog, and I guess yours too, is quite a sophisticated creature; he seems to have a set of interests and concerns and acts in ways that, by and large, tend to further those interests and concerns; he is equipped with a fine sensory apparatus and quite clearly enjoys certain experiences and loathes others. I find it very hard to make any kind of sense of his behaviour without ascribing to him certain desires and beliefs. But ascribing to him any particular desire or belief is hugely problematic. Does he believe that there are three treats on the grass? Though I often say he does, precisely, believe this, it is, on reflection, hard to maintain because I don't think he has the concept of *three*. Let me elaborate. Suppose the following occurs, as once it did. I have three treats clearly in my hand and am about to give them to Pepper. In his eagerness to take them he knocks my hand and the treats fall amidst the grass. He sniffs around and finds first one treat, sniffs a little more and finds another and finally sniffs around and finds the last. And then, quite marvellously, doesn't bother sniffing again. So in some sense he seems to have had a belief very similar to my belief that there are three treats in the grass; he has some sort of representation of the number of treats.

Yet as Frege reminded us dogs cannot have the same thought as us because our thought involves the concept *three* but Pepper doesn't have this concept. Can he see what is common between a group of three treats, a group of three large dogs and three pats? It is hard to see how he might do so without using symbols, that is, without deploying language. Why? Because to see what is common between those groups of three things he would have to think of it being possible to pair one member of each group with a unique member of each of the other groups. So he would have to represent the pairing somehow—the only way of doing this absolutely generally is by means of system of counting and that is to use symbols.

Thus it seems Pepper has *non-conceptual* beliefs that can't accurately be represented by my conceptual beliefs. One way of coping with this is to change the mode of my ascribing beliefs to him, instead of saying, for instance, that he believes that the garbage truck is approaching I might say that he believes, of the garbage truck, that it is approaching. Here I don't presume that he represents the garbage truck to himself *as* the garbage truck, indeed I make no assumption about how he represents it to himself, and this is limited progress: it enables me to make sense of some of his behaviour, to make sense partially of his perspective, yet it doesn't involve ascribing a belief that I can interpret. To interpret the belief I would need to echo his representation of the truck and that is just what I cannot do. However I need to say more since I need to say that he can have the belief about the truck yet need have no particular representation of the truck. For to suppose otherwise is to suppose that he *conceives* of the truck somehow and that I've admitted to being sceptical about. Can one have contentful but non-conceptual thought? My guess is that we can and I take it that my guess is buttressed by our ordinary practice of talking about the behaviour of animals and pre-linguistic children.

At least one thought that would have motivated Wittgenstein's remark about the lion is the following. We could not understand the talking lion because we don't share enough with the lion: we don't share a 'form of life'. But another thought might also be that, though we acknowledge that the lion has contentful states of mind, states of mind that somewhat tendentiously one might say are about the world, the content of those states is not apt to be articulated in a language that resembles our own. And that is just the sort of position I outlined in the last paragraph.

So what's the answer to the question of the title? To be honest, I don't know. But what I *want* to say is that, yes, we walk together because we share a world. We share a world, not because there is a perspective-free world but because I can make sense of Pepper having a perspective different to mine and thus don't need to think that our differences conjure up different worlds. I can make sense of Pepper having a perspective because he exhibits behaviour that needs to be made sense of by thinking of him as having contentful states—beliefs. Those, however, are states that I can't accurately interpret—I don't understand them 'from the inside'—though there is much that I can say about them—I can make sense of them 'from the outside'.

So I've claimed three things: first, that we can make sense of perspectives externally; second, that making sense of the idea of difference of perspective is given by what it is to make sense of a perspective purely from the outside; and, finally, that having such a notion entitles me to say that very different beings may share a world—that Pepper and I share a world—even if I cannot make sense of the idea of the world as it is from no particular point of view.[6]

---

[6] My thanks to Steven Hales, Christine Jacobsen and Steve Shapiro for their critical comment and to Pepper for providing food for thought.

16

The Varieties of Canine Experience

RANDALL E. AUXIER

The Bloodhound has never gotten the respect that it deserves in the dog community, I don't think. Nobody can beat a Bloodhound nose. It's just that you cannot do it. You know, scientifically they have proven if you could measure that, that would be like taking a, a, rocket, you know, and going to space. You know, and if you travel around Venus. And if you mathematically divide that in terms of air speed. If you, if you, calculate that with the, with a nose scent. If it could be compared in any way. The nose on a Bloodhound is going to beat any NASA rocket. Not that it's the same thing 'cause it's a nose and a rocket. But if, if you could, if you could make a table of numbers that would meet. Well the Bloodhound would be up here and I'll tell you that any rocket would be down here. So I'll tell you that would be true.

—CHRISTOPHER GUEST, *Best in Show* [1]

The wonderful little discourse above was uttered by the character Harlan Pepper in the film *Best in Show*. He's a thinker, as you can see, if not a very clear one. Surely all dog people saw this movie. If you haven't seen it, run don't walk to the video store. This film, directed by Christopher Guest (who plays Harlan) and written by Guest and Eugene Levy won the Golden Globe in 2001 for Best Motion Picture: Comedy/Musical, among many other awards.

The Guest and Levy story depends upon striking that nerve in all of us, that ineffable something all too *human* that, with only

---

[1] This bit of dialogue did not make it into the final cut of the film. To see it, consult the "Deleted Scenes" on the DVD.

slight exaggeration, shows us the pathos which accompanies our passion—for dogs in this case—and enables us to enjoy our own weakness, our sentiment, our fallibility. And there, but for the grace of Lassie, go I. The point is that we all get a little crazy when something really moves our souls. Dog people come in many varieties, and only a small group of them ever comes to the point of thinking that dog shows are a good idea, or that winning them is important. But in the extremes we find clearer images of the more muted versions, the silent passion of the ordinary owner for his or her dog.

Think of this. If you wanted to explain the color "red" to someone who had never seen it, would you choose a muted *shade* of red to demonstrate it? Of course not. You would choose the brightest, purest example you could find, and then only later mention that red comes in a million muted shades, but the real thing, the exemplar, is this pure, unmixed attack-on-the-senses called "RED."

This leads to a philosophical question. If you wanted to show someone what a dog is, what dog would you choose? What exemplifies "dog" while all of the others are shades of variation? I know what I would choose, but I will save that for the end. For now I just want you to turn over the question in your mind. But consider also that when the judge in a dog show determines Best in Show, he or she has to do something a little bit uncomfortable, which is to ignore the differences among the breeds—these exemplars of purity—and to form a judgment about, well "dogness," the essence of "dog." Is this Norwich terrier a *better* Norwich terrier than that standard poodle is a standard poodle? How can one decide such a question? It's apples and oranges, isn't it?

The Order of Dogs

Michel Foucault (1926–1984), a notorious French philosopher, began his most famous book with a passage from a certain "Chinese Dictionary":

> Animals are divided into: (a) belonging to the Emperor, (b) embalmed, (c) tame, (d) sucking pigs, (e) sirens, (f) fabulous, (g) stray dogs, (h) included in the present classification, (i) frenzied, (j) innumerable, (k) drawn with a very fine camel hair brush, (l) et cetera, (m) having just broken the water pitcher, and (n) that from a long way off look like flies. (*The Order of Things*, p. xv)

Foucault copped from the Argentine writer Jorge Luis Borges (1899–1986), who cited a certain "Chinese dictionary" he had supposedly "found." It's difficult to know when to *believe* what Borges says, and that is how he wanted it.

Oh really? Are *those* the real classifications of types of animals? It's dizzying. By my count, dogs show up in every category except (d) and (e), and I am uncertain about (e), if the howl is seductive enough to other dogs. Of course, the same dog may show up in several categories at once—for example, a tame dog belonging to the Emperor, viewed from a long way off. At different times, the same dog may belong to contrary categories—for example, a stray dog, later adopted by the Emperor, which then broke the water pitcher in a frenzy, and ended up embalmed. The lesson here is don't decide too quickly what kinds of dogs there are—or anything else for that matter. You may miss some types, and it is best to remember that there are lots of ways of looking at "order." So with that as a warning to us all, I must now plow ahead.

There may be lots of ways to arrange dogs, but there are exactly *two* kinds of dog people, those who want breeds, and those who want just want a dawg. Breed people are themselves a breed apart. If they were only looking for certain features of temperament and appearance, they could just go to the shelter and look for any old dawg having those traits. No, breed people are seeking a certain ineffable something, some approximation of an ideal. Of course they want their own individual and beloved dogs to be happy, unique beings whom they love exclusively, but if that's *all* a person wants, a dawg will do. These people are looking for something of the DOG, just like you wanted to show a person who has never seen red, not some shade of it, but RED, pure and unmixed. There's an unstated conviction among breed people that DOG is the key to grasping shades of dog-dom, just as RED is the key to grasping shades of red.

So I think breed people are on a (minor) quest for the essence of dogness. Of course they love individual dogs, but they cannot quite help seeing them as examples of a *type* of dog, and for them, praising the *breed* is praise for the individual dog(s) they love. Philosophers might say that these people are "dog-idealists," which means that they understand particular dogs through universal ideals *about* dogs, ideas inherited from history and language and culture—human culture.

Dog-idealists are a little strange. I mean, most of them wouldn't dream of praising a person *just* for being, say, French, but I guess some might. And we are all a bit more willing to *criticize* people for being, say, French, or black, or female—or, unfortunately, for being different from ourselves in lots of other ways. But they will praise breeds as though their beloved companions can be adequately complimented thereby.

On the other side are "dog-realists." Dawg people don't care very much about dogness *as such*; they understand it, if at all, by generalizing from their own first-hand experiences with actual dawgs. Where dog-idealists like to discuss breed traits and the blood-lines, dog-realists like to tell stories about, say, the time when their canine companion treed a cat person, or saved them from a cat burglar.

Now, a pure-bred dog can *be* a dawg, but *that* depends on the owner, not on the pooch. In *Best in Show*, Harlan Pepper's Bloodhound, Hubert, is definitely a dawg, and Harlan stumbles every time he tries to describe the abstract features of the breed, because to him, Hubert is an individual person (yes, a person), that he *happens* to take to shows. Harlan doesn't quite belong among the owners and trainers at the show. And Harlan is a good loser; he wouldn't dream of replacing Hubert with a "winner" (although his faith in the perfection of his dawg is complete; he just doesn't assume anyone else will see it—he is a realist). Yes, Hubert *is* a Bloodhound, but mostly he's just Hubert.

So there are these two kinds of dog people. Among dog-idealists, individual breeds appeal to different types of breed people, and the breed people are as varied as the dogs. The old saw that the dogs "look like their owners" is just a way of putting an outward appearance on a more intense connection. It's not just the *appearance* of the dog that connects breed type and human type, it is something deeply embedded in the breed that calls out to something just as profound in the souls of their people. Dog shows are mainly for dog-idealists, with judges looking for exemplary instances of a breed, the very perfection of what is peculiar to that breed. Only when it comes time for "Best in Show" are the judges seeking "perfect dogness" in more general terms. Along those lines, a few philosophical observations will be in order.

Let a Thousand Breeds . . . er, umm . . . Breed: Pluralism Doggie Style

Pluralism is the philosophical doctrine that reality consists of many types of order (even more than Foucault mentions), many modalities of existence and experience, and that these cannot be reduced (by us, with our limited understanding) to a single principle, or law, or substance. Pluralistic philosophers are more inclined to *describe* the many aspects of reality than to attempt to *explain* why they all exist. The most renowned pluralist in recent times was the American philosopher William James (1842–1910). He wrote books like *A Pluralistic Universe*, and most famously, *The Varieties of Religious Experience*. James was the popularizer of the philosophy called "pragmatism," which is a pluralistic *method* for doing philosophy.

And William James was, almost certainly, a dog person. He could observe each person, see individual virtues and needs, and engage socially on just those terms. James discerned character traits the way a Bloodhound discerns scents. It was a gift, and thousands of people loved him—which is what he wanted and *needed* (another endearing characteristic of dog people). For all his many friends, however, James's *best* friend was not a dog, but another philosopher named Josiah Royce (1855–1916). This is notable because Royce was a cat person, and a *cat-like* person. He was also an idealist who criticized pragmatism, which was maddening to James, but they were friends, and they fought like, well, cats and dogs.

For most of their lives, James and Royce resided one house apart, just two blocks from Harvard where they taught. James had to walk past Royce's house to get home. One day Royce was standing on his front porch, with a kitten, as James approached on the sidewalk. Royce said to his feline companion "Puss, pussy, here comes a *pragmatist.*" The kitten took a look at James and *snarled.* James purportedly said "Royce, that's no kitten, that's your familiar spirit." There is something deep and complex that binds us to our animal companions, and to one another, and there is just no reducing it to a single principle or "law of the universe." We underestimate the subtlety of life when we imagine we can get to the bottom of it. There is a bit of mystery and magic about what holds us together. And yet, we do want to *know*, not just to describe. I will return to this point later.

One thing I find admirable about dogs, and dog people (I confess I am an interloper here, because I am a cat person, but please don't judge me yet—many dogs like cats just fine, and occasionally it's even mutual) is that dog people are almost instinctively pluralistic—much more so than cats or cat people. Dogs and their people are nearly always open to the virtues of what philosophers call "alterity," or abiding and befuddling differences and "otherness" in their environment. Dogs are sometimes suspicious of persons they do not recognize, but it's not the "otherness"; it's usually just temporary unfamiliarity. But to be a pluralist, it isn't enough to *respect* differences; rather, one must be positively intrigued by them, and greet them with an adventurous spirit.

For example, notice the way a dog will explore the variations of smells available in a given place, *whatever* the place. When something smells truly interesting, it's difficult to dissuade our dogs from making a full investigation. In their best moments, pluralists are like that about ideas and differences among the people who think them. To pluralists, *some* differences among experiences and people simply demand further sniffing. Cats are certainly curious about various smells, but they are narrowly selective and won't pursue any scent very far (the effect of catnip is an exception, God knows why, except that I have seen the same effect on cat *people* when it comes to, well, *cats*). Dogs, on the other paw, find so many smells irresistibly interesting that they could forget to eat or sleep when something grabs their noses. Cats never forget to eat or sleep.

Thus, dogs are by their deepest nature pluralists, especially about other dogs. The world is simply too exciting and too interesting to exclude any possible sensory experience without first rolling in it a little. This dogged approach to life is what James calls "radical empiricism," by which he means that a *good* inquirer (and dogs are very good inquirers) must take *every* aspect of experience seriously as a source of evidence, and never rule anything out in advance as unimportant. This is a sort of norm that some philosophers freely adopt as a way of ensuring that they are doing philosophy *well.* Radical empiricists don't try to get to the bottom of everything in the world, they just try not to ignore anything that might be important later.

Cats, on the other hand, make an art of ignoring most things, including dogs, until impelled by circumstances to a high threshold of immediate concern. Cats may be moderately pluralistic, they may accept "tolerate" differences, but differences are a bother to

cats, whereas they are they very joy of a dog's life. To be truly pluralistic, one needs more than tolerance, one needs a genuine gusto
for the varieties of experience. Cats aren't empiricists of any kind,
let alone radical ones; their curiosity is disorganized, unpredictable,
fleeting, and often dangerous to their well-being. But dogs can
organize an investigation, pursue it deliberately, and yes, doggedly.
So our pups teach us pluralism and radical empiricism. I want to
examine two more such "varieties" in dog experience, but first, a
story.

It's a Dog's Life

Cats have nine lives (which is a good thing, given their dangerous
proclivities), but dogs have only one. This is a story about the life
of one dog. I have confessed to being a cat person. Some of what
I have to say is unflattering to dog people. I want to offer something of my credentials for making such observations, in hopes that
you dog people may take this, well, not seriously (this is supposed
to be fun), but take it to heart.

My father is a veterinarian and a dog person, more specifically,
a dawg person. We always had dawgs, even when they were pure
bred. You may think that it would be "just great" to be a veterinarian's kid, and it was, but such "lucky" ones do spend precious
youth cleaning up huge gobs and piles of dog poop. Working at
my father's office felt like, to me, being the one cat in a house full
of dogs. I tried to find a perch the dogs couldn't reach and just
watched the insanity. But sometimes the cat has to come down
from the perch, and so did I. I saw thousands of dogs, and their
people, come through that place. I saw what the dogs were like
when their people were gone, and I assisted in many examinations
and operations, and I have bathed more dogs than I care to recall.
I *like* dogs, very much. They grew on me. How can they not? A cat
(person) won't get curious about something until it crosses a certain threshold of immediate concern, but dogs crossed my threshold early, and remained there through all the formative years. I
could tell many stories about dogs from my perch, but I will be
content with one now, and one towards the end of this chapter.
This first one will be difficult for you if you love dogs, or even have
a shred of humanity. Afterwards, I think you will trust me.

I was twenty-one and working as my father's receptionist—and
pooper scooper. One day a woman came into the clinic with her

two children, a boy and a girl about eight and nine years old. They had a small dog, a Pekingese and poodle mix, by the look of it, cute dog, about nine months old. She placed the pup on the counter, and drew her children near to her side. The dog looked fine, but the kids were anxious and distraught. I soon learned why. "I want the doctor to put this dog down." The children began to cry openly. "Is he sick?" I asked. "No," she replied, "these children promised to take care of this dog, and they didn't do it. Now I want them to watch the doctor put him to sleep." The dog was happily panting; I think he licked the woman's hand once. I want you to pause now and consider her request.

I was in over my head. "Dad . . . ," I called. He emerged from an examining room, wiping his hands. I sat slack-jawed as the woman explained what she had in mind. This was demonic. I simply *could not* take in all the varieties of sick cruelty at work in this woman. But things like this happen in the veterinarian's office, more often than you may realize. What would my father do? What would *you* do? The answer was not what I expected, and it has given me a lot to think about in later years.

"No," my father said, it was against clinic policy to euthanize an animal in the presence of children. He was making this up. I had seen him do what he was now forbidding, but what he *meant* is "It is against the moral law of the universe to do what you are asking, so it's clinic policy in this case." But to my astonishment, "yes," he said, he *would* put the dog to sleep. He offered a release form for the "procedure" and said, "You will have to sign this. I will take care of the rest." Recognizing the slightly less severe substitute for her original plan, the mother said "I think *they* should sign it," indicating her "irresponsible" children. "The signer has to be a legal adult," he said. So the mother required her children to watch her sign it, with words of terrible admonishment—they had left her no choice, and this dog's death was their responsibility. The kids were whining inconsolably, I was cringing, but my father was poker-faced. She handed him the form, paid him ten dollars—I couldn't take it, so he did—and left with the children in utter despair.

I picked up the dog. "You aren't really going to put this dog to sleep are you? Can't we take it home or something?" We often took on dogs until we could find other homes for them—keeping the best ones for ourselves, of course. Suddenly the life of this particular dog was of transcendent importance to me, even after having watched innumerable dogs die. I couldn't save those kids from *their* cruel fate, but there was a hope of redemption in defying the woman's wishes for the dog. My father didn't hesitate: "I have to put the dog to sleep; I am bound by the document, and the exchange of fees for services." That wasn't the answer I wanted. "But why did you take her money for this?" I knew he was going to put the dog down. "She would have gone somewhere else if I didn't," was his answer.

Now veterinarians come in many sorts, but the vast majority of them are compassionate people, and often they are very wise. I don't want you to misunderstand my father's answer. He didn't care about the money, and he knew he would never see this woman again. This wasn't a "business decision." He knew that the woman would be hard-pressed to find a vet who would actually do what she was requesting—in front of the children—but she might. And that would be worse, for sure. But Dad was really thinking about the children. They would have to go through the whole thing again, and maybe several times, unless he persuaded the woman to *leave* the dog. The children were already being scarred, and the question was how to minimize the damage. My father is a dog-realist, and the dog in my arms was an individual dog, to be sure, but individual dogs get caught up in human affairs, and where the humans are less than perfect, the dogs suffer the consequences.

But surely, *surely*, I thought, a promise or even a legal obligation to such a woman is *not* binding. My dad wouldn't be convicted by a jury of his peers, or even his inferiors, for violating such a promise *on principle*. But honesty is more important, in the long run, than the life of this little pup. It's not a matter of whether that awful woman had earned any loyalty. "You know it's painless," he reminded me. And he put the dog down. And I assisted. It was painless—for the dog, but not for me. I wanted to call DHS and report an unfit mother. The rage ran deep. It still does. God help her children. My father may not even remember this episode. But I will never, never forget.

I could tell so many stories like this one, stories that would move the innards of any dog person, or anyone with even an ounce of compassion. James Herriot's books are bursting with such experiences as these. This is a cautionary tale. I'm going to make some generalizations about dogs and dog people below. I may be a cat person, but I do not generalize lightly or from the outside; it comes from the heart and from long experience, albeit often perched and only watching. Please forestall your estimation of these generalizations until you reach the reasons for them, near the end.

The Breed People

I admit that I have a problem with breed people, dog-idealists. Dogs deserve better than to be examples of a classification that means nothing to them. Because the practice of breeding originated from very real human needs, the "breeds" are not all just examples of our own human vanity—although some are. Yet, breeding has created some of the most loyal and uncannily smart dogs that exist—Border Collies, Australian Shepherds, and Siberian Huskies, for example. But too often, breeding is the imposition of human pride upon the cunning of evolution. Over-breeding for profit has destroyed the genetic stock of Cocker Spaniels, Dobermans, Dalmatians, and many others. The sort of person who decides "I want an *x*," whatever *x* may be, and then goes to the pet store or the breeder for that category of dog is a part of the *problem*, not part of the solution. The only proper way, in my not so humble opinion, to choose a dog *by breed* is to be able to answer the question "I *need* an *x*," with a pretty convincing argument. You got some sheep to herd? Yes, I agree, you probably *need* a Border Collie. But I get a little more squeamish when I hear "I need a guard dog," and the speaker has his eye on a Pit Bull terrier.

Our horror at pro footballer Michael Vick's recent fall from grace is an object lesson. I'm not at all certain that Pit Bulls should even exist—I am well aware of their virtues, and have assisted in many ear-trims and tail-dockings of said beasts. I fully grasp their sweetness and loyalty. And terriers never give up; the most tenacious breed there is. The trouble is that their humans cannot be trusted to refrain from the temptation to exploit Pit Bull virtues for the gratification of human vices. The results are ugly.

The time finally came when my father refused to accept Pit Bulls for treatment—and he would not trim their ears or dock their tails. Why establish a client relationship with a person who probably has the wrong motives? And who can really tell the difference between Michael Vick and someone who has merely convinced himself he needs a Pit Bull for some other reason? Ear trims and tail docks are done not merely to alter the dogs' appearance, but to prepare them for the ring. Long tails and floppy ears are a terrible liability in the ring. Dad sent these prospective clients elsewhere, knowing that some more "business-conscious" vet would do the owner's bidding. And presumably that vet would get the return business when the dog was chewed up. Let conscience convict those vets, if they have consciences—these are the same ones, I do not doubt, who would have put that little dog to sleep in front of the children for a ten dollar fee. And I'm sure Michael Vick has a regular vet who, in my opinion, ought to have his tail docked, his ears trimmed and his damn license revoked.

I know this is an extreme, but it's a more common problem than most people realize. And it comes from distorted dog-idealism. Now I am something of a philosophical idealist myself, but a responsible idealist must cultivate self-doubt, humility, and a host of other difficult virtues that require much work—I admit I don't possess those virtues in adequate measure. Idealism is a dangerous philosophy, and dog-idealism is too dangerous to be wise, in a world of less than perfect people. Philosophical idealism gave us the fascists of Nazi Germany, and dog-idealism gives us people far worse than Michael Vick. It's a beautiful philosophy, but frankly, our reach exceeds our grasp with idealism unless we take a lot of precautions, especially against narcissism.

Thus, to generalize, I think that no one *needs* a Silky Yorkshire Terrier (interesting little mops), no one *needs* a Great Dane, and above all, no one *needs* a Pit Bull. Even *wanting* such a pooch ought to be an occasion for some pretty heavy self-questioning. There are a hundred dawgs at the pound right now for your *genuine* needs. If you want something other than a dawg, *you* probably have a problem. There are about twenty ranchers in rural Montana who still *need* a Border Collie, but even they should check the shelters before it would make sense *to me*. And certain police officers do *need* exceptional noses on their dogs, but frankly, exceptional noses can be found at the dog pound, if one knows what to look for.

If you're a dog-idealist, I would gladly dissuade you from your habits of thinking. Respect for our most loyal and amazing companions requires that we refrain from using them as props for our own egos. This is a hard saying, I know. But be aware that your dog learns *you* as an individual. You're not an example of a breed of humans to your dog—God help most of us if our dogs really befriended us on such terms. That's the real tragedy in Michael Vick's story—his dogs probably loved him, and only him, in a way he most certainly didn't deserve. So the least you can do is return the favor your dog has already done for you, which is to treat you as a unique being whose love and affection is the very elixir of life. Your dog deserves better than to be praised for being an exemplary case of some "breed." Praise your dog for the virtues that are individual to him or her, not the vacuous abstraction of "breed" that motivated you to make some purchase. And the next time you want a dog, for heaven's sake go to the pound.

Sirens

Enough preaching. We learned about pluralism and radical empiricism, but how do our dogs experience *us*. Let's *apply* "radical empiricism" to dog experience. In thinking about how dogs experience *their* world in general, one thing that struck me long ago was how dogs hear things we don't hear, and then they process sounds differently when they hear them. I mentioned that dogs might end up among the sirens in the passage from Foucault I quoted above. It's time to make good on that remark.

Think about the implications of this simple point: light *exists* beyond the humanly visible spectrum, and sound *exists* beyond our audible range. There's a whole domain of visual and auditory experience, that objectively exists, and of which our sensory apparatus can make no use. We learn about the existence of these things indirectly, for example, as we ponder and discover the causes of sunburn, and find that ultraviolet light carries a kind of radiant heat that, well, cooks us. I wonder, do dogs ever get sunburned? I will have to research that one. I've never seen a sunburned dog. Maybe dog hair blocks UV rays? I mean, if they don't sunburn, why not? Do I need fur? Oh, nevermind.

There are "colors" you cannot see, and a whole painting could be painted using *only* ultraviolet and infrared "colors." That "work of art" would *be there*, but you couldn't even see it. If I could develop a set of paints for that project, I could claim to be as good as Picasso or something, and no one could say I *wasn't*. To a being whose eyes can see ultraviolet and infrared light, even the paintings that you currently recognize would look very different. It's difficult for us to imagine the alterations in the visible spectrum that might result from the addition of other kinds of light to the canvass. I hope that sort of being doesn't show up and ruin my Picasso scam.

We can more easily imagine what a *reduction* of the visible spectrum does to a painting—you can imagine the *Mona Lisa* in shades of black and white and gray, for example. But considering the difference in effect between a black and white version, and the version you're *used* to seeing, in the full human visible spectrum, try to imagine a change of that same magnitude when ultraviolet and infrared light are added in. It could be a very big difference. The *Mona Lisa* might not be so great in that light, while *my* paintings might be pretty impressive. It's hard to know. Maybe I would have just the right touch for ultraviolet-infrared blending, if I could only get some of those fancy paints. Anyway, I think I might, you think whatever you want to. Ultraviolet has always been my favorite color anyway, so rich, so very subtle . . .

This is not just a thought experiment. When it comes to seeing things, your beloved pooch cannot do as well as you can with the *Mona Lisa*—indeed, dog vision is close to being as *focused* as ours, in many cases, but most of the colors aren't there. They don't see in black and white exactly, it's more like red and green—so it's Christmas all the time in doggie-land. But dogs don't "make sense" of their world visually. They use their eyes as a supporting sense for their ears and their noses (more on noses in a minute), while humans tend to use their ears and noses to support their eyes. It's a delightful difference, and I don't think our best friends envy us our visual spectrum, because dogs don't really succumb to envy, at least not very much. I have seen one dog envy another dog's toy, or bone, but not his master. There is a lesson there worth contemplating, as we consider our own religious differences in the human world.

I make this point about what *we* see that our dogs *can't* to make us mindful of what *they* hear that *we* can't. We hear changes in air pressure between about twenty Hz. and twenty kHz. (in terms of frequency), while dogs can hear things as low as sixteen Hz. in the subsonic range and up to forty-five kHz. in the ultrasonic range. It's not just that their audible range is greater than ours, their brains also process the greater range of sound with an emphasis on other sonic features than we notice. Among other things, they *recognize* voices—from tiny sonic clues and characteristics, some of which we can hear, but don't notice, and others that we can't even hear. Humans recognize voices, some can even recognize the individual bark of their own dawg, but dogs are far better at this than we are. You have no idea what your voice sounds like when the ultrasonic and subsonic frequencies are added in, but your *dog* does. Fido hears you better than you hear yourself, which is something to remember the next time you're singing in the shower.

But that brings me to an interesting point. Dogs sing to each other. And we hear only the midrange of the song, and we don't know how to process the "lyrics." For all we know, this is the most beautiful music in the world, but we can't hear some of it, and cannot process the rest of it with attention to the right aspects. When a police car wails down the road and all the neighborhood dogs join in, what do they hear? Accidentally, we sometimes seem to tap the musical root of canine existence, and they respond with their songs. Dogs sing together and create community choruses across fences and fields that we can't even understand. For all I know they're singing the friggin' Dog *Messiah.*

I stretched my brain to try to find something analogous in human experience to the phenomenon of dogs singing, and that level of sonic discernment. Here's an idea: dogs hear sounds the way humans read words. If you just look at a page of words in a language you don't know, you can certainly see them, but processing them for what they mean requires a lot more than visual acuity. It requires an ability to select and discern all sorts of complex relationships between the marks and their meaning. I think dogs do something like that in processing sounds and discriminating relationships and past experiences. It's like they read our voices, and each other's, and recognize a voice they have heard many times, sort of like you recognize a passage you have read many times. Our dogs do not read our voices like a magazine, they hear them like a favorite song, or like we re-read a special letter from a lover. These aren't just any words, they are the words that make us who we are, and to your dog, your voice isn't just any sound, it's the very music of the spheres. Next time you think you can't sing, ask your dog. She thinks you're better than Pavarotti. You are a siren to your dog, just as surely as they are sirens to one another.

The lesson here is how our limits can be understood and can teach us about the world beyond our sensory powers. The world is far richer than our experience of it, which means that we should never get too uppity about taking our own experience as the measuring rod of reality. But it also means that in every limitation is an invitation to explore, in imagination, what is possible for beings different from us. This is a very strong reason to be a pluralist. If you want to know what a completely different world is like, one you can barely imagine, listen to your dog sing, but more importantly, imagine how she hears *you.* And try to stay on key. She'll tell you when you wander too far from the music she wants to hear. Watch the tail.

I Can't Recall Your Face, but Your Breath Is Familiar

Continuing our little foray into radical empiricism, I just covered "dog aesthetics," but it was only a prelude, so to speak, to what *really* boggles my mind about dog experience. Some scientists estimate that on average, dogs' noses are *ten thousand times* more sensitive than ours. This comes from a serious analysis of the concentration and complexity of nerve ganglia, and the neural pathways devoted to processing smells, as well as the level of neural activity that can be detected in magnetic resonance imaging. A dog's world is foremost a world of smells, plain and simple. In the little discourse with which this essay began, Harlan Pepper was trying desperately to find an analogy for this unimaginable power. I have tried for years to find one too, to locate something in human experience that might be comparable to a dog's olfactory sensitivity. The rocket analogy makes some sense, but that isn't it. I finally found the right analogy, I think. You'll have to be the judge.

Knowing that humans rely more upon sight than the other senses, I first tried to imagine what it would be like to *see* a few thousand times better than I currently do. What would the world look like then? I wondered. But this is the wrong course of thinking. It's not simply a matter of increasing the sensitivity of the sense organ, but also of altering the brain's way of processing that experience, and the effects of such processing on the sense of self, of well-being, of belonging to and in the world, as affected by this increase. That was the clue. You'll see.

I have to confess that I don't think the world smells very good as it is, with my own dull nose. I appreciate as well as anyone does the smell of bread baking, fresh cut grass, and that sort of thing. But for the most part, I don't find myself wishing my nose was any more sensitive than it is. And then I see dogs rolling around in putrifying dead things and digging through the cat box for turds to eat, with a full understanding that if I could sniff ten thousand times better than I currently do, this might seem appealing. I'm sorry, but it's off the human scale.

Then I remember other things. I remember the cherished special scent of loved ones I have lost. I consider how, upon losing people we love, one of the most difficult tasks is to clean out a closet full of clothes that retain the scent of a person we will never smell again. In those moments, if I could increase my power of smell by ten thousand, I would almost trade my soul for it. And that, my dog-loving friends, is what you should consider. Your dog inhabits a world in which all of her deepest sensibilities about what is important in life depend upon that same moment. A dog's moral character is formed by smelling the world, because it is here that every judgment of what counts and what doesn't is formed in her experience. And while you have no idea what you smell like to your dog, it's everything good and noble that a dog can imagine. I personally do not wish to smell *you* at this level, but I can think of other people regarding whom I might just desire it—the people I love the most. I'm sure you smell fine to your dog and your spouse (I certainly hope so), but this is so intimate. Don't be offended if I reserve my wishful desires for someone I already know.

And holy cod. Dogs are just olfactory gypsies aren't they? I mean, they will sniff after any old thing like there's no tomorrow. There is something human beings do that really *is* similar. We recognize *faces*. We are the only animals that do this. According to the brain scientists, facial recognition is one of the most complex things we do with our big old brains. MRI patterns show a stunning flurry of neural activity all over the brain when we are engaged in this task, and it strains our abilities to their very maximum (and sadly, as the brain deteriorates with age, this is one of the first things we lose the ability to do).

So why do we strain ourselves to our utmost limits when it comes to this task? I think you already understand it. It is of absolute importance to us, for our social existence. And the rewards for the effort are inexpressible. The face of the loved one, of the old friend, of the parents who gave us life, *these* are the most meaningful sights we ever see. What can replace the faces of the ones we love? If you had to give up everything else, isn't this the thing you would *keep*? Isn't it a fact that one of the most distressing parts of grieving a loss is when we can no longer bring the face to our memories? Is not the loss of the face the loss of the person? Do we not study the faces of those we have not seen recently to connect what *was* with what *is*?

There was a philosopher named Emmanuel Levinas (1906–1995) who noticed the significance of faces in our whole way of grasping the world. He said that the face of the other person is where we learn about the infinite, about God, about ourselves. He was right. And it is not just the face of my beloved, it is the face of anyone at all that presents me with the existential decision about whether to step beyond my narcissistic little world and encounter others. Human moral development depends upon what we decide to do with and about the faces of others. Our bodies and our eyes and our brains strain to their uppermost to achieve recognition, compassion, and to be the best we can be, for we do not see our own faces in the act, and yet we are aware that they are being seen by those we meet.

Your dog does this with her nose. And she's loyal to you because she knows you in a way that you can never even know yourself, in a way that is so important to her that her whole world depends on getting this right. Yes, it's natural to her, just as recognizing faces is natural to you, but that doesn't mean she doesn't work at it. Remember this when she sniffs your crotch in public. It isn't any different to her than you taking a long gaze at your beloved. So the next time you look long and lovingly into the eyes of your beloved, I think you should feel free to say "if I were a dog, I would sniff your crotch right now . . ." It would be pretty close to the truth. I hope you don't get slapped for it, but if you do, your beloved is not a dog person.

And remember this next time you are inclined to praise whatever breed she may belong to (your pooch, not your beloved). To her, no one in the world smells like you, and she will bask in that infinity of *eau de you* even if you are so insensitive as to think she is just a really great Beagle. Your dog is not a Beagle or a Boston Terrier or a Greyhound. Your dog is an individual. And for all your prowess in facial recognition, you wouldn't be able to pick her out of a line-up of a hundred Beagles—but she would know you. Earlier I said there is a bit of mystery and magic about what holds us together—us and our dogs, and us with one another—and that we do want to *know*, not just to describe. We cannot know, with certainty and exhaustively, what binds us to our dogs any more than we can know what binds us to one another, but this much we can know: it is not just what we have in common, it is, more deeply I think, the ways in which we are infinitely different, and in this sense of difference, or alterity, we find *ourselves* through the recognition of our limits. Your dog shows you your limits in ways you cannot learn elsewhere. And she will know you even when you don't know her, and even when you don't know very much about yourself.

The Will to Believe

I promised a second story. Where I grew up, there was a dog track just across the river. Occasionally Greyhounds would be brought in to the clinic. When I was about ten, some men brought in a Greyhound to be put down—they would sometimes bring several at a time, but just one on this occasion. I was not there when this happened, so I didn't hear exactly what my father said to them, but I know what happened. He talked them out of putting her down, and *we* got a Greyhound. So if you wondered whether these stories always have the same ending, I can tell you that they *don't*. Her name was China Doll, and she was only two years old. But she was a little too gangly and slow for the track, and for the same reason, no good for breeding. In the world of dog racers, she was expendable. Now, for those of you who have never been close-up on a Greyhound, and at the risk of praising a *breed*, I have to say that they are simply amazing. They are larger than they appear from the stands or on television, and the musculature and power and speed will simply take your breath away. And they are sweet dogs, happy dogs, highly intelligent, and so bursting with *joie de vivre* as to shame Zorba the Greek. So there is a bone for you unreformed dog-idealists.

But I want to tell you about China Doll, not about Greyhounds. We lived in the suburbs, and even though we had a big yard, well, she needed a lot of room to run. Indoors she was clumsy. Her long tail would knock over every glass bauble that was below four feet from the floor. Our house was roomy, but this sweet dog seemed to take up most of it. Yet, we planned to keep her. She was a good 'un, as Harlan Pepper would say. But we lived on a very busy road, and China Doll could chase a car and *win the race*—even though she was slow *for a Greyhound*. I think Harlan's rocket analogy is more apt here, since "slow for a Greyhound" is like saying "slow *for a rocket*." These were the days before leash laws and ordinances, and everyone pretty much let their dogs out to play, just as they once let their children to do the same. We couldn't prevent China Doll from racing with cars, we weren't willing to fence the yard, and we certainly couldn't keep her in the house all the time. Eventually she lost a race—with a step van as I recall.

But she wasn't dead. My mother had seen the accident from a window, and we got to her fast. She was terribly beat up (China Doll, not my mother), in fact, her neck was broken, but she was alive, and my dad brought to bear all he knew to save her life—for us, his children, who loved the dog, and because, well, that is what good veterinarians do. She tottered on the edge of life and death for days. My sister and I visited her at the clinic. We watched my father treat her. She was a pitiful wreck. But she just wouldn't give up. Eventually she moved past the immediate danger from bleeding and trauma, but the road ahead would be long. She lay in the cage so long that she developed bed sores and had to be physically turned over to minimize them—and this was a huge dog. She lost weight, could not eat and had to be hydrated artificially and fed liquified food, while one attendant held her head up and another gave her a nutritional minimum. A child's sense of time is extended, like waiting for Christmas, so I don't recall the duration of all this, but it went on and on. It may have been two months, I just don't know.

One day I asked my dad, "Why doesn't she die?" Kids are natural philosophers, you know. He said that "she has a very strong will to live," that "she wasn't willing to give up." I can remember other dogs over the years whose will to live was astonishing, but I cannot recall another one going through what China Doll endured, for the simple sake of living. I learned a lot from this. Later, as a sophomore in college, I read a famous essay by William James called "The Will to Believe," in which he said that, for radical empiricists (such as I became), when the evidence does not decide for us what we should believe, we are free to believe any live option, indeed, it is our very right to, as fallible, pluralistic, pragmatic human beings.

This is difficult for humans. We want to form our beliefs based on evidence. We think we are so clever as to be able to use evidence to see the future. But sometimes we actually catch the car we are chasing, and learn otherwise. As I was trying to take to heart what James was saying, I thought of China Doll. She had no idea at all what her future might be like—dogs are blessed with a more robust sense of the present in proportion to their willingness to let go of the future and let it take care of itself. I am not as wise as the dogs I have known, because I have a hard time appreciating the present. I'll bet you do too. China Doll, on the other hand, was reduced to nothing but will. To the men who bred her, she was a liability, and even to the people who cared for her, she was a beloved problem. Whatever drove her, it wasn't in her past, and it wasn't in her future.

China Doll finished her recovery at our home, stumbling around on shaky long legs, and putting a little flesh back on her boney frame. The day came when she was healthy enough that we had to face the inevitable. My dad told us that China Doll couldn't stay. Our postman had a big place in the country where she could run and chase rabbits instead of step vans. Dad took her to the clinic and the postman came to get her. We would get occasional reports that she was happy. And I learned what the "will to believe" really comes down to, from a dog—or, may I say, from a dawg. It has to do with recognizing that your past injuries are not enough evidence to draw conclusions about the value of life, and that your speculations about the future aren't evidence for anything at all. If you would find the source of your life, you will need to look beyond the evidence and discover your will to believe that life is worth living, no matter how much it may stink right now.

So when I consider what a judge is doing when the moment arrives to name "Best in Show," I hope he is saying to himself, "now that, *that* Norwich Terrier *right there*, that's a *dawg*." That is certainly what I would be saying to myself if the chore ever fell to me.

V

Canine Ethics

17

Humanity Is a Prejudice

KAREN C. ADKINS

There's a famous anecdote concerning Friedrich Nietzsche's 1889 stay in Turin before madness overtakes him, in which he embraces a pack horse that is being cruelly beaten by its master. For those who find his philosophy antihumanist, this anecdote might seem telling—he directs impulsive public care to an animal, and implicitly ignores the human (there's no record of Nietzsche making a "teachable moment" out of the abuse and trying to educate the horse's owner). Another story from this same period that might make that charge even sharper; a child who peeps at Nietzsche as he dances in his room is driven away by Nietzsche's shouts that she is an ugly beast.[1]

Our modern sensibilities would interpret these stories as evidence of Nietzsche's moral inferiority; he places love and care for animals on a higher plane than love and care for his fellow humans, even than defenseless children. But this is far too simple a view. Nietzsche's philosophy is grounded in his understanding of the tragedy of culture; the same culture that gives us the grandeur of the arts and music can do so only by changing our natures, by abstracting us away from inescapable physical immanence. Domesticated animals, especially dogs, are central to Nietzsche's philosophy, because they most concretely represent that hopelessly problematic relationship that Nietzsche's philosophy exposes. Like dogs, horses are domesticated animals; 'broken', tamed for human

---

[1] Anacleto Verecchia, "Nietzsche's Breakdown in Turin," in Thomas Harrison, ed., *Nietzsche in Italy* (Saratoga: Anma Libri, 1988), p. 107.

purposes. David Miller describes domesticated horses as bearing the brunt "both of the flogging and the embrace."[2] We train dogs, and we spoil them; their wildness is shaped and adapted, if only partially, to our particular purposes. It's the duality of domesticated animals, more so than purely wild animals, that seems to capture Nietzsche's imagination; they are both with us and fundamentally other. Domesticated animals like dogs are emotionally and cognitively adjacent to us. Their presence reminds us of the artifice and temporariness of human existence and culture.

This, of course, is an unwelcome reminder. As humans, we seek identity in our uniqueness among beings, our special self-consciousness. We fetishize our dogs for their psychological resemblance to us; dog kitsch—fashionable canine clothing, dog-friendly stores and coffee houses, furniture and accessories designed for dogs, professional holiday photos of pets with Santa, the Easter Bunny—speaks to nothing as much as our desire to demonstrate our dogs' emotional closeness to ourselves. Indeed, many dog owners (called "guardians" by legal decree in some American cities) refer only semi-ironically to their dogs as children. And yet, we dissemble from that same obsession by consciously devaluing our relationships with our dogs against the more serious human relationships.

When I was pregnant with the first of my two daughters, several of my fellow dog-owners-cum-parents made a point of alerting me that once children are born, dogs are "just dogs," that upon becoming a parent I would discover true love and the ultimate meaning of existence. Raising children, of course, is also (among other things) a way to stake a claim to a meager immortality; your genes, virtues, vices, unconscious habits, reflexive sayings, and embarrassing stories all have a reasonable shot of continuing on in time, whereas individually we are pathetically mortal. This assumption that the love of human children is more important than the love of dogs sometimes gets a concrete application; it's not entirely uncommon for the care of dogs to be seen as practice in nurturing, training for the undeniably more serious work of nurturing a human.

As he does with so many things, Nietzsche challenges us on this comfortable contrast between serious human love and more trivial

---

[2] "Nietzsche's Horse and Other Tracings of the Gods," in *Nietzsche in Italy*, p. 167.

animal love. Nietzsche's personal (and theoretical) embrace of animals, and especially his comments on domesticated animals like dogs, reflects his real preoccupation with our own self-obsession.

The Dual Nature of Dogs

Dogs are pitiless in Nietzsche's masterpiece *Zarathustra*; they look "over the backs of swarming flocks of sheep" (Part 4, Section 7). He's describing the working dogs (like my own Bouvier Bruno was bred by generations of Belgians to be, though all he ever herded was toddlers); dogs manipulated by human culture. In one quick move Nietzsche's reminding us of the dual nature of the dogs; naturally pitiless (sheep are "backs" only, not worth notice), even when acculturated by humans for our own purposes. In this way at least, Nietzsche claims they are superior to us; they are closer to nature. David Miller argues that Nietzsche's embrace of the horse in Turin—one of the last times Nietzsche speaks before his descent into madness—suggests that Nietzsche's embrace of the animal indicates his return to the world of the animal, his departing from the tragic world of the human.[3] Nietzsche's Zarathustra thinks the companionship of humans is feebler than the companionship of animals; "May my animals lead me! More dangerous I found it among human beings than among beasts. *That* was loneliness" (Part 3, section 9). When you look at Nietzsche's prolific writing career, it's towards the end of his writing career that he starts including animals more seriously into his writing. His later books—*Thus Spoke Zarathustra, Beyond Good and Evil*—incorporate frequent references to animals; his earlier books few or none. As he becomes more skeptical about the merit and future of human culture, animal references are more important.

Nietzsche's reading of Darwin's *The Origin of Species* clearly motivates this analysis on his part; humans are fundamentally animals. The adjacency of dogs, their living with us, allows us to remember our animal selves. Dog domestication is often so extreme as call attention to their otherness instead of making them seem more like us—the extensive wardrobes and Halloween costumes, the training that serves no purpose (such as President Bush's press secretary Dana Perino, who trained her dog to fetch a

---

[3] *Nietzsche in Italy*, p. 161.

flip-flop from the closet at the mention of John Kerry's name). While Nietzsche disagrees with some aspects of Darwin's theory, there's no doubt that Darwin's general challenge to a completely orderly and purposive nature is hugely influential to Nietzsche's own views on nature. Nietzsche endlessly reminds us that nature is not orderly, tidy, circular (*The Lion King* aside); rather, nature is "wasteful beyond measure, indifferent beyond measure, without purposes and consideration, without mercy and justice, fertile and desolate and uncertain at the same time" (*Beyond Good and Evil*, Section 15). We ignore the chaos in nature, and in ourselves, at our own peril.

The False Contrast between Humans and Canines

Typically, we value the parent-child relationship because of its mutuality and development; the continual change of the relationship is part of its challenge and value. Children's needs are different from year to year, and as parents, we have to respond to those changing needs (which often requires uncomfortable adjustments to our ideas of ourselves). We value the parent-child relationship because of the demands of consciousness; children's demands are higher than those that companion animals make upon us.

Nietzsche challenges us on our cozy and casual egotism. His reminders of our animal existence are instructive; the demands of consciousness can become convenient distractions and rationalizations away from more basic injustices and demands. Dogs' needs are almost laughably the same on a perennial basis (kibble, walks, pets, chew toys). Instead of seeing that as a limit, Nietzsche would remind us that there's something fundamentally universal in their constancy, and we diminish it in favor of 'higher' needs without basis. While our human needs, and our human wants recast as needs, may be larger in number, Nietzsche would remind us that they are similarly repetitive, and many of them similarly fundamental. I hope I don't sound like a negligent mother by saying that I did not have the epiphany predicted for me that the love of children was worlds away from the love of a dog. While I adore both my children, I've found many more similarities than differences in the repetition, joys and absurdities of raising small children and living with a dog, even considering the differences in language. Just to give one example, anyone who wants to say that there's a remarkable difference between reading *A Very Hungry Caterpillar* for the tenth time in a row, versus playing "fetch"—put in quotations depending on whether or not your dog's version actually involves the dog returning the ball; ours did not—is putting themselves on. We falsely elevate ourselves in importance.

Indeed, Nietzsche takes the flip side of this argument as well, sharply cautioning us not to make too much of human-all-too-human love. He notes that romantic, sexual, or neighborly love—which can easily be extended to familial love—is really about possession; it disguises itself as altruism when in fact it is a truer form of egoism (*The Gay Science*, Section 14). It certainly requires no great stretch of the imagination to think of parents whose treatment of their children far exceeds even the most obsessed dog owner's as a kind of pathetic projection of their own interests, needs, and anxieties onto the child. Some of our more human vanities (our pride in human wit, for instance), Nietzsche mocks as sub-animal; what we see as refined, Nietzsche sees as uselessly debased (*Human, All-Too-Human*, Section 553). Nietzsche's parable of "The Leech" in *Zarathustra* demonstrates this as well; in the tale, the man and dog recognize each other as solitaries. The hearer of the tale dislikes it because it comes too close, revealing him as animal like in a way, as opposed to his sense of himself as stern and impartial (part 4, section 4).

Whistling Past the Graveyard

We make these false elevations mainly to comfort ourselves not simply about our fabulous uniqueness, but about our human endurance; we reproduce, we write history, we continue. Here again, Nietzsche uses animals to wave the yellow flag. By overvaluing our brains, Nietzsche says we commit a fundamental error; we place ourselves "in a false order or rank in relation to animals and nature" (*Gay Science*, section 115). In a *New York Times* commentary ("My Life as a Dog," November 27th, 2006), Jonathan Safran Foer echoes this idea, when he notes that the very otherness of dogs from humans makes the relationship necessary for our humanness. Dogs remind us of the abstractedness of our own lives; that's why, Foer argues, it's good to have dog parks in cities. They make it harder for us to see the accomplishments of culture as all-consuming.

We fetishize cultural achievements because we can't escape symbolic thinking. Nietzsche's philosophy starts in large part from his understanding of the history of concepts and values, and his scholarship in the history of language. One of his most powerful books, *On the Genealogy of Morals*, both challenges our false ascriptions of universality to moral judgments by showing the contradictory ideas of "good" throughout history, and refutes the idea that moral judgments can take us away from the tenuous existence of the body. The sickness of Christian morality, for Nietzsche, lies in its ascetic values; paradoxically, for Nietzsche, it makes the denial of physical existence and physical appetites the apogee of human existence. Temple Grandin's comparison of autistic and animal thinking in *Animals in Translation* issues a gentler version of Nietzsche's challenge that symbolic thinking is natural to humans, or always good. She argues that animals are like autistic people because they "don't see their *ideas* of things, they see the actual things themselves" (Simon and Schuster, 2005, p. 30). While in the days prior to the Americans with Disabilities Act we might have seen autistic people as more limited in their grasp of experience, Grandin's book offers a spirited defense: in their different experience of the world, autistic people actually are *closer* to lived experience than those of us locked in language.

Abstraction gives us meaning because we can compare, we can value. Autistic individuals, like dogs, remind us that that value is always already after the fact. The value in being with dogs is immediate and pre-cognitive—you feel the comfort of their bodies pressed against yours on the sofa, the heaviness of their heads as they flop on your lap, the quiet rhythm of their panting, and the steady odor of their breath as they merely exist with you. That value shouldn't require tabulating, or comparing.

Herds of Humans, and of Dogs

And yet dogs aren't idols for Nietzsche; nothing can be. He is distinctly critical of the acculturation of herd and pack animals like dogs. He famously assails Christianity as a 'herd morality' that sacrifices excellence for the safety of the meek in the crowd. He describes free spirits as living in nature, and being without sullenness, "those familiar bothersome traits of old dogs and men who have lain a long time chained up" (*Human*, section 34). Christians are tame domestic animals for Nietzsche (*Beyond*, section 52).

Dogs aren't simply symbols of pure nature for Nietzsche; their very domestication makes them troublesome—they reveal our worst traits to ourselves. The ability of dogs to submit to and endure neglect and abuse, for example, reminds us of our own bovine passivity. On the banal side, we rightly and revealingly call the beginning of dog-training "socialization"; getting dogs used to interacting with other animals or other members of the household. The most successful socializers—those who quickly learn that being friendly to waitstaff, store clerks, and government bureaucrats works far more reliably than berating—are essentially training themselves with the reward method we utilize with dogs. (The beraters, I suppose, are old school and still use corporal punishment on their dogs who don't sit.) Our ease at adapting to changing behaviors in public spaces—our patient endurance of security lines in post-9/11 airports, our comfort with omnipresent noisy cellphone users around us—shows our animal ability to adapt to changing circumstances. There are darker examples of this behavior—dogs and humans can adapt to domestic abuse and neglect with terrifying speed.

Because dogs are both like and unlike us, Nietzsche uses them occasionally as omens or prophets—they reveal the most unnatural extremes of our human culture. When Nietzsche's character Zarathustra describes a dog howling at night, he is astonished at the fervency of the howl; he hasn't heard it since childhood. The dog howls at a symbol of Western culture, Christianity, which Nietzsche caustically represents as a shepherd with a snake in its mouth. Zarathustra notes that dogs "believe in thieves and ghosts," which in this case is Christianity itself (part 3, section 2). The dog occupies a marginal position—it recognizes the vision of Christianity as something unnatural and threatening, but can do nothing or than stand witness and call our attention to it—much like Nietzsche himself. The "fire-dog" in *Zarathustra* seems to fulfill the same function of mirroring, and revealing, our weaknesses to ourselves (part 2, section 18).

While Nietzsche's pen is especially sharp for Christianity, he sees this herd impulse everywhere in the nineteenth century; democratizing movements in education, politics, and women's suffrage all reek of the barnyard to him. And his use of animals to characterize our protection of the meek is instructive. Herds have leaders, but the leaders aren't visionaries, merely instruments. Herds don't progress; they waddle. Herds don't explore; they relocate. And herds, of course, are the result of human breeding and selection of animals to do their productive bidding. Herds falsely equalize, Nietzsche notes in *Beyond Good and Evil* (section 202). While dogs themselves don't move in herds (unless it's a crowded dog park), they have a comparable pack mentality (more or less) with their family units. Some dogs are less pack-oriented than others (Labradors' fondness for anyone holding any kind of ball comes to mind), but even this is because they are excessively social, not because they are iconoclastic. Dogs adapt easily to the rule of the crowd.

Nietzsche's reading of Darwin allows him to see this herd impulse as something that's a biological selection; he attributes the origins of justice to animal behavior. In *Daybreak* (Section 26), he argues that animals adapt themselves to their surroundings, and to the rule of humans (learning to disguise themselves, control their behavior); humans do the same thing to live with other humans. Adaptations for herd and species survival are the origins of justice, he counterintuitively argues. Our understanding of justice as impartial fairness, in other words, is a retrospective rewriting. Originally, justice is highly partial—the will to survive—and often quite unfair: animals select out, sometimes violently, the weaker members of the herd, though their weakness is the randomness of nature.

These adaptations finally allow us to rewrite cruelty as kindness or justice—we restrict and punish in the name of a higher good or God. Nietzsche punctures this self-deceiving hypocrisy with his usual terseness: "misery is a sign of being chosen by God; one beats the dogs one likes the best" (*Genealogy of Morals*, Essay 1, Section 14). Our need to see our own social and public violence as thoughtful, deliberate, and unnatural leads us ultimately to seek pleasure, or at least absolution, in ultimately inexplicable violence—a difficult life, an untimely death, is a sign of holy favoritism, and not simply a bad roll of nature's dice.

Our Conflicted Response to the Duality of Dogs

We make these contradictory social responses to the vagaries of existence because our much-praised logic in fact has a basic flaw. Human logic tends to value things and ideas as singular entitities; arguments are valid or invalid, statements are true or false. While there's some value, and certainly much efficiency, in these judgments, they leave us ill-suited to making complex assessments.

Similarly, we respond to the two-sided nature of dogs by ignoring either of the unwelcome ideas; we tend to verge to one of two psychological extremes when thinking about our dogs. One extreme is not only anthropomorphizing our dogs, but apotheosizing (Lassieizing) them—they become the embodiment of all that's good in humanity, and have none of the ills.

Praises of dogs' gentleness, loyalty, patience, and devotion typically leave out the full picture of dogs, such as their goofiness, their unreliability, their curious inability to remember commands, and their equally curious ability to find garbage on every single walk no matter how deviously you design the route. In the other direction, we can over-anthropomorphize our dogs, psychoanalyzing their every behavior as if they really were like the poker-playing dogs in the famous Coolidge paintings.

Perhaps more commonly we treat our dogs as thinly veiled projections of our own anxieties, excitements, and bad habits. We talk about our dogs' jealousy, what makes them angry, and what gets them excited. At my most pathetic, I used to argue seriously that my dog Bruno would really think about which plastic chew toy he would select from his bin of toys (making far too much neurologically out of his pauses at the bin, which lasted maybe three seconds and could be explained by him trying to see through his shaggy mane of Bouvier bangs).

Nietzsche himself is aware of this tendency of ours, and indeed lampoons it in *The Gay Science* when he writes that "I have given a name to my pain and call it 'dog'. It is just as faithful, just as obtrusive and shameless, just as entertaining, just as clever as any other dog—and I can scold it and vent my bad mood on it, as others do with their dogs, servants, and wives" (Section 312). Instead of projecting himself onto a dog, he projects our shameless use of dogs back onto ourselves, and in so doing reveals our self-obsession to us.

Painful Temporality

Part of what Nietzsche finds so worthwhile about Darwin's theory of natural selection is its implication that *Homo sapiens* isn't the apotheosis of biological existence; just as apes mutated and selected into humans, humans could mutate and select into another form of biological existence. He notes this about non-human animals as well; in *The Gay Science* he predicts the development of new domestic animals—lion and eagle, "so that I always have hints and omens that help me to know how great or small my strength is" (Section 314). Conversely, he argues in *Human All-Too-Human* that we might discover humans to be a temporary way station on the way to a more apelike form of development (Section 247).

Nietzsche resists other nineteenth-century thinkers who maintain that humans can change while still remaining recognizably domestic—independent and free of culture, yet still merciful.[4] Nietzsche wants us to remain skeptical of our control over our existence, to recognize consciousness as a tragic trap.

This is why end-of-life decisions for dogs are as hard as they are for us; we are painfully and finally cognizant of the ways in which dogs are both like and unlike us. When American dogs started getting sick from industrially poisoned dog foods in the last few months, there were quotations from agonized dog owners in newspapers. What devastated these owners was not just that their dogs were sick, or unnaturally sick, or might have to be put to sleep well before their expected lifespan, but that they would die a death that reveals the worst of human culture, visited upon its innocents. Deborah Blum reminds us that "we're all poisoners in our way," using pesticides when it's convenient.[5] We mourn only when it seems unjust. Its injustice is all the more painful, because it is incommunicable.

This fall, my ten-year-old Bouvier, Bruno, was diagnosed with lymphoma. He was a candidate for chemotherapy, but my husband and I, after much agonizing, decided simply to give him steroids, so that his final few weeks would be as painless as possible. Chemotherapy would not have cured his lymphoma, merely given him another half-year or year. It would have taken 6 months of weekly treatments, which would have meant twelve-hour days at the vet's. The hardest thing for me to realize was that I would have been doing chemotherapy more for my own purposes than for Bruno's. Longevity for longevity's sake doesn't seem meaningful for creatures who can't count or read a calendar. Since Bruno was already at breed lifespan, his greatest pleasures, like romping in snow, play-fighting, and playing with tug toys, had already been abandoned in the last year or two. He spent most of his time nap-

---

[4] Rüdiger Safranski, *Nietzsche: A Philosophical Biography* (Norton, 2002), p. 262.

[5] "Who Killed Fido? We All Did," *New York Times* (March 28th, 2007).

ping, going on placid walks, or simply sitting with us. To put him through months of isolating and painful treatment simply to buy more time for us to sit with him seemed incomparably selfish to me. But as the weeks passed and Bruno became more and more inert, needing to be carried in and out of the house, not following us from room to room, and responding less to petting, I certainly wondered what was in his mind, if he had any sense of my choice over his life.

When I came home from work a few days after Thanksgiving to find Bruno dead on our bed, his body stiffening but still warm to the touch, I wept from sadness, but also from shame. I hated not being there for his death; I hated wondering that he died alone, being abandoned, being rejected. I cried the way Nietzsche wept for that horse being whipped in Turin. My biologist friend tells me that the evidence suggests he died in his sleep. My response isn't singular, as I know from several difficult discussions with friends whose dogs have died. We struggle with what seems to be the right decision for the dog's life, and feel like murderers. Other friends have reported experiences similar to mine; dogs dying when everyone else is asleep, or out of the house. This doesn't do much to counter the pain.

Rory Stewart's gripping account of his trek by foot across a recently de-Talibanized Afghanistan, *The Places in Between* (Harcourt, 2004), gets much of its force not just from the personalities and dangers Stewart meets, but from his rescued dog companion, Babur. Babur survives the physically draining trek (saving and being saved by Stewart), and then dies a day before his scheduled flight to Stewart's home, by eating lamb bones. Stewart writes "I don't imagine Babur would have been very impressed to see me crying now, trying to bring back five weeks' walking alone together, with my hand on a grizzled golden head, which is Babur, beside me and alive" (p. 297). Stewart's pain is appropriately, and indeed movingly, tempered with the reminder of the otherness of Babur; while dogs seem to have many emotions, pity is one they lack (and one of the ones that, as Nietzsche notes, makes humans most tragically human).

Stewart's sentiment is presaged by Nietzsche's imagining animals' view of us; "animals consider man as a being like themselves that has lost in a most dangerous way its sound animal common sense; they consider him the insane animal, the laughing animal, the weeping animal, the miserable animal" (*Gay Science*, Section

224). It would be slightly cheerier for me to end with Stewart's comment; he reminds me of what's best and most powerful about dogs, why we continue to live with and care for dogs even after they go and die on us. But Nietzsche's observation reminds me of how the duality of dogs keeps us painfully honest about ourselves. This is the most difficult task.[6]

---

[6] The title of this chapter is a quote from Nietzsche's *Daybreak*, Section 333. Thanks to Steven Hales for his incisive comments and questions, and to my fellow dog-obsessives Debbie Gaensbauer and Mike Ghedotti for their support. Brian, Audrey, and Cassandra are delightful and distracting, as always.

18

Dog Dignity

ANDERS SCHINKEL

If you are of a skeptical bent of mind, I can imagine your reaction to the title above. You're cocking your head, perhaps, in disbelief. Surely, you're raising a brow.

"*What* dignity?", you're asking.

"*Whose* dignity?"

Thinking about this some more you might continue in this vein:

"Dog dignity? Are you really suggesting that dogs have dignity? (Let me sneak in an answer: Yes, I am.) When did you come up with that idea? One time when the dog was wallowing in mud, perhaps, while you were standing in the pouring rain with nothing better to do than come up with silly ideas? Or maybe you were struck by this flash of insight on another occasion, when she was contentedly swallowing bite after bite of some herbivore's (or even worse: some other dog's) pile of feces? No, it must have been that time when she ignored all your increasingly desperate commands to take some time off for rolling over in a particularly smelly dead fish! I'm sorry, but it is surely an anthropomorphism to say that dogs have dignity. You're applying to dogs a word that only fits us humans!"

An understandable reaction. Moreover, it almost seems self-evident—except for the fact that it isn't, of course. Let me just review what was said here: dogs do all kinds of dirty and disgusting things. They roll around in mud, eat dung, and if they get the opportunity they even shroud themselves in the odor of rotting sea creatures. None of this is very dignified. *Ergo*: dog behaviour is incompatible with the notion of dignity. Something smells fishy about this argument, and it's not the dog.

From whose point of view, we should ask, is this behaviour disgusting? Exactly. From *our*—human—point of view. And for whom would such behaviour be undignified? Again, for *us*, humans. If *I* were to roll over backwards and forwards in a dead fish or a puddle of mud, people would surely and rightly say that I had lost my sense of decorum, if not my mind. They would feel that my behavior was undignified. Therefore, we believe it goes against human dignity to force anyone to do any of the above things that dogs take so much pleasure in. It's against *human* dignity—but that doesn't affect dogs or their dignity at all. So who is guilty of anthropomorphism now? Do you, dear sceptic, still think it's me, or is it perhaps you, who measures dogs by human standards?

That dogs like to welter in mud doesn't mean they don't or can't have dignity. I believe that they do have dignity, their own kind of dignity: *dog dignity*. If you bear with me, you will—ideally!—find yourself agreeing with me after just a few pages. You will say: "Yes, of course dogs have dignity," and you will be able to explain to all your dog-hating friends (if you have any) exactly why this is so. If you were not a sceptic to begin with, you'll agree with me already and are now probably impatiently waiting to find out why. As you are most likely a dog lover, I'm sure I'm not barking up the wrong tree here in thinking that you'll find this worth your while.

Dignity and Dignity Make (at Least) Two

Imagine: a man, forty years old, single, unremarkable in everything except for the fact that he still lives with his mother. She's the stern, bossy type. She sits on her throne in front of her kingsized (or queensized) TV all day, while her son earns the rent and the food on the table, which he also prepares according to her exacting Michelin-star standards. Every evening he cleans the house (she's very precise about these things), trying not to block her view. Every now and then she barks a command at him, and he shrinks further and further between his shoulderblades.

What would you say about this? Perhaps you're thinking: "She treats him like a dog!" Why would you think that? Well, because she treats her son horribly, of course. No man deserves to be treated like that. He is in fact treated like a slave, and this, obviously, violates human dignity.

Now imagine that he reads something about human dignity and decides that he's not going to put up with it anymore. He comes home from work with two take-away pizzas, throws one into his mother's lap, and crashes onto the coach with his own Cheese and Pineapple (extra cheese). His mother's eyeballs are on the verge of dropping from their sockets. Steam escapes from her ears. She ticks a few more times, then she explodes. The whole neighbourhood gathers on the street in front of the house that is the epicenter of the commotion.

Let's say this is a rather backward town they're living in, where our poor 'slave' is mocked for being such a wuss that he lets himself be bossed around by his mother. Inside the house, this wuss is actually standing up to his mother, which, however, results in his being ejected from the premises. He doesn't care about that, though. He has decided to start living his own life. Turning his back on his mother's curses, he walks down the driveway. Some of the people gathered there ridicule him, even spit at him. They show an utter lack of respect for his dignity. And yet, he ignores them and walks away with his head held high—in a *dignified* manner. They may violate his dignity as a human being, but he still *has* his dignity.

How is this possible? Well, this is simply another way to use the word 'dignity'. The concept may serve as a protective device, entitling everyone to a certain minimum of respect. Hence we ascribe dignity to every individual human being in virtue of their membership of the species *Homo sapiens sapiens*. But we also speak of 'dignity' as an attitude, or a quality of a person's attitude. No matter how many people violate your dignity (in the first sense), you may still undergo all this with dignity (in this second sense). Note that the first kind of dignity is also independent from the second: we don't reserve the concept of human dignity for those who show dignity in their attitude. No matter how undignified someone behaves, we still owe this person the respect (s)he is entitled to as a human being.

So dignity and dignity make two. In fact, there are other uses of the term, so that there will be more than two 'kinds' of dignity, but that doesn't matter here. The point is that when I speak of dog dignity I'm not saying dogs have dignity in the second sense. It may be a debatable point to some, but I'm not arguing that dogs can have the attitude we call 'dignity'. (Arguably, this would entail respect for the dignity [in the first sense] of oneself and others, and therefore require a level of reflexivity that dogs don't have.) My point is that dogs have dignity in the first sense: that *as dogs* they're entitled to a certain minimum of respect (from us).

Humans with Attitudes

Human beings know the attitude called 'dignity'. Well, some of us, anyway. So we're the ones with the attitude. Perhaps there are examples of this attitude or something analogous to it in the animal kingdom. For instance, sometimes it seems that animals bear their own suffering and death with dignity – perhaps dogs are also capable of this. But it's very debatable whether this is the same thing we call 'dignity' in humans. If you think I have an attitude for saying this, for reserving 'attitude dignity' to humans, so be it.

I think people have an attitude when they say that dignity in the *first* sense is a peculiarly human thing. I believe that when people say that, they're mixing up the two kinds of dignity. But many people have in fact said this, including the illustrious eighteenth-century German philosopher Immanuel Kant.

For Kant, human dignity had to do with human rationality. On the one hand, there was nature, the realm of blind, purposeless causality, where everything was strictly determined by what preceded it. On the other hand, there was . . . well, us, really: a rational, and therefore free, autonomous and moral creature, unique in its ability to escape the clutches of causality. To be free, moral, autonomous, constituted the highest attainable value. Therefore, all human beings are of equal worth; all human beings are (and must recognize each other as) *ends in themselves*. In other words: you should never treat another human being solely as a means to some other purpose, but always also as an end in itself. What's wrong with the mother's behaviour in our previous example is that she treats her son solely as a means, an instrument, a piece of equipment to be used and then discarded.

With no special intention to make Kant the bitten dog here, let me mention one more thing he said, because it concerns a dog. If a dog that has served you loyally becomes too old to continue doing so, are you morally allowed to shoot it? His answer was: no, you're not. But don't cheer too soon! The moral problem, for Kant, was not that you *owe* it to your dog to let him live out his days in peace. You don't owe anything to your dog; you have no duties towards it. The point is that treating your dog like this might incline you towards less than proper behaviour towards fellow *humans*, and you *do* have duties towards *them*![1]

---

[1] Richard Sorabji, *Animal Minds and Human Morals: The Origins of the Western Debate*, (London: Duckworth, 1993), p. 129.

So dogs (and all other animals, for that matter) are *fundamentally* different from us humans, so Kant thought (and many philosophers through the ages with him). Humans are placed on an incomparably higher plane. We're on one side of the divide, and all the rest are on the other. It's this kind of thinking that led certain philosophers to think, in various periods in history, that animals do not matter morally. I think this is plain wrong. It is not okay to treat your dog as a mere instrument. *Dogs* (and animals, generally) *are ends in themselves, just like us.*

Why is that? Well, because this depends on something much more basic than the exalted faculties Kant made central to his notion of dignity. Just think: is it really true that what is evil about slavery depends on the slaves' being rational and moral creatures? Or is it simply that we have no right to deprive people of the opportunity to lead their own lives, make their own decisions, pursue their own goods? This is what being human means and we should respect that. If the mother in our example would respect this, she would probably lose her source of income, her housemaid, and her cook. How likely is it that he would *choose* such a life for himself?

Like us, many animals are capable of autonomously pursuing their own good. When I say 'autonomously' here, I *don't* mean what Kant meant; I don't mean 'in accordance with Reason and morality'. I'm merely referring to the ability to initiate one's own actions, to be the source of one's actions. Some years ago, scientists 'created' a remote-controlled rat. This illustrates the difference between an autonomous animal (in my sense of the word 'autonomous') and a non-autonomous one very well. A remote-controlled rat has no control over its own actions. Someone else decides for the rat. A remote-controlled rat lacks the autonomy that normal rats have.

Animals have needs and desires and can initiate action to satisfy these. That's why I feel ashamed when I'm in the zoo, looking into the eyes (if I can bear it) of a gorilla, with me on the right side of the glass and him on the wrong side. That's why it's wrong to treat an old dog like a broken piece of equipment. And this is why I claim that dogs have dignity—not in the attitude sense, but in the sense that they deserve respect as creatures living their own lives and pursuing their own ends.[2]

---

[2] For those interested in the more technical philosophical aspects, let me add

Treating a Dog Like a Dog

When we say that a human being is being treated 'like a dog', the implication seems to be that dogs are necessarily inferior and impossible to disrespect. But what if *dogs* are being treated 'like dogs'? How do we express the idea that some treatment may be beneath the dog's dignity when the very expression we use to convey the idea of undignified, disrespectful treatment has their 'inferiority' built into it?!" (Suzanne Laba Cataldi, "Animals and the Concept of Dignity: Critical Reflections on a Circus Performance," in *Ethics and the Environment*, 2002, pp. 104–126)

If I treat my dog (well, actually, its my parents-in-law's dog that's 'the dog in my life') like a dog, am I doing the right thing or not? Well, that depends. If I treat humans like humans, cats like cats, and dogs like dogs, that seems to be okay. (Assuming we know what 'like humans', 'like cats', and 'like dogs' means.) But if I treat my dog like a dog in the sense in which the mother in our example treats her son like a dog, this is surely wrong! Dogs deserve to be treated with respect, and if 'treating a dog like a dog' means that I treat it disrespectfully, I am committing a moral wrong.

When do I treat a dog disrespectfully? Kant provided us with one example: we treat a dog disrespectfully if we use it solely as a means to our own ends and kill it as soon as it can no longer function as such a means. A dog is not a machine that you might throw away when it's broken beyond repair. It is a living, sentient being with a life of its own. Dogs have needs, and they have their ways of reminding us of them.

---

that the difference between Kantian autonomy and 'autonomy' as I use the term here is that the first is meant to ground moral *subjectivity*, whereas the second only serves to help explain how beings can be moral *objects*. Moral subjects *have* moral concerns and considerations, and moral objects are the *objects* of such concerns and considerations; they are what such concerns and considerations can meaningfully be about. (Moral subjects are *also* moral objects; they can also be the object of moral concerns and considerations themselves.) Kant reserved dignity to moral subjects alone—but this was not 'attitude-dignity'. He failed to distinguish between moral objects and moral subjects (something that we have to do all the time when discussing animals, babies, or others who are not moral subjects, in ethical theory); one can be a moral object without being a moral subject. I would say, then, that dignity in the first sense (the protective device) belongs to moral objects, while attitude-dignity is something only moral subjects *can* have, and only some *do* have.

Bo[3] ('the dog in my life') sits looking at me for a while, then walks into the hall, where I can't see her, but where I know she's sitting by the door. That's her way of telling me she needs to 'powder her nose' (well, her nose is definitely more involved than with us humans). If I don't respond soon enough, she may choose either of two options: make some soft, heart-melting, high-pitched sounds, or come back into the room and look at me again, penetratingly, and perhaps lick my hand once as well. Or when it's Bo's dinner time, but for some reason there's no food in the bowl yet, she will look at me in what I interpret as a surprised and expectant way. "Where's the grub?" she seems to be asking.

Dogs also have desires beyond their needs. Bo often walks up to me with some toy in her mouth—a clear way of telling me she feels like playing. When I stop playing, she often drops the toy, gets another one, and returns, obviously thinking that if I don't feel like playing with the rope anymore, I might enjoy playing with a rubber ball with her.

Of course many of the things dogs need to and like to do involve other dogs, rather than humans. Dogs that can never run around in a field with other dogs are certainly deprived of something that belongs to 'being a dog'. When there are no dogs around for Bo to play with, I sometimes sit down with her in a field. She will then roll around in the grass, walk this way and that a bit, but never stray far from me. The simple fact that I am sitting, that I am at her level, makes her feel better. When I am sitting on the ground, we form a pack; when I'm standing, it's not the same—I'm the boss, the one holding the leash, deciding where we're going, where to sniff and where not to sniff.

Treating a dog like a dog should mean: letting her do what dogs do. (This involves rolling around in the dirt—even if we can't always allow that.) But it also means: treating a dog like a dog would treat a dog—to some extent, anyway. So I regularly 'stoop to her level' (in a literal sense) to play with her, push her around a bit as a dog would do, and let myself be pushed. I find this highly enjoyable, and it is the best way to discover (as far as we can) the dog's world, the dog's perspective on things.

---

[3] Actually: Anna Bo van Vierambacht, a black Labrador. I would like to take this opportunity to thank her for inspiring me, and for just being herself, basically.

Perhaps you're thinking: "Okay, dogs have needs, desires, pleasure and pain, their own perspective on things. But I still don't see where dignity enters the picture." Remember that I'm not talking about dignity as an attitude. When we speak of human dignity, we mean that all humans are ends in themselves, who deserve respect as such. What I've been trying to express is that dogs (but the same goes for other animals) are ends in themselves, too, who deserve the same kind of respect for the same reason. Taking the dog's perspective helps us see that (if we need help).

Show Dogs' Dignity

This is a dangerous section. I'm going to say things that may upset some dog loving readers. I ask them to bear in mind that I know they love dogs, even if they make them do things that . . . well, let's not run ahead of myself.

As a dog lover, you're almost bound to know Crufts, the world's largest dog show, organized annually by The Kennel Club UK. Now, I'm Dutch and though Dutch television doesn't broadcast any dog shows, I can also receive BBC1 and 2, which I watch quite often. So I've seen rather a lot of Crufts over the last few years, and it evoked mixed feelings. Let's start with the positive feelings.

There's a competition element in Crufts called 'Agility', where dogs run an obstacle course as fast as they can, guided by their 'handlers', who try to make sure the dogs make no mistakes (and lose no points). Border Collies are usually quite good at this, but dogs don't have to be pedigree dogs to compete. As it says on the Crufts website: "Many people think that Agility is the most enjoyable of all the canine sports for both dogs and humans" (http://www.thekennelclub.org.uk/activities/agility.html).

Agility is exciting for the spectators, the handlers, *and* the dogs. They're as tense as sprint athletes before the sixty meters. At the signal, they shoot away like an arrow from a bow. They *want* to achieve. They're doing what they do best, and I'm sure they enjoy it. In a sense, they're just doing what comes naturally to them. No, they don't 'naturally' lie down in the middle of a seesaw, or zigzag through a row of sticks. But everything they do is an extension of their natural behaviour and relies on natural capacities: their speed, their ability to jump, their *agility* of course.

Winning this might not mean to the dogs what it means to their handlers (and trainers, and owners—not necessarily the same people), but it is a joint effort. The handlers are working *with* the dogs, trying to achieve something *together*. In other words: they respect the dogs' dignity.

Now comes the hard part. The culmination of Crufts is the 'Best in Show' final. Here, the winning dogs from all categories (Gundog, Working, Pastoral, Terrier, Hound, Toy, and Utility) are showed (off) once more in front of the single man or woman on whom was bestowed the honour of judging this event. The dogs are judged according to their own 'Breed Standard'. (The Breed Standard, so the website tells us 'is the prescribed blueprint of the particular breed of dog', and specifies 'for every breed of dog The Kennel Club recognises, the ideal conformation and characteristics for that breed'.) So the winning dog, supposedly, is the 'best' dog in view of its own Breed Standard.

Now, when I'm watching Crufts, this is where I stop wagging my tail and my ears start drooping. Phrases are used that make my hair stand up straight. I learn that some dogs are 'better' than others—not better at fetching the newspaper, not better at listening, just 'better'. They're 'better', because they conform more to the 'prescribed blueprint of the particular breed of dog'. I've seen a disappointed handler, whose dog had not become Best in Show, admit that hers was indeed not the 'best' dog, though still a nice one.

I don't get this. This boggles my mind. The Kennel Club studies 'the historical background, health and temperament' of dog breeds, then draws up a Breed Standard which subsequently becomes the norm according to which dogs are divided into better and poorer examples of their breed. In my book, this is a gross violation of dog dignity. All dogs are of equal worth. No dog is simply 'better' than another—only more friendly, faster, stronger, perhaps, but not 'better' *period*. (Imagine some people studying 'the historical background, health and temperament' of the various human races in order to set up a Racial Standard which would be 'the precribed blueprint of the particular human race'. What do you think? Wouldn't that be a violation of human dignity? I'll let you make up your own mind as to how far the analogy goes.)

Another way to see how exhibiting dogs conflicts with dog dignity is to use the means-ends distinction as a criterion. In 'Agility', people and dogs work together. The dogs are not (or at least not *merely*, which is enough) used as means to an end. But in show elements, it seems to me that dogs are seen as raw material for the creation of something approximating as closely as possible some ideal of racial excellence and purity. In Best in Show dogs are used as a vehicle for certain pedigree qualities. The goal of this element is reached *through*, rather than *with* the dog. Yes, the handler still needs the dog's cooperation. No showing off of pedigree qualities is possible if the dog sits down and scratches herself. (Things that are beyond the dog's cooperative abilities are fixed by the handler, who will hold up the tail with one hand, push up the chin with the other, and puff up the fur in between.) But if the dog cooperates, the judge no longer sees the dog. She sees the Breed Standard, or the deviations from it.

(But) I Love My Dog!

Some of you may be saying: "I love my dog, and therefore I don't exhibit her in dog shows." But I can hear some other readers say: "I love my dog, and that's why I take her to dog shows."

There's no point in denying either of these claims. Several kinds of love may be mixed up in them, but this is not the place to investigate that. I don't doubt that people who show off their dogs in events like Crufts love their dogs, take care of them extremely well, and so on—they even *have to* care for them in a better than average way, or their dogs won't look the part.

All I'm saying is: it makes sense to talk about dog dignity, and if you agree with that, you can see that some things we do with (or to) dogs may conflict with their dignity. There are far worse things one could do to dogs than exhibiting them. Shooting them when they are no longer of use to you is one example. Making them fight each other or some other animal is another. But some things are wrong, even though there's no pain or serious discomfort involved. This has to do with the attitude we take to dogs. Do we respect them as living creatures, with their own will and character? If we do, and we plan to do something with the dog (like exhibiting her), we should also ask ourselves: "Is this even remotely related to what she would choose to do herself?"

If you love your dog, is it because she exhibits all those qualities that make her an excellent example of her breed? Is it because she matches 'the prescribed blueprint of her breed'? Surely not! You love your dog for who she is.

19
"Who's My Special Beagle?"

WENDY LYNNE LEE

Animals come when their names are called. Just like human beings.
—LUDWIG WITTGENSTEIN, *Culture and Value*

Thanksgiving Day, 2006: All revelry comes to an abrupt halt when
Bagel, my ancient and much loved Beagle, tries to pull herself up
and out of her doggy bed, falls, struggles to get up on her right
front leg, lurches forward, and bumps her nose. I all but panic.
Before she can collapse again, I pick her up (quite the heifer of a
beagle she is) and carry her out to "go potty-time" in the yard. I
hold her up while she pees and silently commit myself to doing this
for the rest of her life. The next morning, I build a doggy disability ramp off the back porch complete with no-skid carpet. My veterinarian meets me at her office door, Bagel in my arms, worry on
my face. X-rays confirm what I already know. Arthritis. It's her
knee, but—thankfully—not her hip joint (yet). Doggy meds.
Hurrah a thousand times over for doggy meds.

As I draft these words, Bagel asleep at my feet, snoring like
an outboard motor, I consider whether the emotional claim she
has on my heartstrings can be translated into anything more
binding, anything that has the form of a moral obligation. Do we
owe (at least some) nonhuman animals moral consideration? In
virtue of what? It certainly *feels* like we do, but I don't think so,
not at least in the ways we philosophers have typically formulated such obligations. Moreover, the problem isn't just that feeling can't be readily converted into duty, but that what we have
to believe in order to get principles made for people to work for

animals just isn't obviously true enough to ground real honest-to-goodness obligation.

The Similarity Claim

A view typical of mainstream animal rights activism is that our moral obligations to nonhuman animals derive from behaviorally detectable similarities we seem to have in common with at least some of them, for example those with whom we appear to enjoy communicative, emotional, and social bonds, like our dogs.

Our pooches, in other words, behave in many of the ways we do, so to whatever extent this is true, we take ourselves to owe them what we owe to other human beings, or something like it. Dogs respond to hunger, distraction, exhaustion, play, and so on in ways that remind us of the responses of fellow human beings, so we infer that they must entertain similar psychological, emotional, cognitive—mental—states. I'll call this *the similarity claim*. That we can infer moral obligation from this claim finds a voice in animal rights theorist Tom Regan who, appealing to eighteenth-century philosopher Immanuel Kant, argues that one of the most important values for reasoning creatures like ourselves is consistency; that is, we ought to treat apparently similar cases similarly because anything less is incompatible with reason (an insult to our smarts).

So when Bagel began limping, the right inference to draw is not only that her leg hurts somewhere but—following Regan—that I'm morally obligated to act so as to relieve her pain. Why? Because I would act in just such a fashion (assuming I'm in a position to do so) were my friend Katie limping on her right front leg. If Regan's right, I am duty-bound to act consistently in virtue of my presumed knowledge that both cases are cases of pain (and I can do something about it). The only difference is that while Katie can tell me her leg hurts, I must infer it from Bagel's behavior. It's not difficult, however, to envision a situation where, rendered unable to speak by trauma or injury, I might have to infer Katie's pain from other clues, say limping; and—assuming I'm right—I must then act to relieve Katie's pain. What I take for granted in both cases is that I can correctly infer *relevant* similarities from the evidence, that is, that I can distinguish bits of behavior that signify pain from bits that don't, or that signify something else like "I'm pulling your leg" as opposed to "My legs's hurting here."

This seems pretty obvious; but think about it. What this "obvious" sorting of relevant from irrelevant behavior assumes is that I know (1) what a relevant similarity is, (2) to what species of creature inferences like "X is in pain" apply, and (3) what bits of behavior indicate similarity of state. An entire view of the *reality* of mental states, in other words, is built into these inferences, and the problem is that there are cases—and not just a few weird ones—where making the inference that "X" is in pain is just wrong, no matter what the behavioral evidence seems to say. In fact, the very possibility that we could be wrong raises at least two questions: (1) can we be as sure *as we need to be* to ground moral *obligation* to nonhuman animals that seeming similarity is real similarity? How do we know, in other words, that we're not just *anthropomorphizing?* That is, how do we know we're not just attributing human feelings and human qualities, to creatures that don't have them?

Given their writhing about, for instance, we think that lobsters must be in terrible pain when they're plunged into the pot of boiling bay-seasoned water. But they're not. "No brain, no pain" is a good rule of the mind, and lobsters don't have brains. So, can we be sure we aren't guilty of the same mistake when our Beagles start limping? Maybe, but I don't think it's obvious *enough*. To be precise: I don't think the similarity claim is as obviously true as we need it to be to establish moral obligation. After all, obligation doesn't just mean "It would be nice if you got around to helping me out here." It means "you gotta help me out here, and if you don't you're morally deficient." Obligation, in other words, implies a "must do" that requires a "must be the case."

It won't do to counter with something like "brain, so then pain" in order to let in dogs and leave out lobsters. Goldfish have teeny brains. Can goldfish experience pain? Unlikely. Plus, size in this case really is only a relative consideration. Maybe goldfish brains are just too teeny to support pain sensations, but this doesn't necessarily mean that *just* because you've got a bigger brain, you get to feel pain.

Consider Terry Schiavo. Her parents believed that she could feel pain, hear voices, and respond to them even when the physical evidence said otherwise. Why? Because they interpreted her behavior according to the similarity claim. But they were just wrong, and it didn't matter what size her brain was. What mattered was the damage it sustained. It won't do, moreover, to point to physical, anatomical or genetic similarities to establish the similarity claim, say, for creatures more like us than goldfish. If the Terry Schiavo case taught us anything, it was that the behavioral evidence—what we *think* we see—isn't necessarily evidence of similarity of mental state.

Lastly, if it seems like what I'm raising is just a "mental states" version of that old chestnut that the only "minds" we can know are our own—no matter who the other minds belong to—so be it. Given that we make the same assumptions, (1)–(3) above, for people, say, Katie and Terry Schiavo, as we do for Bagel, perhaps moral obligation can't be established for any creature. This is a bullet we might have to bite, but, I'll argue that it's not a teeth-crushing one if my alternative works. What these considerations bring us to is question (2): if I'm right that the similarity claim can't be nailed down well enough to establish moral obligation does this mean that we are just out of luck when it comes to establishing any grounds for at least the moral consideration of (if not obligation to) nonhuman animals? No, in fact what we need is neither luck nor appeals to principles (that haven't even worked all that well for us), just a clearer idea about *why* we anthropomorphize in the first place.

Whoa Be to the Similarity Claim

One of the best examples of the similarity claim in action can be found in Tom Regan's "The Case for Animal Rights." Here, Regan implicitly appeals to it when he distinguishes moral *agents* from moral *patients*. He argues that

> Moral agents are individuals who have a variety of sophisticated abilities, including, in particular, the ability to bring impartial moral principles to bear on the determination of what, all considered, ought to be done . . . In contrast to moral agents, *moral patients* lack the prerequisites that would enable them to control their own behavior in ways that would make them morally accountable for what they do. ("The Case for Animal Rights," in *The Animal Ethics Reader*, p. 17)

Setting aside questions about the validity of the distinction itself, what Regan must assume in making it is that what kinds of creature count as moral agents and what count as moral patients is fairly unmysterious (or can be settled in some straightforward way). He goes on to draw a further distinction among moral patients:

Of particular importance is the distinction between (a) those individuals who are conscious and sentient (i.e., can experience pleasure and pain) but who lack other mental abilities, and (b) those individuals who are conscious, sentient, and possess other cognitive and volitional abilities . . . Some animals . . . belong in category (b); other animals *quite probably* belong in category (a) . . . Our primary interest . . . concerns the moral status of animals in category (b). (Regan, p. 17–18, my italics)

What matters here is that Regan assumes we can tell which creatures "quite probably" belong to (a) and which to (b), but he no more gives an argument for this than he does for the agent-patient distinction. Instead, Regan implicitly appeals to the similarity claim: moral patients are those whose behavior just is more like that of a human being—even while falling short of that of a moral agent.

While Bagel, in other words, may not be an agent, she "quite probably" qualifies as a moral patient since her behavior fits with at least some of the criteria on Regan's list—*and we can tell.* Regan's aim, of course, is to argue that we have obligations to moral patients. Unfortunately, we will have obligations to moral patients only if Regan can defend the implicit appeal to the similarity claim, and I don't think the similarity claim is defensible.

In his central argument for moral obligation Regan appeals to the concept of *inherent value.* Inherent value is that value something has solely in virtue of being the thing that it is; in other words, it's that value independent of any *use* anyone can make of it. A light bulb, for example, has only use-value, but a Beagle, argues Regan, has inherent value in virtue of its capacity for mental states like consciousness. This moral patient's inherent value converts it from being a mere something into what Regan calls the *subject-of-a-life.* Such a subject can

have beliefs and desires; perception, memory, and a sense of the future, including their own future; an emotional life together with feelings of pleasure and pain; preference and welfare interests; the ability to initiate action in pursuit of their desires and goals; a psychophysical identity over time; and an individual welfare in the sense that their experiential life fares ill or well for them. (Regan, p. 20)

So, says Regan, a subject-of-a-life is a creature who can *really have* beliefs, desires, and so on such that when it seems to me that

"Bagel wants a treat," I'm not anthropomorphizing when I head for the "treat time" shelf, but am acting to satisfy a real want that I can be sure about. If Regan's right, then Bagel's behavior implies that she just is the sort of creature whose value inheres—is part and parcel—of her being a subject-of-a-life. I'm morally duty bound not only to recognize this fact—and the value-independent-of-use that comes with it—but to act for the welfare of creatures, like Bagel, who seem to have these wants and desires.

The trouble is how I can know what's an example of such a subject and what's not. Sure, it's easy to let out viruses, bacteria, and moss, but consider another example: my elderly Cockatiel, "Bird," gets all worked up when I open the "bird stuff drawer" that she can see from her favorite perch outside her habitat. Should I infer from this that Bird *wants* some millet? What does this inference depend on? Bird's not a mammal, and her brain is pretty teeny. So is Bird deprived when I forget (rarely, I'd point out) Saturday night "millet time"? Only if Bird is a moral patient capable of experiencing something as fancy as not-getting-what-she-wants. But how do I know she can? Why should I count her behavior as sufficient evidence? How do I firmly establish her as a subject-of-a-life?

It's just not *that* obvious, yet nothing could matter more for a view like Regan's since being such a subject is what qualifies a creature for having value beyond mere use. But this is precisely why language like "quite probably" doesn't cut it: if a creature's value, hence our moral obligation to it, derives from the capacities that make it a subject-of-a-life, then it's crucial that we be able to determine whether it *really* has them. But unless we have a principled way of doing this, we aren't going to be able to say which creatures have inherent value and which don't. Regan, in other words, needs not only to be able to make this distinction clearly—not just "quite probably"—but he needs to spell out how we know to what the similarity claim really applies. Nothing else will do if what we want is obligation.

In other words, whatever Regan's intentions, "quite probably" still leaves it up to us in the end to decide to what we have a moral duty. Why? Because without criteria for telling which creatures' value is inherent—and not assigned by, well, us—we end up the "assigners" anyway; and we don't have a pretty track record. Consider, for example, racism, anti-Semitism, each its own ugly version of human chauvinism, each its own variety of "we're more human than you are, and we have the power to say so." The similarity claim, in other words, has a dark side. By the same token we get to decide what's a candidate for inherent value since, according to us, it makes the grade on the similarity claim, we also get to decide to what we have fewer moral duties since they're "less like us," that is, less like us in whatever ways we regard as morally significant.

Bats may be mammals, but while we can and do attribute mental states to bats, we might be less committed to the notion that they are really thinking things like "I like apples more than pears." Hence we are likely to be less concerned about, for example, whether bats in zoos enjoy variety in their diets than we might be for animals we think to be more like ourselves, like Bagel. But "like Bagel," is pretty relative too; after all, a good pet for some is just "good eats" for others. The point is that without good criteria for distinguishing patients (a) from (b), appealing to the similarity claim is just plain arbitrary; it amounts to "what critters we like" or "what critters remind us of things we like about ourselves," and there's no way of cranking moral obligation out of *that*.

What We're Stuck with, and Why It's a Good Thing

The project of establishing solid grounds for moral obligation to nonhuman animals, even those for whom we have strong feelings, (like Bagel) is forlorn. The trouble, however, isn't that we human beings aren't the ultimate arbiters of what counts as valuable; we are. In fact, we're stuck with this job in that every judgment we make is inescapably anthropocentric or human-centered all the way down to the weeny bits and pieces of our ordinary experience.

Short of a mind or soul that could afford us a "god's eye" objectivity, ours is just one more story from the annals of evolution. Hence, we can safely assume that our points of view are as limited by our perceptual, motor, physical, psychological, and cognitive gear as are those of any other species of creature. That, for example, we have eyes only on the fronts of our heads implies a host of perceptual and cognitive limitations that inform the way we see and interpret the world. So too Bagel, whose limited color vision means she relies on smell to find her dinner bowl (call her point of view "poochocentric").

Does this mean that every time we insist a creature (including a human being) has inherent value—is the subject-of-a-life—we're guilty of denial? Yes, at least insofar as we deny that we are in a position to cancel recognition of that value at any time by, say, deciding dogs are "good eats." This is just what comes with being the most powerful and smartest critters on the planet. We get to decide. That our points of view, judgments of value, foibles and fears are as human-centered as we are members of *Homo sapiens* does imply self-interest. But—and here's the mistake I think we make—it needn't result in the chauvinistic history we've produced so far. Considering how much more we now know about, for instance, the interdependence of living things like beagles and people, we're also in a position to reconceive our anthropocentrism as an opportunity to take responsibility for our actions precisely because we're the most powerful and strongest critters, that is, because we're the only ones who can. Perhaps the trouble with establishing ground rules for the moral consideration of nonhuman animals lies then not so much in our human-centeredness, but in (1) what we think we're doing when we use anthropomorphizing language to describe behavior, and (2) what we think human-centeredness means.

According to folks like Regan, what we're doing when we say that "Bagel *wants* a treat" is recognizing the mental states she really has as indicated by her behavior; we're appealing, in other words, to the similarity claim. We might well think that since she has these states, we're morally obliged to respond to them. Yet, as we've seen, it's just not as obvious as we need it to be that Bagel really does have such states, hence it's not obvious that we actually have any such obligations. The mistake, however, is to think that it's *only* if Bagel does have such states that we can defend *any* notion of moral consideration with respect to her. We think that if Bagel doesn't have these mental states (or possibly any that we'd recognize in her behavior) that the use of anthropomorphizing language is without purpose. As philosopher Daniel Dennett shows, however, nothing could be further from the truth.

In his 1981 essay "True Believers," (included in his 1987 book, *The Intentional Stance*) Dennett argues for an anthropomorphizing that offers a new shine to an old concept by showing how it can be transformed into a credible strategy for understanding and making predictions about behavior. It can, that is, be drafted to the pursuit of scientific knowledge. Whatever the case about the reality of mental states, argues Dennett, one virtue of what he calls the *"intentional strategy"* is that it permits its user (us) to remain agnostic about whether something really has mental states.

It doesn't matter whether Bagel really "wants a treat." What matters is that by treating her *as if* she were a rational agent who could have wants, and whose wants can be made sense of given other factors, for example, that she's a Beagle, we can craft predictions of future "Bagel-behaviors" that are likely to be true. As Dennett explains,

> First you decide to treat the object whose behavior is to be predicted as a rational agent; then you figure out what beliefs that agent ought to have . . . Then you figure out what desires it ought to have on the same considerations, and finally you predict that this rational agent will act to further its goals in light of its beliefs. (Dennett, p. 17)

Voilà! Anthropomorphizing made credible not because it appeals to the similarity claim, but because it's useful to us in predicting future behavior.

Now, it may be tempting to think that the next task, as Dennett puts it, is to distinguish "those intentional systems that *really* have beliefs and desires from those we may find it handy to treat *as if* they had beliefs and desires" (Dennett, p. 22). But, he goes on, "that would be a Sisyphean labor, or else would be terminated by fiat" (Dennett, p. 22). In other words, making the "really has"–"as if" distinction is so hard that doing it would be like shoving a boulder up a hill for eternity—*and it doesn't matter*, not one iota's added to predicting why Bagel hobbles happily in front of the treat shelf by insisting that she really wants a treat—even if it's useful to treat her as if she did. "So one rule for attributing beliefs is this," writes Dennett, "attribute as beliefs all the truths relevant to the system's interests (or desires) that the system's experience to date has made available" (p. 18). It makes good sense, in other words, to attribute to Bagel the belief that the treat shelf is over the washer, that the water bowl's under the kitchen window, that table scraps are the best of all possible treats, and so on. These are true, available to Bagel, and relevant to her interests; attributing them gets us to reliable predictions even though the likelihood that she has *these* sophisticated beliefs (if she has any) is pretty much zero.

According to Dennett's view we need a "special genealogy," that is, a special story for attributing false beliefs—and even these will mostly be built out of true ones (p. 18). So if Bagel suddenly stopped her happy hobbling, fell, and struggled to stand—like she did last Thanksgiving—the best way to understand her behavior is to treat her as if she's doing what any rational self-interested creature—*like one of us*—would be doing under the circumstances, trying to regain composure (and safety) with respect to abilities that, up to this moment, she "knows" she's had. According to the intentional strategy, we'd say that Bagel falsely "believes" her leg will support her; our "special genealogy" would include the diagnosis of her arthritis.

But notice: anthropomorphizing is anthropocentric. When we ascribe human qualities to other things, we're ascribing our own, *human*, qualities. What the intentional strategy achieves is the transformation of a human-centeredness rightly criticized for its chauvinistic history into a credible method for understanding behavior, a sow's ear into a silk purse. If we didn't take ourselves to be the standard of comparison, the strategy wouldn't be useful since it's only in relation to what we understand about ourselves that we can make the predictions that we do. What matters, then, is the strategy's usefulness to understanding the behavior of those creatures to whom we attribute the only mental states with which we are familiar—ours. Dennett's argument isn't just another swan song for the similarity claim, it's an opportunity. In fact, it's a chance to hew an argument for the moral consideration of nonhuman animals that may be more practically compelling than appeals to obligation. There are two remaining questions to consider: Why does the intentional strategy work? Why do we want it to?

Who's My Special Beagle?

The intentional strategy works because we human beings have enough in common with at least some of our nonhuman relations that we can make predictions that turn out to be true. With more of the evolutionary puzzle pieces falling into place, the clearer it is in just what ways we're connected to other species of creature, and ultimately even to the primordial ooze. While we have less in common with barracudas than we do with beagles, the intentional strategy offers us a better understanding of both than can a science without it in its toolbox. It works precisely *because* it's anthropocentric.

An unmistakable (if coincidental) consequence of the intentional strategy is that it reminds us of the interdependency of our connections to other species of animal. It's hard in fact to imagine how anthropomorphizing could be predictively successful were we creatures whose needs and desires were radically unlike those to whom we applied it. (Would the strategy even have occurred to us under these circumstances? Unlikely).

What this interdependence suggests, however, is that the resources that fulfill those needs and desires are more or less the same, that is, that the environment upon which, say, beagles depend is the same as what sustains us. Such observations are hardly earth-shattering, of course, but they do put the lie to a history that offers precious little recognition of it. We mostly act like we own the place, and now we're beginning to reap the consequences of that chauvinism. Global climate change, pollution, species extinction, deforestation, acid rain all point to an interdependency we've ignored and to a future that may not include us. From our point of view the prospect of such an "ecocide" is catastrophic. But isn't "from our point of view" just what's at issue?

Consider: We human beings anthropomorphize nearly everything. From forks to oaks to beagles, our self-understanding is enhanced by imagining talking utensils, talking trees, and beagles who want treats. It's through the possibility of such objects of comparison that we come to comprehend what it means to be a human being (as opposed to, say, a door stop). This is why we want the intentional strategy to work. Objective scientific knowledge? Sure. We want that too. Yet most of us don't care about knowledge that fails to connect directly with our ordinary self-interests.

Anthropomorphizing contributes to a valuable human activity—self-understanding—and provides us just the reason we need for taking seriously the welfare of those "objects of comparison" that become candidates for the intentional strategy. We don't need to conjure up murky notions like "inherent worth" in order to make a compelling argument for the moral consideration of nonhuman animals; all we need is to recognize that the *desire* to anthropomorphize—to pan out the similarity claim—stems from a centeredness which owes its own self-understanding, at least in part, to those creatures without whom such an understanding would be far less lush and three-dimensional than it is. Who fits this bill better than our dogs?

It's tempting to object that, given our history, there's little reason to hope that even the most universal recognition of the relationship between our desires and what they entail will persuade us to do better by nonhuman animals. Possible. Still, I think that science, the intentional strategy among its tools, has shown us that our desire to see ourselves in the eyes of these others suggests something more than mere self-interest; it demonstrates an aspect of our interdependence in that, unless we're just fated to be the chauvinists of our history (and if we believe that, we might as well just give it up) we can't fail to see some bit of the world upon which we're all dependent. Notice, however, such claims aren't about feelings; rather, they're about what the intentional strategy can show us about why it works so well if we're paying attention.

Nothing, of course, can make us pay attention. Still, our dogs offer something special in that they represent this interdependence in a deeply intimate way. They're our companions; they occupy our human-made spaces. They can make us mean something of tremendous value to ourselves. Recently my local newspaper ran a story about eighty dogs living off the carcasses of thirty of their dead mates in the home of an elderly, senile, couple. A request had been made for donations to the local shelter. My kids and I took over some food. A thin, old, matted, and very pregnant Pomeranian peeked out at us from one of the holding pens.

Without the notion of inherent worth, nothing obligates me to take home that dog, and I don't know for sure—however much it feels like it—that she's the subject-of-a-life. Nevertheless, as soon as her puppies are weaned, I'll bring her home. Why? Because offering her moral compassion makes of my own human-centeredness something a bit more ennobled, a bit more in keeping with a human recognition that we really are all in this together. While that's as much as I think we can expect out of morality, it's not nothing. Bagel, who will eventually need me to hold her up for "potty time" and to put her down when that doesn't work, reminds me of just about everything that can be good in human beings.

It pretty much says it all, doesn't it? Dogs. They meet us at the door.

20

What Aristotle Can Teach You about Your Dog

GARY GABOR

According to René Descartes, the great seventeenth-century French philosopher and Father of Modern Philosophy, your dog has no soul.

It's not that Descartes has anything against dogs in particular. He doesn't think any animal has a soul. In his introspective *Meditations on First Philosophy*, Descartes lays the foundation for a conception of the soul, rooted in the famous phrase *cogito ergo sum*, "I think therefore I am," in which it's only possible for thinking beings such as humans to possess a soul. Since dogs lack such activity, Descartes believes, they're out of luck.

I would be lying if I didn't admit feeling a twang of regret the first time I reflected upon Descartes's argument, elicited by the still fresh memory of my childhood Golden Retriever, Sandy. I clearly wasn't the only one in class that day struck by such thoughts, because I also distinctly remember my classmate Derrick forcefully pipe up:

"What do you mean dogs don't have souls?"

"Well," our professor said in reply, "Descartes thinks that only mental substances have souls. So if something isn't a mental substance—if something doesn't have a mind—then that also means it doesn't have a soul."

"But how does Descartes know that—how does he know my dog doesn't have a mind?"

"Well," he continued, "can your dog speak to you?"

"No," Derrick replied.

"Can he write?"

"No."

"Can he compose a poem? Arrange a symphony? Engage in higher mathematics?"

"No."

"So is there any evidence that your dog is able to think or possesses an ability to reason?"

"I guess not."

"Then that means it doesn't have a mind. And since it doesn't have a mind, it doesn't qualify as a mental substance. And since it doesn't qualify as a mental substance, then, for Descartes, that also means it doesn't have a soul. So that's why he thinks as he does. Any questions?"

But neither Derrick nor any of the rest of us had anything we could definitely say against our professor, while still accepting what Descartes had said about the soul.

Some of the students mentioned love—even though dogs may not be able to think, it seems pretty clear that they can, and do, love their masters very much—so doesn't that indicate they have a soul?

"Conditioning," our professor replied. "It's a survival mechanism, an automatic reflex, exhibited towards a source of food. You can teach a machine the exact same thing, and that's exactly what Descartes thinks an animal is—a finely honed, automatic machine."

It isn't that Descartes had anything personal against dogs. The fact is that for him, no animal, outside of a human being, has a soul, because none other has the capacity for reason. And if reason is the only stable indicator of the presence of an immaterial soul, then it would seem that every other animal is out of luck—dogs included.

But this still leaves us with a lot of questions. If animals don't have a soul, then why do we think that it's wrong to harm them? Why do we pass laws against animal cruelty, if they're nothing more than machines in furry clothing? And if animals—dogs especially—don't have a soul, why is it that so many of us feel such a close bond with them?

Aristotle on the Soul

Enough of Descartes. While one might admire the consistency of his argument, I can't really bring myself to agree with his opinions about the existence of the animal soul. That's because I think that there is another option when it comes to considering the soul, one which I think does a better job when it comes to explaining the human-canine bond. That option comes from one of the most famous philosophers of all time: Aristotle.

At times, Aristotle says very similar things to Descartes on the soul. Aristotle too thinks that reason sets human beings apart from other animals, and because of this he doesn't think that a non-human animal can truly be 'happy'. As he says, "other animals have no share in happiness" because they are deprived of the end of "contemplation." (*Nicomachean Ethics* 1178b24; this, as well as all other works from which I will be quoting from Aristotle are available in *The Basic Works of Aristotle*, New York: Modern Library, 2001).

Some things that Aristotle says might seem even more objectionable to a devoted dog-lover. For instance, he writes in the *Politics* that an ox is "a poor man's slave," (1252b12) and it would seem that his view of all other domesticated animals (including dogs) is mostly the same.

So—at first—it seems that Aristotle doesn't provide any more help when it comes to understanding the often deep bond that exists between canines and humans.

But appearances can be deceiving. One important key feature of his philosophy is that, unlike Descartes, Aristotle believes that a dog does, indeed, possess a soul. It's not the 'rational' soul that human beings possess, but rather a different type of soul—an 'animal' or 'appetitive' one. Aristotle calls it this because it reflects the key fact that all animals *move*. This causes them to sniff out, hear, chase, pant after, pursue, and seek things outside of themselves—that is, to possess *appetites* which they in turn *move* towards satisfying.

Where motion was a purely mechanical process for Descartes, for Aristotle it is an indicator of life, and hence also the possession of a soul. *Psuchi*, the Greek word for soul—think 'psychology'—refers to any and all things possessing life.

This is not how most people think of the soul today. Many people, often because they believe it is what their religion teaches, conceive of the soul as an immaterial, immortal 'self', which is distinct from the body and hence can continue to live on even after a person's death. Aristotle's teacher Plato, for instance, mythically described the soul as analogous to charioteer driving a chariot, which many have interpreted as representing the distinction between the soul and the body (*Phaedrus* 246a–b). Descartes conceives of the soul as an immaterial, thinking thing, which we come to know through our thoughts, emotions, fears, and joys. Since Descartes believes (perhaps rightly, perhaps wrongly) that none of these depend upon the body, he reasons that the soul, which performs them, can also exist apart from the body.

Aristotle doesn't believe the soul to be so easily separable from the body. Indeed, Aristotle is usually much more comfortable speaking about the whole body-soul compound as one's primary self. Thus it is the individual horse, or the individual human being that is primary for Aristotle, not its matter or its 'form' (that is, soul) considered in isolation. So Aristotle says that one can "wholly dismiss the question whether the soul and the body are one: it is as meaningless as to ask whether wax and the shape given it by a stamp are one" (*de Anima*, 412b6–8).

For Aristotle, all living things possess souls, because he does not conceive of a soul merely as a thinking, or even as a human, thing for that matter, and this includes dogs. A soul also need not necessarily be *immortal* for Aristotle, because, since it is so closely unified with the body, it dies along with it. Nevertheless, all living things, by virtue of the very fact that they are alive, possess souls.

Because of this, each animal would also have a particular 'good' or 'end' appropriate to it. Unpacking what this appropriate end is, in the case of dogs, amounts to unpacking what it means for a dog to be a 'good dog'.

Aristotle spends most of his time in his ethical works explaining what it means to be a good human being. This makes sense, since the most important part of ethics (as Aristotle understands it) is to identify what a good human life is. Yet when it comes to identifying what a good *animal* life would consist in, Aristotle doesn't consider the question. It is generally thought that for Aristotle animals don't have any moral qualities.

I think, however, that we can stretch Aristotle a bit here. While he himself doesn't address it, I think that a lot of what Aristotle says in his *Ethics* can actually be applied to many animal species, not just the human. And that's what I hope to show.

What Does It Mean to Be a Good Dog?

If you asked the question, 'What does it mean to be a good dog?', you would probably get as many different answers as you would get dog-owners. Maybe, for a child or an elderly person who lives alone, it is to be a faithful and devoted companion. Maybe, if you're a single person who lives alone in the city, it's to provide safety and security. If you work on a farm or a ranch, perhaps it's to help with the chores and take care of the other animals. For a member of a police or fire department, it's to save lives in cases of emergency. Or one might (rather frivolously) even say that for some it's no more than to provide a fashionable canine accessory.

We instinctively say things like *"Good dog!"* and *"Good boy!"* after our dog's done something well, usually accompanied by a good amount of playful ear-scratching and petting, almost automatically. Why is it that we only do this with our dogs? Why don't we as often hear *"Good cat!"* or *"Good bird!"*? What is it that makes a good dog so 'good'?

When it comes to what constitutes a 'good' human life, Aristotle acknowledges that there are a lot of contenders (many of which sound quite contemporary): It could be wealth. Maybe it's a life of pleasure. Perhaps it's a life devoted to honors in one's profession. Or maybe it's a life of service to one's state. Aristotle notes that it seems just about every person has a different answer to the question, 'Which is the best human life?' But it is asking this question, and determining which answers are better than others, which serves as the beginning of ethics for Aristotle.

What a Human Wants—Happiness

Aristotle doesn't leave us in suspense or confusion for long. In the *Nicomachean Ethics* he offers one of the most famous and influential answers to this question in the history of human thought. What every single human being wants, and the answer with which each would agree, Aristotle says, is one very simple word—happiness.

You might think that answer requires a bit more elaboration. Aristotle agrees. It all depends, he says, upon what you take happiness to be. In Chapter 13 of the first book of the *Ethics*, Aristotle offers his own definition: "happiness is an activity of the soul, in accordance with perfect virtue." He then goes on to divide virtue into two parts, corresponding to a similar two-part division of the soul.

One part of the soul is distinctively 'human'—the rational part of the soul. As such, Aristotle suggests that there is a distinctive type of virtue corresponding to it, "intellectual virtue." This would include things like science, contemplation, wisdom, and all the other 'activities of the soul' that set us apart from animals. Like Descartes, Aristotle believes that no other animal possesses these traits, as well as the pleasures and joys that come along with them. Since rationality is the most important part of being human, that's why Aristotle said before that "other animals have no share in happiness"; they are deprived of the end of "contemplation."

What Does a Dog Want?

There's another part of the soul that Aristotle discusses. This component—the 'animal' or appetitive part of the soul—while lacking reason, is itself receptive to reason. It has a capacity to be shaped and molded by reason, to listen to it, to perhaps be led by or reject it. Let's let Aristotle himself speak here:

> There seems to be also another irrational element in the soul—one which in a sense, however, shares in a rational principle . . . (even though it) naturally fights against and resists it. For exactly as paralyzed limbs when we intend to move them to the right instead turn to the left, so it is with the soul . . . But even this seems to have a share in a rational principle, as we said; at any rate in the continent man it obeys the rational principle—and presumably in the temperate and the brave man it is still more obedient. (1102b13–28)

Aristotle is explicitly talking about the *human* soul here. While there is no mention of animals or dogs in these pages, or anywhere else in the *Nicomachean Ethics*, however, it seems to me that much of what Aristotle says about virtue and happiness and being a good man can also roughly be applied to animals by analogy. Even though Aristotle himself might never have intended this, I think that the *Nicomachean Ethics* can tell us a lot when it comes to educating the animal soul.

The appetitive, or animal part of our soul, Aristotle says, is a creature of habit. It stands or falls based on the presence or absence of good or bad habits, and this is what moral virtue flourishes in: the ability of our animal instincts and impulses to become receptive to reason through the course of developing good habits. This is only true of 'moral' virtue. Intellectual virtue, as we saw above, is dependent only upon the capacity to learn and discover truth about the world—that's why it's the special province of human beings only. But that's not the case with moral virtue.

Just as there's an animal soul in man, which is 'receptive' to reason and hence can develop the virtues, so I would suggest that one of the 'virtues' of a being good dog is a similar ability to be receptive to reason. In the case of the dog, the reason that it is receptive to is not its own, but that of its master. It's just that where before the relationship between 'animal' and 'rational' existed within the soul of one being, a human, now we are considering it between two things—dog and human.

If this is true, then it would imply that dogs, if properly guided, can develop some (if not all) of the moral virtues which Aristotle attributes to human beings—virtues like courage, temperance, honor, and pride—perhaps even capstone virtues like friendliness and 'greatness of soul'.

The Canine Virtues

But how does one instill such desirable qualities as friendliness or courage into your dog? It seems difficult enough for many people to come by such habits, let alone impart them to their pets. The key, Aristotle says, is not to be satisfied by merely general accounts of virtue; one must know what the nature of virtue is specifically.

The first main feature that defines moral virtue, according to Aristotle, is that it always has the structure of a mean between two opposed extremes. Take, for instance, courage. Many people might think that a courageous person is one who has absolutely no fear of death, and is ready to rush into danger at a moment's notice. Aristotle, however, thinks that this account of courage is as, at best, incomplete. While some might think so, rushing into danger without any consideration of the outcome is not in fact courageous, since the outcome may very well be worse after the fact for both oneself and others. The truly courageous person, Aristotle says, is the one who hits the proper mean between complete fear and cowardice on the one hand, and excessive rashness and recklessness on the other. And while courage might be closer to fearlessness than cowardice, the real virtue is always somewhere between the two.

The case is the same when it comes to analogous canine moral virtues. Some might think that a dog which is raised to be completely vicious and ferocious is the correctly 'courageous' way for a dog to be, but Aristotle would likely criticize its owner for erring towards one extreme at the expense of another. In addition to the moral virtue of courage, there are many others Aristotle thinks that we should develop, and which it would seem natural to also transfer to dogs. Courage, temperance, friendliness, and good temper all seem to be virtues that we would like to find in our dogs, if in a slightly transformed and dog-appropriate way.

While some human virtues like generosity with money or truthfulness in speech may not appropriately apply to dogs, others, like temperance, courage, and friendliness, would apply. If one's dog over-ate to the point that its health was threatened, then it would certainly seem appropriate to give the dog a more temperate diet. If, in the hopes of training a good watch-dog, you caused your dog to become so hostile to strangers that it could no longer be taken for a walk down the street, then it clearly would need training to temper its hostility.

That isn't to say that there might not be some difference between a virtue in humanity and its equivalent amongst dogs. Humans seem much more susceptible to excesses of pleasure than the natural temperance that seems to reign in dogs, say, and a person seems much more likely than a dog to be afraid when family or friend is attacked. But this wouldn't prove anything against an Aristotelian-style account of canine 'virtues', because Aristotle himself says that each particular mean will differ from virtue to virtue, and indeed from person to person. So it should come as no surprise that such differences might also occur across species.

This Aristotelian account of canine virtues also helps us to understand what would otherwise be somewhat perplexing talk about dogs and their behavior. Unless we had some idea in mind of how a dog should act in society with other people, how else could we make sense of what is means to be a 'good' dog? Where else could the unspoken bond connecting owner and pet come from, and how else could we explain why we call dogs "man's best friend"?

The Flip Side of the Coin—
Human Responsibility

But if one's dog has the potential to share in some form of life that is mutually beneficial to both canine and human, then this also places a great deal of responsibility upon its human master. Not only does this mean providing food, water, and safe shelter for the pet. These essentials, while not providing them would be cruel, are not the main contributions of a human master to a canine pet; after all, a dog, if left to its own devices, has the ability to see to its own natural needs. No, the real, distinctively *human* contribution of a dog's owner is that of possessing the greater share of reason, and hence looking out for the future good of both. This is what makes the relationship between a human being and a dog so dynamic and unique, mutually beneficial when done right, cruel and terrible when exercised poorly.

With a greater share of reason between the two, it is the responsibility of the human master to look out for the greatest good of both. But this does not mean that, as 'master', the human half of the pair can simply control or dominate his pet. Rather than deliberating about and acting for the greater good of both creatures, such a relationship would really be no better than an animal form of slavery. In such a way, even the word 'owner' is too strong to describe the type of relationship that should exist between a human and its pet. Rather, one should not look upon one's dog merely as something owned or used, but rather, in a deep and important way, as sharing certain faculties in common, and hence as a kind of extension of one's very own soul, much as Aristotle says we consider a friend as a 'second self.'

If one neglects the unique responsibilities on the human side of the relationship, and doesn't act in such a way as to be truly worthy of the title 'master', bad things can result. The animal soul is a creature of habit, as Aristotle says, and it's important to instill good habits in both master and pet. Like a tree which grows crooked if left unwatered or placed in the blistering wind or sun, so does the animal soul in humans become twisted and distorted if bad habits take seed.

Experience shows that bad habits regularly repeated become bad dispositions. A broken and wounded dog is almost always paired with an abusive and neglectful master. And just as Aristotle thinks there is no more dangerous animal than a vicious human being, it seems that dogs develop a capacity for viciousness that far exceeds their natural potential if placed in the hands of an abusive or neglectful master.

So it seems reasonable to hold a dog's master responsible for bad actions done by the dog, if that happens as a result of abuse or neglect by the master. It's important, therefore, to get clear on what a 'good' dog and a 'good' master truly is, because, as Aristotle says about a 'good' life, it not only makes a little difference; it makes all the difference.

A Dog's Behavior—Is It All Just Instinct?

Some—perhaps my old philosophy professor, or a professional dog trainer or animal biologist—might object to this whole idea of canine 'virtues' and the special relationship between humans and their dogs. Could it be that what appears to be 'friendship' is not some bond felt between human and animal, but is in fact just a function of *instinct?* Perhaps these supposedly 'human' interactions are really an anthropomorphization on our part of a certain instinctual canine pack-mentality in canines. Maybe, as my professor suggested, the 'friendliness' of a dog or its 'happiness' at seeing its master again is nothing more than a conditioned response sparked by the return of the dog's regularly-supplying source of food.

My friend Kalee tells an interesting story here. At one time she was having behavioral problems with her two dogs, Flipper and Luna, two large mutts. Whenever anyone came to visit, the dogs would rush upon their guests, sometimes knocking them to the ground. So she took them to a dog training school. The trainer's attributed Flipper and Luna's reckless behavior to the fact that Kalee and her husband Andrew were being too 'gentle' with them—overly cuddly, speaking in cutesy high-toned voices all the time, ineffectively reacting with anxious high-pitched shouts whenever their dogs would rush towards their houseguests.

According to this trainer, the root of the problem was that neither Kalee nor Andrew had effectively asserted their dominance over their dogs, and this weak behavior was instinctually interpreted by Luna and Flipper as evidence of their owners' weakness. And thus since Kalee and Andrew were too weak to protect themselves, that meant that it was the responsibility of the dogs—Flipper and Luna—to protect them. This explained the uncontrollable and over-aggressive behavior of the two dogs; it seemed to them necessary to provide for the safety of the 'pack'. All because Kalee and Andrew had appeared too ineffectual to do it themselves.

So what was the solution? Kalee and Andrew needed to reassert their dominant position in the pack, and to abandon all behavior that could be interpreted as a sign of weakness. No more cute high-pitched voices around the dogs. They would tussle with them more. They would growl at them from time to time (yes, they would 'bark' at them on their way out the door). And you know what? In the end, the training worked.

Two Social Animals

So does this story show that the Aristotelian-style analysis of the human-canine relationship is wrong? Is it perhaps the case that dogs really are just driven by an instinctual pack mentality, one which is really at the root of every dog's behavior, even after millennia of domestication, and hence something which can never be wiped away or altered, even through the development of good habits? Does this prove that Aristotle's framework must be wrong?

I actually think that the exact opposite is true, that the story of my friend Kalee and her dogs really confirms what I've been saying all along. According to Aristotle, it's important to maintain the proper relationship between 'ruler' and 'ruled' in any such structure (remembering that 'ruler' does not mean 'owner'); for instance, that between parents and children, rulers and subjects, and the rational part of the soul and the more animal appetitive part of the soul.

To maintain this proper relationship, proper habits have to be developed. The more animal part of the soul, Aristotle believes, has to learn to be receptive to the reason of the rational part of the soul. The same is true in the case of dogs. The main 'virtue' of a dog consists in having the character of being receptive to the reason of its master.

That is the whole wonder of the process of domestication. Two animals, from two different species—human and canine—come together to forge a relationship which can be mutually beneficial. We get something out of the relationship: the devotion, strength, courage, power, and companionship of our dogs. These virtues are often far more evident in a truly devoted dog than in many of our friends.

The dog gets something out of the contract too: not just food, shelter, and security, but also the possibility to cooperate, to work towards something higher. Think about the intricacy of a sheep dog's task. Could she ever accomplish it by herself? If you ever get to view a sheepdog at her work, I think that you'll see one of the clearest examples of an element which is 'receptive to reason' within her soul. It's true that dogs would never have developed these abilities and more had it not been for their interaction with the human species. But the same could be said for us; we never could have accomplished all that we have, both now and throughout the course of human history, had it not been for the relationship we've developed with *Canis lupus familiaris*.

To maintain the fruitfulness of such a relationship (to allow it to 'flourish' as Aristotle would say), each needs to serve its own role well—the human master as the one providing reason, and his canine partner as the one receptive to his master's direction. When the human part of the pair doesn't take on the responsibility to be a good master, then his pet will never develop into a good dog.

Truly Man's Best Friend

All this grows out of a common feature shared between humans and dogs that is often overlooked: sociability. As Aristotle says, man is naturally a social animal (a '*zÿon politikon*' in Aristotle's Greek). 'Pack mentality', far from being something distant and foreign between dog and humans, is actually something that we in fact share, and hence it gives rise to the possibility of developing close relationships with dogs, even across the deep chasms of nature that divide the two species from one another.

Friendship, Aristotle says, is the highest political virtue. It's also one of the most fulfilling parts of our lives. In Book Nine of the *Nicomachean Ethics*, Aristotle asks whether any of us would consider the good man happy, if he lacked friends (1169b4). Might we not ask the same thing about our dog? While we may not be able to share higher rational activities like contemplation or linguistic communication with our dogs, we can share in something almost as deep, and much more tangible in substance—friendship.

This may not be the highest form of friendship. One must never discount the depth of bonds between siblings, parents, children, true friends, or lovers. But perhaps it helps to answer that question which we started with, namely, why it is that there is often such a deep bond felt between people and their dogs.

By considering Aristotle's account of the cultivation of moral virtue in his *Nicomachean Ethics*, we've gone part of the way in explaining why, alone among all the other animals in the world, dogs most deserve the title of 'man's best friend.'

No matter what Descartes says.

21

Utilitarianism for the Dog Who Has Everything

JOHN HADLEY and SIOBHAN O'SULLIVAN

Many dog lovers think of themselves as good global citizens. For most dog owners, showering your canine friend with affection comes as naturally as donating money to your school's fundraising drive or conserving energy to minimise your 'ecological footprint'.

Companion animal ownership is increasingly popular among the well-educated middle class. Such people are often the backbone of their local community and consistent contributors to charitable organizations. As part of their moral world-view, many modern dog owners increasingly consider their dog to be an integral part of their home and personal life. As such, many dogs receive a level of care, love, and attention befitting a fully-fledged member of the family.

The dedication shown towards many dogs in affluent countries raises important ethical questions. Do dog owners act with moral integrity when they lavish benefits upon their dog? Or, do some acts of generosity towards dogs actually compromise the dog owner ethically, because finite resources are directed away from more pressing matters such as global poverty, and towards dogs – an animal whose needs can be satisfied reasonably simply?

Those Privileged Pooches

Dog lovers demonstrate their dedication to their animal companions in a variety of ways. Canine veterinary medicine continues to expand. Service providers specializing in doggy day-care, grooming and dog walking persistently spring up in an already crowded marketplace. Gone are the days when dog owners rewarded their animal's loyalty with the odd bone or shelter in the laundry on a rainy night.

The dog consumables industry is one of the fastest growing sections of the American economy, and a similar trend is occurring in other rich countries such as Canada, Britain, and Australia. Nowhere is the phenomenon more pronounced than at the high end of the dog-luxury market, catering to wealthy owners for whom price is no object.

In 2006, *New York Dog Lover Magazine* carried an advertisement for a $5,500 Swarovski crystal dog vest.[1] The fashion conscious dog owner can now adorn their pet in designer dog clothes with celebrity brand names, or doggie nail polish. For a cool ten thousand bucks a dog's ailing kidney can be replaced with a donor kidney. Ongoing treatment for a kidney transplant dog is between $150.00 and $2,000.00 per month, for the rest of the animal's life.[2]

For many dog owners who love their four-legged friend, and who have a significant disposable income to call upon, consumer goods and costly veterinary treatment may be a way of demonstrating their affection; both to their dog and to the world. But for those who strive to live an ethical life, what does utilitarianism, the moral theory that seeks to generate the greatest happiness for the greatest number, have to say about the luxury dog market? Is it possible that in our rush to shower our dogs with affection we are inadvertently wronging people who could significantly benefit from the energy and resources currently being directed towards individual animals?

Utilitarianism Is a Philosophy for Dogs

Moral theories are a service to the community because they provide people with guidelines or rules to follow if they are concerned about leading an ethical life. Moral theories give us an opportunity to bring our actions into line with values that, upon reflection, we regard as important.

---

[1] Mindy Fetterman, "Pampered Pooches Nestle in Lap of Luxury," *USA Today* (February 11th, 2005), http://www.azcentral.com/families/articles/0211Dogs-ON.html (accessed February 13th, 2006).

[2] University of California, Davis, "Information Brochures: Canine Renal Transplant" (2007), http://www.vmth.ucdavis.edu/vmth/clientinfo/info/sasurg/k9rentrans.html (accessed February 13th, 2006).

Yet moral theories do not agree: they offer differing accounts of what makes an action right or wrong. While the plethora of rival moral theories may reflect disagreement about what makes an action right or wrong, most theories generally presuppose that ethics is not a futile enterprise and that people can be moved to perform moral actions, even if doing the right thing requires a significant degree of personal sacrifice.

For moral theories influenced by the Judeo-Christian tradition, the morality of an action is determined with reference to what God commands. On that view, an action is right if God approves of it and wrong if God forbids it. Other moral theories don't look to religion for guidance but instead hold that the morality of actions can be determined with reference to reason.

According to Kantianism, for example, the right action is one that passes an elaborate deliberation procedure or thinking test. If a formal statement or maxim of an action does not generate a rational inconsistency or contradiction, then the action is regarded as morally binding, or what Kant calls a 'categorical imperative'. A categorical imperative is considered to have moral authority in virtue of its being the product of a strictly reason-centred deliberation procedure—a process for thinking about moral issues that allows no influence for what a person feels or desires. On this kind of view, moral reasoning boils down to plugging information into your cerebral computer in order to get a green or red light.

Utilitarianism is referred to as a 'consequentialist' moral theory. In contrast to theories that ground the authority of ethics in God or human rationality, consequentialism determines the morality of actions with reference to the real world. Consequentialists are concerned with how things actually are 'on the ground', so to speak. For consequentialists, it's the outcome of an action that determines whether that action is right or wrong.

The exact consequences assessed to determine whether an action is right or wrong will depend on the particular value the consequentialist theory is seeking to promote. Ethical Hedonism, for example, is the consequentialist moral theory that holds that the highest good and the ultimate standard of morality is the realization of happiness. According to hedonism, the right action is the one that serves to bring about the happiest consequence of all the available actions one might perform.

Utilitarianism can rightly be called a hedonistic theory insofar as it is concerned to promote happiness, but it is wrong to think of it as an ego-driven theory. It doesn't entail an ethic of selfishness and is not concerned to promote the realization of a rampant 'sex, drugs and rock 'n' roll' culture of happiness. The egalitarian character of utilitarianism is anchored by the fact that not just any amount of happiness will secure the morality of an action. The mere fact that an action makes the person performing it happy does not make it right; instead, only the action that realizes as much happiness as possible for everyone the action will affect is the right one to perform. In the words of utilitarianism's founder Jeremy Bentham, the right action is the one that brings about "the greatest good for the greatest number."[3]

It's the concern to promote as much happiness in the world as possible that attests to the benevolent or 'other-regarding' character of utilitarianism. Indeed, the thoroughly empathetic character of utilitarianism is evidenced by the theory being the first to identify the consciousness of animals as a legitimate location for the realization of morally relevant states of affairs. It's for this reason that utilitarianism is a philosophy for dogs!

As all dog lovers instinctively know, dogs have an emotional range. They can be happy, sad, excited, exhausted, frustrated or content. In seeking to *maximize* happiness, instead of merely promoting just any amount of happiness, Jeremy Bentham argued that the happiness of animals is an issue of serious moral concern. Other philosophers had called for greater compassion towards animals but until Bentham, none had built animals into the mechanics of a moral theory.

By prescribing a maximising hedonistic theory, Bentham included within the scope of morality any creature that has the capacity to be happy. To include only humans in the circle of moral concern would no doubt promote a lot of happiness, but it would not promote the *greatest* good for the *greatest* number. To truly maximise happiness, therefore, utilitarianism must include animal joy and animal suffering. And as all dog owners know, there is no greater delight than that of a Labrador at dinnertime, a Jack Russell at walk-time, or your dog when you return home from work at the end of a long day.

A moral theory which has as its primary objective to make all sentient creatures as happy as possible makes a strong claim for the

---

[3] Jeremy Bentham, *An Introduction to the Principles of Morals and Legislation* (Oxford: Clarendon, 1996).

allegiance of dog lovers. Ask yourself this, what could be a better life for your dog than for him or her to be as happy as possible? Even if you think that human beings are more morally important than animals, isn't a world with as much human *and* animal happiness as possible, better than a world with merely the maximum amount of *human* happiness?

It's utilitarianism's ability to readily include animal satisfaction that made it the ideal moral framework for Australian philosopher Peter Singer to deploy in his famous defence of animals. Some two hundred years after Bentham, Singer argued in his influential book *Animal Liberation*, that when humans assess the consequences of their actions they should seriously reflect on how those actions affect animals.[4] Although Singer focused on animals used in agriculture and scientific research, his philosophy also has implications for our closest animal friends: dogs.

The Dog Luxury Market

The dog services and consumables market has changed rapidly since the 1990s. Commentators argue that a combination of some sections of the community experiencing a rise in their disposable income, declining birth rates, and feelings of alienation associated with living in large urban jungles, has resulted in a sizable expansion in the number of people who own dogs, and in turn, the dog product market.

In 2006, sixty-nine million American households owned a pet. That's a jump of five million animals in only four years.[5] In addition to the rise in companion animal ownership, in the ten years since 1995, the American pet industry has doubled in size. By 2005, it was generating $34 billion a year in revenue.[6] A similar trend has occurred in other affluent Western nations, with no end in sight. And what's more, everyone seems to be getting in on the act!

Most people are familiar with the concept of the professional dog walker. But it doesn't end there. Doggy day care offers long

---

[4] Peter Singer, *Animal Liberation* (London: Pimlico, 1995).

[5] Alison Rosen, "Pet Mania . . . Unleashed!" *Time Out New York* (March 30th–April 5th, 2006), http://www.timeoutny.com/newyork/Details.do?xyurl=xyl://TONYWebArticles1/548/features/pet_mania_unleashed.xml (accessed February 13th, 2006).

[6] Fetterman, "Pampered Pooches."

day care for dogs in luxurious surrounds. For around forty dollars a day, your dog can attend a day care centre in the heart of Manhattan. Facilities include toys, beds and TVs so your four-legged friend can watch his or her favourite show. For an additional $60.00 your dog can enjoy an hour long massage. Starting from $175.00 per night, medium-sized dogs can also board. Hotel guests will be tantalised by meals prepared on site by the in-house chief, and some dog day and night programs include webcams, so you can keep an eye on your best friend while you work. At one of America's many dog holiday resorts, your pet can sign up for hiking and swimming lessons. Moreover, for the right price, a professional dog party planner will conceptualise and host your dog's next birthday party.

But when it comes to the dog luxury market, services are only the thin edge of the wedge. For close to six thousand dollars you can buy a crocodile-leather travel bag for your dog. A matching purse for humans is also available from the same exclusive boutique on New York City's Fifth Avenue. The motorcycle manufacturers Harley-Davidson have a doggie-leather jacket on the market and well established brands such as Ralph Lauren, Lord and Taylor, and Swarovski have all have begun manufacturing clothing products especially for dogs. Pet furniture is also readily available. Dog beds start at a hundred dollars, and for four and a half thousand dollars, your dog can be the proud owner of the 'Louis XVI Palace' dog bed.

While there has been an upturn in the availability of consumables for dogs, there has also been a surge in canine health care. Insurance policies for dogs are selling at three times the rate they were in 2000.[7] For some dog owners pet insurance may be money well spent as the cost of specialised treatments rises. With improved canine health care has come increased longevity. As a result, the instance of cancer in dogs is also increasing. Treating cancer in dogs costs between two thousand and nine thousand dollars per dog.[8] But not all dog veterinary medicine is targeted at good health. Cosmetic surgery for dogs is becoming more widely available. Neuticles are testicular implants for pets. They allow a

---

[7] Fetterman, "Pampered Pooches."

[8] Erin Kirk, "Dog's Tale of Survival Opens Doors in Cancer Research," *USA Today* (July 24th, 2002), http://www.usatoday.com/news/health/2002-07-24-cover-cancer_x.htm (accessed February 13th, 2006).

dog to be neutered while still maintaining an 'intact' look. Hundreds of thousands of neuticles are selling around the world. It seems that fashion-conscious dog owners want their pets to look as good as themselves.

The Utilitarian Case Against Indulging Your Dog

In a recent article in the *New York Times Magazine* Peter Singer reminds us that there are many people suffering and dying from diseases that could be prevented by the money we spend on luxury items for ourselves or our canine friends.[9] It's tempting to ignore this kind of argument, especially when we consider how overwhelming the problems associated with global poverty appear to be. If what Singer claims is true, then for any reasonably civic-minded person, the fact that as many as ten million children are dying every year from diseases that could be prevented by increased aid donations from individuals just like us, is going to be difficult to digest.

The utilitarian injunction to promote the greatest good for the greatest number compels us to consider our responsibility for the suffering of others, so long as we are in a position to have a tangible impact upon helping to alleviate their plight. And most interested observers, whether they be utilitarians or not, accept the efficacy of aid provision, even though it may be imperfect. As Peter Singer points out, giving money to charity may be a solution that has its flaws, but in comparison to spending money on luxuries, it is a highly effective means of alleviating suffering and reducing the number of unnecessary deaths.

But could utilitarianism be wrong about our obligations to help distant strangers in dire need? Why should we be responsible for helping others simply because we are in a position to do so? Some anti-utilitarian philosophers argue that we're only responsible for harm we personally and intentionally cause through our actions. On this kind of view, if the average dog owner keeps to his or her self, and does not infringe upon others, he or she has no further moral duties and is entitled to spend as much as they like on their canine companion.

---

[9] Peter Singer, 'What Billionaires Should Give—and What You Should Give,' *New York Times Magazine* (December 17th, 2006).

Utilitarians like Singer and his American counterpart Peter Unger, however, present a very simple yet compelling argument for the view that we are responsible for what we don't do, as much as what we do.[10] Imagine if you were walking past a shallow pond in which a small child was drowning; wouldn't it be wrong for you to fail to help the child if it was reasonably easy for you to do so, at no great financial imposition? If you think that a passer-by who failed to help a person in dire need, when they easily could have done so, has done something wrong, then, just like utilitarians from Bentham to Singer, you agree that people are morally responsible for harm they fail to stop.

A common criticism of this implication of utilitarianism is that it makes leading an ethical life too demanding. Some argue that utilitarianism asks too much of us by requiring that we take into consideration the happiness of everyone, near and far, human and sentient nonhuman. But, while the sacrifices called for by utilitarianism may at first glance seem difficult, they should not be overstated. Even though people do seem to frequently put their own interests, or the interests of their nearest and dearest, first and foremost; an overly pessimistic outlook of what people are capable of overlooks how closely our thinking about ethical issues reflect the attitudes and judgments of others, at least this is what utilitarians think.

The Scottish utilitarian philosopher, David Hume, thought that there was great scope for agreement among people because he believed it's part of our nature to approve or disapprove of much the same things. Hume famously said, "The minds of all men are similar in their feeling and operations, nor can anyone be actuated by any affection, of which all others are not, in some degree, susceptible."[11] His basic point is that while it may not be easy to be compassionate to distant strangers, it's not something that we have

---

[10] Peter Singer, "Famine, Affluence, and Morality," *Philosophy and Public Affairs* (1972), and Peter Unger, *Living High and Letting Die* (Oxford University Press, 1996).

[11] David Hume, *A Treatise of Human Nature*, (Oxford University Press, 1978). Originally published 1739), p. 575. Consistent with Hume's moral psychology, the contemporary utilitarian Jack Smart says people have a natural propensity to support utilitarianism in virtue of having "an ultimate pro-attitude to human happiness in general". See J.J.C. Smart and Bernard Williams, *Utilitarianism: For and Against* (Cambridge: Cambridge University Press, 2005), p. 31.

to do in spite of ourselves; instead, we have a capacity for sympathy that can be nurtured or suppressed. Helping others comes naturally to us because we can all imagine ourselves being in need of another person's assistance. Inherent in our innate capacity to put ourselves in another's shoes, is our instinctive willingness to extend the hand of friendship to others when required. Observing the plight of others we call to mind feelings that are similar in character to those experienced by the sufferer. Such is an unavoidable aspect of our nature, according to Hume, much like our feeling of love and companionship for our canine friends.

Sharing the Wealth

Luxury goods are by definition surplus to a dog's needs. Just as humans do not need an expensive car or designer watch to live a reasonably good life, so our dogs do not need diamond encrusted jackets or pedicures in order to be happy. The law of diminishing returns suggests that we get very little happiness from luxury items; and empirical evidence from animal cognition research suggests our canine friends get no enjoyment at all from luxury products.[12] Indeed, they are most likely irritated or made anxious by being made to wear unfamiliar materials or by being compelled to endure unusual practices.

The dogs we live with today are in fact domesticated wolves. Dogs have the same number of chromosomes as wolves, and retain a number of wolf-like features such as a similar skeletal structure, sensory range, social organization, and communication patterns. The domestication process has generated some notable differences. For example, the domestic dog has a small jaw and teeth compared to wolves.[13] But the domestication process has not instilled dogs with a love of luxuries. A dog jacket does not provide greater protection against the cold when it is designed by Paris Hilton and

---

[12] See Colin Allen, "Animal Consciousness," *Stanford Encyclopedia of Philosophy* (Winter 2006 edition), http://plato.stanford.edu/archives/win2006/entries/consciousness-animal/ (accessed June 6th, 2007). The deep disagreement about the qualitative aspects of animal consciousness supports taking a parsimonious view about their mental states. This entails that while we can say, on the basis of available evidence, that they experience pleasure and pain, we have little basis for claiming they experience pleasure in unusual or unnatural surroundings.

[13] Linda P. Case, *The Dog: Its Behavior, Nutrition, and Health* (Iowa State University Press, 1999).

priced at ten times its material worth. Even if a designer dog vest does not cause irritation, its luxury status means nothing to a dog.

The most famous utilitarian of all, John Stuart Mill, provides us with a reason for thinking that when we choose to refrain from buying dog luxuries, and instead use the money helping people in dire need, we do not in any way compromise the happiness of our canine loved ones. Mill once said "It is indisputable that the being whose capacities of enjoyment are low has the greatest chance of having them fully satisfied."[14] Implied in this statement is the idea that dogs experience no discernable improvement in their quality of life when we indulge them with luxuries; instead, we can provide them with the best possible life simply by being good companions to them.

Fully satisfying dogs' capacities for enjoyment entails some level of commitment, but it does not require us to shower them with services and accoutrements they cannot understand and have no particular preference for. A dog is just as easily satisfied by going for a walk at the local park as by going for a run at a luxury dog retreat, spied on by webcam. It seems appropriate to wonder whose needs are really being satisfied by the luxury dog market. If a dog gets no discernable increased enjoyment out of a visit to an exclusive Manhattan dog spa—but the dog's owner feels comforted in the belief that he or she is doing everything in their power to make their canine friend's life as wonderful as possible—it may in fact be human pleasure that is increased by dog consumables! Yet the human pleasure generated by spoiling a dog pails into insignificance when considered in light of the joy humans living in dire poverty experience when their suffering is relieved.

---

[14] John Stuart Mill, *The Basic Writings of John Stuart Mill: Utilitarianism* (Modern Library, 2002. First published 1861), p. 242.

Sniff Our Butts

ANDREW ABERDEIN divides his time between England and Florida, where he is Associate Professor of Logic and Humanities at Florida Institute of Technology. One price he pays for this jet-setting lifestyle is that he is presently dogless. However, he grew up alongside a Pekinese, a Dachshund, an Airedale, and a Labrador Cross.

RANDALL AUXIER grew up around dogs, spending many years cleaning up their poop at his father's veterinary office in Memphis. Dogs have licked him, bitten him, sniffed him, barked at him, and once in a while, hunted him in packs in the Mississippi River bottoms. Having brought their impressive sensory complement to bear on his person, they have decided he smells interesting, except for a lingering *eau de chat*. He is professor of philosophy at Southern Illinois University in Carbondale, so the Governor of Illinois is his current master.

KAREN C. ADKINS is Associate Professor of Philosophy and Associate Dean of Regis College in Denver, Colorado. After years of fieldwork in coffee-houses and bars, her dissertation work on the cognitive status of gossip and rumor has been published in *Social Epistemology*. She's cohabited with dogs most of her life; their ability to keep secrets has been part of their appeal. She is just starting to think about getting another dog.

JIRI BENOVSKY is seriously worried that the world, contrary to the way it seems to us, does not really exist. Instead of ending up in a clinic for the mentally disordered, he got employed by the philosophy department of the University of Fribourg in Switzerland as an expert on metaphysics (the branch of philosophy that studies the nature of the world). His publications include his book *Persistence through Time and Across Possible Worlds* and a number of articles. He would really like dogs if they existed, of which he is still not fully certain. •

293

Owing her existence to a case of frozen penguins, **HEATHER DOUGLAS** was born to an animal physiologist and a Swedish polyglot. While living on the plains of Northern Illinois, Heather got her first dog at the age of seven, a keeshond named Yorick. Alas, poor Yorick died in 1989 and Heather was sadly dogless when she completed her B.A. in Philosophy and Physics from the University of Delaware. She remained dogless through her graduate education at Pittsburgh's History and Philosophy of Science Department. Happily, once having a real job as the Phillip M. Phibbs Assistant Professor of Science and Ethics at the University of Puget Sound, she and her husband Ted were finally able to properly raise a puppy, Corin, a black lab mix adopted from the pound. With her move to the Department of Philosophy at the University of Tennessee in Knoxville, and the ability to buy some land, they have adopted their second pound dog, Jade, a vizsla mix. Together, Corin and Jade terrorize the local chipmunks and keep Heather as sane as possible.

LAURA DUHAU is a philosophy professor at the National University in Mexico. She has been studying animal thought for some time. She is an avid lover of dogs and cats, regardless of whether or not they can think. Both she and her dog Kibbles are indifferent with regard to bees.

GARY GABOR is a Ph.D. candidate studying ancient philosophy at Fordham University. He is co-organizer of the transatlantic Philosophical Red Star Line collaboration between the University of Antwerp and Fordham, and is co-editor of its upcoming book *Rethinking Secularization*. Until a space opens up on the Iditarod Great Sled Race, Gary is content to go jogging with his family's two miniature Alaskan Eskimos, Wendy and Tinkerbell, much to the amusement of their Floridean neighbors.

MICKEY GJERRIS is a theologian with a Ph.D. in bioethics, working within the area of applied ethics at the Faculty for Life Sciences at the University of Copenhagen. He has written about ethics and nature in many context and is currently seeking ways to make the idea of the integrity of life understandable beyond a narrow group of long-bearded philosophers. Believing firmly in the idea that ethics should be understood as the collective hesitation of our culture in front of technological opportunities, he works within a phenomenological, hermeneutical, and critical framework. This basically means he asks a lot of "why"-questions. He has three children and a part-time dog.

MARCIN GOKIELI is a young philosopher from Warsaw, Poland, interested in the philosophy of mind, ethics, and metaphysics. Additionally he works as a journalist, plays noisy improvised music, and writes weird tales. As he travels quite a lot, he can't own a dog; though he often takes care of his friends' dogs when they go away.

JOHN HADLEY is Lecturer in Communication Ethics in the School of Communication and a Research Fellow at the Centre for Applied Philosophy and Public Ethics (CAPPE) at Charles Sturt University, Australia. He has a number of recent publications on animal rights and is currently working on the contemporary relevance of J.S. Mill's views about freedom of speech. While John grew up in a cat household (his parents once had eleven cats!), he enjoys spending time with his friends' dogs whenever he gets the chance. His only animal companion however, is a human one.

STEVEN D. HALES is Professor of Philosophy at Bloomsburg University. His official interests are epistemology and metaphysics, but he also publishes books like *Beer and Philosophy* and the companion to the volume you are holding, *What Philosophy Can Tell You about Your Cat.* Steve has had numerous dogs over the years, including Freckles, Patches, and Brenna. Presently the family dog is a one-year-old Golden Retriever mix named Sophie.

MIKOLAJ HERNIK is a cognitive developmental psychologist working at the University of Warsaw, Poland. By now he probably has just finished his PhD studies. His work concerns the ability to understand others' thoughts and actions. Usually he studies children and adults, but by now he might have run some dog-studies as well. Certainly he'd love to.

SARAH JONES is Assistant Professor of Philosophy at Northern Michigan University. She's a frequent contributor at the American Philosophical Association's annual Central Division meeting. She is the Chair of the Philosophy Division of the Michigan Academy of Science, Arts, and Letters. She lives in a town that time has all but forgotten. It's not quite Lake Wobegon, but all the philosophers are good looking and all the dogs are above average.

WENDY LYNNE LEE is professor of philosophy at Bloomsburg University, Pennsylvania. She writes on contemporary philosophy of mind, philosophy of language, feminist theory, environmental philosophy, and ecological aesthetics. But really that's just the stuff she does when she's not mixing doggy food, washng doggy bowls, building doggy disability ramps, cleaning up doggy poo, and otherwise attending to her animal family. The "crazy dog lady"? Sure, but only if you include five cats, a cockatiel, an iguana, as well as her four dogs.

PAUL LOADER works as a Disability Officer at a London University. He's also a research student in Philosophy of Cognitive Science. His favourite film is *Dog Day Afternoon*.

CHRISTIAN MAURER is doctoral assistant for research and teaching at the Institute of Philosophy, University of Neuchâtel, Switzerland. He likes many dogs and adores children, even adolescent ones. In spite of the facts that his dog died a while ago, that he does not yet have children of his own, and that his main area of philosophical interest are theories of self-love and egoism, he is a very sociable person and likes to work in teams.

GLEN A. MAZIS is Professor of Philosophy and Humanities at Penn State Harrisburg. Bhakti, his apple-headed Chihuahua has been known to sit in on his courses, especially Critical Theory in which she was voted a regular graduate seminar member. He's the author of several books, essays, and poems, and his latest book *Humans/Animals/Machines: Blurred Boundaries* should just be out by the time you read this.

ED MINAR is professor of philosophy at the University of Arkansas and head dog and people trainer at Canine Connection in Fayetteville, Arkansas. He has written on Wittgenstein, Heidegger, and topics in philosophy of mind and epistemology, and is currently working on and teaching about animal minds. He and his wife Diana Nagel (psychologist and dog trainer) have three Australian Shepherds, the youngest of whom, Staarry Heavens to Bessie, participates with Ed at the highest levels of agility, formal obedience, and rally obedience.

KAMILA PACOVSKÁ is a doctoral student of ethics and philosophy of mathematics at Charles University in Prague, Czech Republic. She has always secretely envied the care bestowed on their dog by her parents. She started to do philosophy to make sense of this fact. Participation in this volume is a crucial step in dealing with her infancy.

WEAVER SANTANIELLO is Professor of Philosophy at Penn State, Berks. She's the editor of *Nietzsche and the Gods* and author of *Nietzsche, God, and the Jews* (1994), and *Zarathustra's Last Supper* (2006). She lives in Berks County, Pennsylvania with her dogs, Turbo and Plato, who have her wrapped around their paws.

ANDERS SCHINKEL, historian and philosopher, currently teaches at the Philosophy Department of Erasmus University in Rotterdam, the Netherlands. Having published his dissertation *Conscience and Conscientious Objections* (2007), he considered writing about dog dignity the obvious next step in his career. Dogless throughout childhood, the first dog Anders really got to know was Floor, his parents in law's first black labrador, who died as an old lady four years ago. Bo, Floor's successor, has taken such a shine to Anders and his girlfriend Eva that Eva's father recently suggested they lease her. They're unsure, however, whether leasing dogs is compatible with dog dignity.

GLENN STATILE teaches philosophy at St. John's University in New York. He's the author of two books on the philosopher René Descartes, the co-editor of *The Tests of Time* and *The Journey of Metaphysics*, and has written various articles. His beloved companion of many years was a border collie–pointer mix named Sanchi. Named after Sancho Panza, the loyal companion of that greatest of all windmill chasers, Don Quixote de la Mancha, his sidekick Sanchi now enjoys eternal rest in the Peaceable Kingdom that is the Hartsdale Pet Cemetery in Westchester, New York.

SIOBHAN O'SULLIVAN is based at the University of Sydney, Australia. Siobhan is also an Associate Fellow of the Oxford Centre for Animal Ethics. Her research focuses on the ethical, legal and political dimensions of animal studies. Siobhan doesn't have a dog of her own. However, Kelly, the neighbour's dog, has realised Siobhan is a soft touch and as a result Kelly spends many hours at Siobhan's house, being sweet and hoping for food.

ANDREW TERJESEN is a visiting Assistant Professor at Rhodes College in Memphis, Tennessee. Previously he has taught at Washington and Lee University, Austin College and Duke University. His interests are in ethics, the philosophy of mind and the philosophers of the Scottish Enlightenment (like David Hume and Adam Smith). Although he grew up without any pets, his life was transformed when Emma entered his life at the beginning of graduate school. He still refers to her as his first Master's Degree (say her name with a long "A" sound). Certainly, his contribution to this volume shows how much she has taught him about how philosophy intersects with our daily lives.

BERNHARD WEISS, educated at the Universities of St Andrews and Durham and by a succession of dogs, now works in Cape Town, South Africa. When not walking his dogs—occasionally when walking them too—he tries to think about the philosophies of logic, language, and mathematics. He has published a book on the philosophy of Michael Dummett and articles in various philosophy journals.

Caninedex

COMPILED BY ABBY L. BURKLAND